VIVEKANANDA
WORLD TEACHER

"May I be born again and again, and suffer thousands of miseries, so that I may worship the only God that exists, the only God I believe in, the sum total of all souls. And above all, my God the wicked, my God the miserable, my God the poor of all races, of all species, is the especial object of my worship."

"It may be that I shall find it good to get outside my body—to cast it off like a worn-out garment. But I shall not cease to work. I shall inspire men everywhere, until the world shall know that it is one with God."

—Swami Vivekananda

VIVEKANANDA
WORLD TEACHER

His Teachings on the Spiritual Unity of Humankind

Edited and with an Introduction by
Swami Adiswarananda

Walking Together, Finding the Way®
SKYLIGHT PATHS®
PUBLISHING
Woodstock, Vermont

**RAMAKRISHNA-VIVEKANANDA
CENTER OF NEW YORK**

"As Many Faiths, So Many Paths"

Vivekananda, World Teacher:
His Teachings on the Spiritual Unity of Humankind

2006 First Printing
© 2006 by Swami Adiswarananda

Library of Congress Cataloging-in-Publication Data
Vivekananda, Swami, 1863–1902.
[Selections. 2006]
Vivekananda, world teacher : his teachings on the spiritual unity of humankind / edited and with an introduction by Swami Adiswarananda.
    p. cm.
ISBN-13: 978-1-59473-210-2 (pbk.)
ISBN-10: 1-59473-210-8 (pbk.)
1. Spiritual life. 2. Vedanta. I. Adiswarananda, Swami, 1925– II. Title.

BL1280.292.V58A25 2006
294.5′4—dc22

2006019076

10   9   8   7   6   5   4   3   2   1

Manufactured in the United States of America
Cover Design: Sara Dismukes
Cover Art: Statue (detail) of Swami Vivekananda by noted American sculptor Malvina Hoffman (commissioned by Swami Nikhilananda in 1950 and presently installed at the Ramakrishna-Vivekananda Center of New York, New York City).

SkyLight Paths Publishing is creating a place where people of different spiritual traditions come together for challenge and inspiration, a place where we can help each other understand the mystery that lies at the heart of our existence.

SkyLight Paths sees both believers and seekers as a community that increasingly transcends traditional boundaries of religion and denomination—people wanting to learn from each other, *walking together, finding the way*.

SkyLight Paths, "Walking Together, Finding the Way," and colophon are trademarks of LongHill Partners, Inc., registered in the U.S. Patent and Trademark Office.

Walking Together, Finding the Way
Published by SkyLight Paths Publishing
A Division of LongHill Partners, Inc.
Sunset Farm Offices, Route 4, P.O. Box 237
Woodstock, VT 05091
Tel: (802) 457-4000   Fax: (802) 457-4004
www.skylightpaths.com

Contents

Introduction

Science and technology have increased our knowledge of the universe. Advances in computer science and telecommunications make it possible for all of us to have immediate access to one another and to the information and knowledge accumulated over many centuries. Satellites constantly orbiting in space provide us with a continuous view of every corner of the earth. The study of genetics has reached the point where the most basic building blocks of life have been revealed to us, presenting the possibility of conquering many diseases and increasing the length and quality of life.

Yet new developments in science and technology have not been an unmixed blessing. The secular culture ushered in by science has broken the unity of existence. It has replaced cooperation and interdependence with competition and the struggle for survival. It has ignored the Socratic teaching that knowledge is virtue and replaced it with its own, knowledge is power. The trend toward globalization that had the prospect of bringing about global peace and shared prosperity has instead greatly increased inequality, injustice, and economic disparity and exploitation. The divinity of the human soul has been completely ignored, and this has set in motion a chain reaction of alienation from reality, from nature, and from our true self. We have lost sight of our highest aspiration of the unity of humankind through love, compassion, and democratic equality. Science and technology have brought the world together, but our minds have not come together. We claim to be more intelligent than our ancestors, yet we cannot say that we are any less selfish or more kind.

We have had crises before in different forms—political, economic, cultural, and religious—but we have never had the total crisis we are facing today. We face a conflict between secular values and faith, between the economically developed and the underdeveloped societies, between generations, between religions, between reason and dogma, between human beings and nature. Politics has become the religion of our times; and wars, civil unrest, and riots based upon religious prejudices have become everyday occurrences.

Against the background of these bleak and fearful developments, Swami Vivekananda's words are more relevant today than ever before. Vivekananda introduced to the world the teachings of Vedanta, the essential message of the oneness of existence, unity of faiths, nonduality of the Godhead, and divinity of the soul. Oneness of existence is the basis of all love, compassion, and charitable feelings. We are like the leaves of a huge, universal tree. Driven by intolerance and greed we disclaim the rights of others. We forget that the leaves cannot survive apart from the tree. No one can be at peace while others are unhappy. No one can enjoy prosperity while surrounded by a world of poverty.

The movement of our life is a search for our true Self. Through acquisition of wealth, education, and fulfillment of desires we are moving toward that ultimate goal. Life evolved from the subhuman stage to the human stage, where physical evolution came to a stop; but evolution continues on the mental, moral, and spiritual planes. Survival of the fittest may be true, but only up to a certain stage of evolution. Beyond that, self-sacrifice for the good of others is the guiding principle of life.

Although there is joy in acquiring and possessing, there is a greater joy in giving and serving. By controlling our raw impulses and urges, we developed the faculty of reasoning. But reason divorced from love and compassion makes a person callous and insensitive. True knowledge teaches a person the spirit of sharing with others. It makes a person see that life is interdependent and not independent. When reason is purified and disciplined there emerges intuition. Through intuition we perceive our true Self—the center of our being. Knowledge of the Self is our birthright.

Vivekananda presents us with a positive view of the human individual and says that education is the manifestation of the perfection already in a person. True peace and fulfillment depend upon this knowledge of our true Self. We do not move from falsehood to truth but from lower truth to higher truth. Ignorance is less knowledge. Impurity is less purity. Darkness of the soul is less enlightenment. The urge for Self-knowledge is irresistible. The master urge of a human individual is not sex-gratification or acquisition of power or wealth but desire for unbounded joy, unrestricted awareness, and eternal life. This desire is the driving force behind all evolution, struggle, and efforts for peace and happiness.

According to Vivekananda, world peace depends upon social peace; social peace upon individual peace; and individual peace upon the spiritual awakening of the individual. No amount of political reform, economic regeneration, or increase in the amenities of life can ever insure the peace and well-being of the world. The Upanishads tell us that we may roll up the sky like a piece of leather yet peace will not be achieved until we know our true Self. Each one of us is called upon to promote these values not only for social and community welfare, but also for our individual peace, happiness, and prosperity. We transform the world by first transforming ourselves, and the key to transformation is the transformation of consciousness. These are the teachings of the great prophets and teachers of humanity. Vivekananda once again affirmed for our age the timeless wisdom of the prophets and saints.

Nonviolence and tolerance are the basic virtues taught by the great teachers of all traditions. While the prophets teach love and tolerance, traders in religion preach division and dissension. "What good is it if we acknowledge in our prayers that God is the Father of us all," asks Vivekananda, "and in our daily lives do not treat every man as a brother?"

The world is in need of a new spiritual revival. Unity in diversity is the natural law, and the core of this unity is not social, cultural, or humanitarian but a spiritual unity that says "the same soul dwells in every one of us." Fear, hatred, bigotry, and war are symptoms of a forgotten spiritual unity. Human unity will never become a social reality unless we realize the fact that the same God dwells in all. Foreseeing the need of our age, at the first World's Parliament of Religions held in Chicago in 1893, Swami Vivekananda made his famous remarks:

> Sectarianism, bigotry, and its horrible descendant, fanaticism, have long possessed this beautiful earth. They have filled the earth with violence, drenched it often and often with human blood, destroyed civilization, and sent whole nations to despair. Had it not been for these horrible demons, human society would be far more advanced than it is now. But their time is come; and I fervently hope that the bell that tolled this morning in honor of this convention may be the death-knell of all fanaticism, of all persecutions with the sword or with the pen, and of all uncharitable feelings between persons wending their way to the same goal.

Swami Vivekananda warned us of the dire consequences we face by forgetting the spiritual unity of all beings and things and called for a recovery of our true Self—the bond of all unity. If we fail to heed this call, our civilization will face the unforgiving law of history. Vivekananda reminded us: "You may not believe in the vengeance of God, but you must believe in the vengeance of history."

Vivekananda is looked upon by many as the world teacher who shows us the way to regain our human dignity. Thoughtful people throughout the world derive inspiration from his life and teachings. His message has found its way into the spiritual current of our times. His all-encompassing, universal message has paved the way for a new generation of spiritual seekers who are interested not merely in religion but in attaining genuine peace and self-fulfillment.

Vivekananda is regarded as a great prophet by millions of people. His birthday is observed throughout India as a national holiday. The present government of India, by an act of Parliament, has established an all-India university in his name—the first time that the secular government of India has created a university in the name of a religious personality. There is no leader in India on whom his shadow has not fallen. His message is the model of education and training presented for the new generation to discover where we fail and how to rise to the need of our time.

Vivekananda's message gives us hope for the future. His love for humanity gave him the mandate for his message, and his innate purity gave him an irresistible power that nobody could match. The same love that was born as Buddha, the Compassionate One, once again assumed human form as Vivekananda. Though he lived only thirty-nine years, he strides like a colossus across the whole of modern history and culture. A versatile genius, Vivekananda's contribution to world thought is immense. His major contributions to world religious thought have been his *spiritual democracy, spiritual humanism,* and an *enduring bond of world unity.*

Vivekananda's teachings foster *spiritual democracy.* Vivekananda offers an infinite variety of ideals and paths to choose from in order to reach the same ultimate goal—Self-knowledge or God-consciousness. Lacking this freedom of spiritual democracy, religion becomes authoritarian and oppressive, insisting on blind obedience to rigid doctrines and dogmas and unquestioning belief in ceremonials and creeds. Spiritual freedom insures individuality, critical inquiry, honest doubt, free choice of the path, and verification of truth through personal experience. The ideas of exclusive salvation, a jealous God, and a chosen people are all alien to Vivekananda's thought.

Vivekananda promoted *spiritual humanism,* as opposed to secular humanism. Spiritual humanism is not simply doing good to others but rendering loving service to the Divine, seeing its presence in all beings. Spiritual humanism embraces the whole of humanity, regardless of race, culture, country, religion, or social affiliation.

World unity based on political considerations, economic interest, cultural ties, or even humanitarian principles is never enduring. The bonds of such kinds of unity are too fragile to withstand the stresses and strains of social diversities. Unity of the world body, in order to be real, must be organic—and this requires a world soul that embraces countless diversities of human experience and human aspirations. Such a world soul must be the soul of all beings. "The God in you is the God in all," Vivekananda says. "If you have not known this, you have known nothing." Unity of the world soul includes not only human beings, but also animals, plants, and every form of life.

The essential teachings of Swami Vivekananda as a world teacher can be summarized as follows:

The fall of a country or culture is caused by its spiritual bankruptcy. In the same way, its rise depends upon spiritual awakening. Spiritual fall brings in its wake moral fall, moral fall brings intellectual blindness, and intellectual blindness brings material downfall.

The meaning of spirituality is the manifestation of the divinity already in a person. "Religion is realization—not talk or doctrines or theories, however beautiful they may be. It is being and becoming—not hearing or acknowledging. It is the whole soul's becoming changed into what it believes." Direct perception of this innate divinity is the core of spirituality. Doctrines, dogmas, theologies, and philosophies are secondary details.

The ultimate reality of the universe is nondual, designated by various traditions by various names. Believers in time call it time; believers in God call it God; believers in consciousness call it consciousness. We attribute names and epithets to this reality for our convenience, and they are symbolic.

"Each soul is a star," wrote Swami Vivekananda, "and all stars are set in the infinite azure, the eternal sky—the Lord. There is the root, the reality, the real individuality, of each and all. Religion began with a search after some of the stars which had passed beyond our horizon, and ended in finding them all in God, with ourselves in the same place." God is not only absolute reality but also the sum total of all souls. When this ultimate reality is ignored or forgotten by us, we confront it in our everyday life in the form of sorrow and suffering. When it is recognized, realized, and adored by us, we overcome all laws of material existence.

The unity of religions is based on direct perception of ultimate reality. The paths are different but the goal remains the same. Even if the whole world becomes converted to one religion or another, it will not enhance the cause of unity. Unity in diversity is the plan of the universe. Unity of religions calls for our paying attention to the basic teachings of all faiths, which provide us with the common ground where we are all rooted. Our scientific age is forcing us to find this common unity. Either we remain in our isolated religious ghettos or we accept the fact of the innate spiritual unity of all faiths.

Realization of the spiritual unity of humankind begins with ourselves. We may not be able to change the whole world but we can change ourselves. "For the world can be good and pure only if our lives are good and pure. It is an effect, and we are the means. Therefore let us purify ourselves. Let us make ourselves perfect." Unless we begin to see God within, we will never see God without. Again, unless we see God in the hearts of all beings, we will never see God inside ourselves. To serve the less fortunate and think of their well-being is a sacred duty of all human beings. This is the basis of all ethics and morality.

When we discover the Self and look upon every being as the embodiment of that Self, we attain the goal of life and become blessed. Swami Vivekananda tells us that we are not living in the final days of our destiny. We can change our destiny by our knowledge and awareness of our true Self and by our selfless work and spiritual humanism. Vivekananda says, "The education which does not help the common mass of people to equip themselves for the struggle for life, which does not bring out strength of character, a spirit of philanthropy, and the courage of a lion—is it worth the name?" Regaining our spiritual balance may seem hard or impossible, but Vivekananda assures us that it is attainable by our determined effort.

Vivekananda's teachings are based on four fundamental principles: *nonduality of ultimate reality, divinity of the soul, unity of existence,* and *harmony of religions.* Ultimate reality is always *nondual,* and the call for overcoming human separateness and human finitude is innate in all beings. *Divinity of the soul* is the most vital aspect of our lives. We do not become divine by making pilgrimages, bathing in sacred waters, or meticulously performing ceremonies and rituals. The foundation of religion is an implicit faith in our own divinity. Ceremonies and rituals only heighten our faith in this divinity. The difference between a saint and a sinner is that the saint has faith in his saintliness and the sinner has faith in his sins. *Unity of existence* is the law of the universe. Individual selfishness and greed disrupt this unity and endanger even one's own existence. *Harmony of religions* is the corollary of the first three principles. When religion loses its spiritual content all dissensions begin—not before that. Unity of religions cannot be promoted merely by lectures and discourses, conferences and workshops. Until we learn the essence of the teachings of all religions, find a common ground, and live according to these principles, harmony and unity will be a far cry.

The present book will give the reader the essential message of Swami Vivekananda as a world teacher. The first chapter is an article by Swami Nikhilananda, "Swami Vivekananda: India and America," written for the *Swami Vivekananda Centenary Memorial Volume* in 1963 and never before published outside India. It presents Vivekananda's major teachings and introduces us to Vivekananda's ideals of spiritual freedom and spiritual democracy.

Chapter 2, "The Ideal of a Universal Religion," consists of Vivekananda's lectures on his universal vision of religion. He tells us that the different religious systems are not contradictory. "Each religion, as it were, takes up one part of the great universal truth.... I accept all the religions that were in the past and worship with them all; I worship God with every one of them, in whatever form they worship him. I shall go to the mosque of the Mohammedan; I shall enter the Christian church and kneel before the Crucifix; I shall enter the Buddhist temple, where I shall take refuge in Buddha and his Law. I shall go into the forest and sit down in meditation with the Hindu, who is trying to see the light which enlightens the hearts of everyone. Not only shall I do all this, but I shall keep my heart open for all the religions that may come in the future."

Chapter 3 presents Swami Vivekananda's most significant lectures on his ideal of the worship of the living God. The one goal of life—Self-knowledge or God-consciousness—is fulfilled only when a person is able to see God with eyes closed and the same God with eyes open. "Let us be no more the worshippers of creeds or sects with small, limited notions of God, but see him in everything in the universe." Swami Vivekananda warns us against the greatest obstacle to the realization of the universal religion—the claim to spiritual privilege of one sect or individual over another. "All are our fellow travelers.... All are in the same stream; each is hurrying towards that infinite freedom.... The cosmic process means the struggle to get back to freedom, the center of our being."

Chapter 4 brings together Swami Vivekananda's lectures on the great spiritual teachers of the world. God as ultimate reality is always one, and all spiritual seekers, regardless of their religious beliefs and traditions, are calling on the same God. Vivekananda presents his views on the life and teachings of Christ, Buddha, Sri Ramakrishna, and the great prophets and saints of all times. "What wonder," he says, "that I should fall at the feet of these men and worship them as God? ... I should better like that each one of you become a prophet of this real New Testament.... Take all the old messages, supplement them with your own realizations, and become a prophet unto others."

It is not always easy to understand or portray the individuals whose personalities have placed them high above ordinary human experience—these great souls who at different periods of history have stood out among all others, who moved and inspired humankind to noble goals. Chapter 5 intends to capture for the reader a close-up, deeper understanding of the personality that was Vivekananda. Newspaper reports of the time help us appreciate the profound impact Vivekananda had on people and society. Another section presents reminiscences by those who came to know him directly. World thinkers express their impressions of the significance of the life and message of Vivekananda. Through a selection of letters and poems of Vivekananda we get another intimate glimpse of the swami and the ideals that motivated him.

The world today faces a serious crisis, and Swami Vivekananda points out that this crisis is essentially spiritual. Vivekananda the world teacher appeals to thinking people of the world to rise to the occasion and bring about a change and a worldwide spiritual regeneration. "That society is the greatest," he says, "where the highest truths become practical. That is my opinion. And if society is not fit for the highest truths, make it so—and the sooner, the better. Stand up, men and women, in this spirit, dare to believe in the truth, dare to practice the truth!"

It is our hope that readers will derive inspiration from Swami Vivekananda's message of love, compassion, and the spiritual unity of humankind.

Swami Vivekananda at the Parliament of Religions, Chicago, 1893

1

Swami Vivekananda:
India and America

Swami Vivekananda's spiritual mission to America, for which the World's Parliament of Religions held in Chicago in 1893 furnished the impetus, fulfilled a deep-seated need of our times for the welfare of India, America, Europe, and humanity in general. What he preached has been slowly entering into the thought-current of both the East and the West.

The immediate compelling purpose of his visit was the improvement of the material condition of Indian humanity. His wide travel in India as a wandering monk after the passing away of Sri Ramakrishna, his intimate contact with people of all classes—high and low, educated and illiterate, maharajas and pariahs—revealed to his highly sensitive mind the pitiable condition of the Indian masses. They lacked the basic needs of food, education, health, and economic security. The descendants of the once proud Indo-Aryans, whose achievements in religion, philosophy, literature, art, science, and the evolution of an enduring social system still draw the admiration of thoughtful people everywhere, were groveling in the dust. Forgetful of their inner strength, they had

From Swami Nikhilananda, "Swami Vivekananda: India and America," in *Swami Vivekananda Centenary Memorial Volume,* edited by R. C. Majumdar (Calcutta: Swami Vivekananda Centenary Committee, 1963).

become the target of exploitation of the rich and the powerful—both indigenous and foreign. "It is for them," Swami Vivekananda said to his devotees in Madras, "that I am going to the West—for the people and the poor." To two of his brother disciples he remarked in the same strain: "I traveled all over India. But, alas, it was agony to me, my brothers, to see with my own eyes the terrible poverty of the masses, and I could not restrain my tears. It is now my firm conviction that to preach religion among them, without first trying to remove their poverty and suffering, is futile. It is for this reason—to find means for the salvation of the poor of India—that I am going to America."

Night after night he spent without sleep, brooding over India's problems. Many other ideas came to his mind. First and foremost, he realized that religion was not the cause of India's downfall. On the contrary, it was religion which created and stabilized the Indian culture, integrated the divergent elements in the nation, and preserved the Hindus from total disintegration in spite of ruthless domination for nearly a thousand years by alien rulers, giving people the patience and fortitude to remain calm in the vicissitudes of fortune. No amount of poverty could take away their faith in dharma and providence.

Secondly, he saw that India would rise again through religion, occupy her rightful place in the comity of nations, and fulfill the expectation of many Western people: *Ex Oriente lux*. How well it has since been recognized that the modern revival of India started from Dakshineswar.[1]

Thirdly, Swami Vivekananda realized that the fundamental truths of Hinduism could be resuscitated by an intense study of the Upanishads, the Bhagavad Gita, the *Ramayana*, the *Mahabharata*, and other secondary writings. The ignorance of the people regarding these basic works made it possible for unscrupulous priests to exercise their power

---

[1] Dakshineswar Temple Garden, where Sri Ramakrishna lived and communed with God.

over them. This also accounted for the encrustations of the eternal truths of Hinduism with many superstitions. The ancient wisdom must be made accessible to the ignorant and the educated alike.

Fourthly, the great swami clearly saw that no philosophy or religion could be understood if the stomach was empty and the body sick. Everyone needs a certain amount of protein and carbohydrate for higher thinking. How to build the sound body and mind through which spiritual truths could be manifested? His insight at once told him that this could be done with the help of science and technology, which had been highly developed in the West during the past three hundred years. The method of science based upon reasoning, experimentation, observation and verification would enable Indians to understand rationally the nature of the physical universe. By means of technology they would apply these scientific truths for the material welfare of the individual and society. The swami felt he must go to the West and appeal to its conscience. He would tell the people of the West that the sickness and health of India were the concern of the whole world.

But Swami Vivekananda was a proud man. He hated begging. He would not go to the West as a beggar. His penetrating mind realized the plight of the West; though of another kind, it was no less poignant. Science and technology no doubt gave the West material prosperity, but they did not give it inner peace. A materialistic culture contains the seeds of its own destruction. In a competitive society, clamoring for material gain, brother raises his hand against brother. The West must deepen its spiritual outlook, and in this it could be helped by the ancient wisdom of India. Hinduism, Swami Vivekananda thought, could especially teach the West universal compassion, the ideal of seeing unity in diversity, and the harmony of religions.

The swami clearly recognized the achievements and limitations of the culture of both East and West. The Indian climate has, it is true, produced a Buddha, a Shankara, a Chaitanya, a Ramakrishna—something which perhaps it alone can do; but Indian history also reveals the tragic facts of how high an individual can rise and how low a nation can fall. The history of the West, too, reveals the fact that a nation as a whole can attain, through science and technology, a high level of physical comfort and intellectual knowledge, but in the absence of knowledge regarding God, the soul, and the spiritual basis of the universe, it can become a victim of anxiety, fear, and suspicion. India has no doubt discovered many eternal spiritual truths, but she has kept them buried in heaps of filth. There is no appropriate jewel box to preserve them. The West has created a jewel box in the form of a wonderful social, political, and economic organization, but where are the jewels? India often worships a phantom in the name of a soul, and the West a corpse from which the spirit has fled. Thus Swami Vivekananda keenly felt that both the West and India needed each other for their mutual welfare and for the ultimate good of humanity. His message was both national and international. His expanding soul could not be cribbed or confined in any narrow cage.

Swami Vivekananda chose America as the place to give his message. The United States appeared to him suitable for this purpose. Making America his base, he would carry his work to Europe. In his journey to Chicago he received the blessings of both Sri Ramakrishna and Holy Mother.[2] He did not have the support of money, or government, or any organization. This lad of barely thirty, totally inexperienced in the ways of the world, had spent the formative period of his life either at the feet of Sri Ramakrishna or as an unknown wandering monk, practicing meditation and prayer. He had received encouragement from a handful of admirers; a prince who was his disciple supplied him with the passage, the clothes, and some pocket money. But Swami Vivekananda carried with him, besides his knowledge of Western and Indian history and

---

[2] Sri Sarada Devi, wife and spiritual companion of Sri Ramakrishna.

culture, a warm heart, which endeared him to sincere and broad-minded people in the West. Needless to say, his deep spiritual experiences were his most priceless asset.

Sri Ramakrishna, while he was alive, pointed out to his beloved disciple the mission of his life. Once when young Narendranath[3] was eager to forget himself and the world in *samadhi* (total absorption in God), the Master asked him why he was anxious to see God with eyes closed and not with open eyes, adding that service to all beings was the best way to worship God. After the Master's death, the young swami resolved many a time to spend the rest of his life in a mountain cave in contemplation, but every time he went into solitude for this purpose, he was thrown out, as it were, by a powerful force. Evidently his was not to be a life of exclusive meditation. No doubt a part of his mind, like that of his Master, soared above the world, but another part bled at the sight of human suffering. It seldom found a point of rest in its oscillation between contemplation of God and service to all beings. "May I be born and reborn," he once exclaimed, "and suffer a thousand miseries, if only I may worship the only God in whom I believe: the sum total of all souls, and above all, my God the wicked, my God the afflicted, my God the poor of all races." It appears that in obedience to a higher call he chose service to all human beings as his mission on earth, and this choice endeared him to people in the West, the Americans in particular.

At the time of the swami's visits to the West, no two countries showed such diverse characteristics as India and America. The United States was free and democratic; India was a colony of England. In America, education was universal; in India, barely ten percent of the people could read and write. Americans were affluent and prosperous; ninety percent of the Indians hardly ate a square meal. America, following the

---

[3] The premonastic name of Swami Vivekananda.

Anglo-Saxon tradition, upheld the ideal of social justice and individual rights, especially for white Americans; Hindus were oppressed by the tyranny of caste, priestcraft, and wealthy landlords. American women enjoyed a social freedom which was denied to their Indian sisters. In America religion, government, science, and technology were harnessed to promote the welfare of the masses; in India the power of religion and the social system was often used to keep the masses down. Indian culture developed a high degree of intellect. Americans were sentimental. Hindus were imaginative and speculative, Americans pragmatic and practical. The general trend of American philosophy was a revolt against the nineteenth-century romanticism of Europe. In American education, science and technology played an important part; in Indian universities, science was studied for a limited purpose mostly in its theoretical aspect. Following the tradition of the frontier days, Americans, as a rule, were adventurous, alert, resourceful, and given to improvisation. Hindus were generally static in their thinking. The atmosphere of India, even during the worst period of material setback, produced saints and mystics given to contemplation. The American soul expressed itself through action. Buddha, Krishna, Shankara, Chaitanya, and Ramakrishna are still among the national heroes of India; a successful person of the world is admired by the American public. Western science investigated the nature of the universe in order to find the human individual's place in it; Indian philosophers, through the study of the universe, realized its ultimate unreality and directed their minds to the exploration of the inner world. The above characterization may be somewhat oversimplified, but it is nonetheless substantially true.

Within a few days of his arrival in America, Swami Vivekananda became aware of her general world outlook. What tumultuous thoughts must have raced through the mind of this mendicant monk from India when he sat on the platform of the Parliament of Religions facing seven thousand men and women representing what was best and noblest in American culture! He saw the Occidental mind to be young, alert, restless, inquisitive, tremendously honest, well disciplined, and at ease with the physical universe, but skeptical about the profundities of the supersensuous world and unwilling to accept any truth without rational proof and pragmatic tests. Behind him lay the ancient world of India, with its diverse creeds and rituals woven into a complex religio-philosophical system called Hinduism, whose principal concept was unity in diversity; with its saints and prophets, who investigated reality through self-control, nonattachment, and contemplation, unruffled by the passing events of the transitory mundane existence, and who were absorbed in meditation on the eternal verities. The swami's education, upbringing, and personal experience seem to have made him the confluence of these two streams of thought whose apparent conflict he sought to remove.

Perhaps at the outset Swami Vivekananda was a little bewildered. Certainly he was seized with stage fright and postponed his address several times. But as soon as he mounted the rostrum, he felt at ease. Even his first few words, "Sisters and Brothers of America," evoked spontaneous applause from the whole audience that took two full minutes to subside. People were deeply moved to see, at last, a person who discarded formalities and addressed them in a natural way, showing the warmth of his heart. Swami Vivekananda's colorful personality, his orange robe, yellow turban, and youthful face through which might be seen a mature mind, could not but impress the audience. Perhaps he was the youngest among the representatives of the great religions of the world, being only thirty years old.

What Swami Vivekananda said at the Parliament of Religions and at numerous meetings afterwards is now mostly on record. Through his lectures, conversations, and writings he tried not only to remove the colossal ignorance of the Americans regarding Hinduism and India but also to present the positive truths of his ancient religion.

Swami Vivekananda on the platform at the
Parliament of Religions, Chicago, 1893

In his opening address the swami spoke about the validity of all religions as means to reach the same goal of perfection, and in his final speech he asked the religions to give up their claim to exclusive salvation. He wanted every religion to inscribe on its banner: "Help and not fight," "Assimilation and not destruction," "Harmony and peace and not dissension." This noble concept, which was propounded in the Vedas, the Upanishads, and the Bhagavad Gita, was ably demonstrated by his master, Sri Ramakrishna, who was the only prophet in recorded history to practice the disciplines of Hinduism, Christianity, and Islam and to realize that all of them, through their different rituals and beliefs, brought out the potential divinity of human nature.

In his numerous lectures delivered throughout the American continent, Swami Vivekananda continually stressed the divinity of the soul, the oneness of existence, the nonduality of the Godhead, and the harmony of religions. In his doctrine of the divinity of the soul, perceptive Americans found the spiritual basis of freedom and respect for others, highly treasured by them. The concept of oneness of existence, which is the principal teaching of Vedanta, was the spiritual basis of love and such ethical injunctions as fellowship and compassion. Through the realization of this oneness one could get rid of fear, suspicion, hatred, and malice. Through the knowledge that God is one without a second and that the same Godhead is the goal of all faiths, religion could give up bigotry and fanaticism, which, more than anything else, have made it an object of criticism for all rational people. Swami Vivekananda taught Vedanta, which in the final analysis is neither religion nor philosophy but an experience, though it accepts both as suited to the different levels of spiritual evolution. Not created by any mind, it is based upon eternal and immutable laws, coeval with the creation, and discovered by the insight of illumined souls in the depths of their contemplation. But Vedanta also recognizes prophets and incarnations as the demonstrators of eternal truths. Vedanta gives the rationale of rituals, which are the concretization of abstract spiritual truths, necessary for mental concentration. Mythology illustrates philosophy through stories of legendary or semi-historical personages, helps in the development of devotion, and enriches literature, sculpture, painting, and architecture. In Swami Vivekananda's view science, philosophy, or art, if pursued to the end, gives one the vision of the Infinite, provided one accepts the Vedantic concept of the oneness of existence.

Swami Vivekananda's instructions for the development of spiritual consciousness can be summed up in the word *yoga*, which means the union of the individual soul and the Universal Soul, called God, and also the method to realize that union. His approach was psychological. Taking into consideration the four broad divisions of the human mind, he taught the yoga of divine love (bhakti-yoga), the yoga of work (karma-yoga), the yoga of philosophical knowledge (jnana-yoga), and the yoga of the suppression of the modifications of the mind (raja-yoga). He wrote four classic books on these four yogas. They are all based on the solid foundation of moral life, without which no spiritual experience is possible. The special reason for the swami's explaining raja-yoga, which he asked people not to practice without the guidance of a competent teacher, seems to be that he wanted to accept the challenge of the Western intellectuals who demanded proof of religious experiences. The teaching of raja-yoga, he contended, was based upon experimentation and verification of the result. Besides describing raja-yoga in his book, the swami taught it to qualified students in person.

Swami Vivekananda explained to Americans that religion was realization and experience, not mere acceptance of dogmas and creeds, and that one could suppress one's lower desires and realize one's divine nature in this life. He always reminded them of the divinity of the soul and the unity of existence. In order to bring out this divinity one might follow any yoga suited to one's temperament. Scriptures, temples, and rituals were of secondary importance.

In the final session of the Parliament he made a grand appeal for the harmony of religious faiths. He said: "The Christian is not to become a Hindu or a Buddhist, nor is a Buddhist or a Hindu to become a Christian. But each must assimilate the spirit of the others and yet preserve his individuality and grow according to his own law of growth. If the Parliament has shown anything to the world, it is this: It has proved to the world that holiness, purity, and charity are not the exclusive possessions of any church in the world, and that every system has produced men and women of the most exalted character. In the face of this evidence, if anybody dreams of the exclusive survival of his own religion and the destruction of the others, I pity him from the bottom of my heart."

Never in the course of his preaching did Swami Vivekananda condemn the true spirit of any religion, though he bitterly attacked hypocrisy and false appearance. In the Parliament of Religions he really stood as a champion of all religions and not just as a preacher of Hinduism. A Jewish intellectual who had attended the Parliament said later to the present writer: "After hearing Swami Vivekananda I realized that my religion was also true." The swami's admiration for Jesus Christ was unbounded. Even before his appearance at the Parliament, when he had been suffering from acute poverty, he wrote to a worried friend in India: "I am here amongst the children of the Son of Man, and the Lord Jesus will help me." He began his famous seminar at Thousand Island Park with a quotation from the Gospel of St. John, as his students belonged to the Christian faith. But he was intolerant of what is often preached in the name of Christianity, especially by missionaries abroad. Bigoted Christians in America, the missionaries, and their patrons savagely attacked Swami Vivekananda, often traducing his personal character. He was equally blunt in his rejoinder. In a speech given in Detroit, he declared angrily: "You train and educate and clothe and pay men to do what?—to come over to my country and abuse all my forefathers, my religion, my everything. They walk near a temple and say, 'You idolaters, you will go to hell.' But the Hindu is mild; he smiles and passes on, saying, 'Let the fools talk.' And then you, who train men to abuse and criticize, if I touch you with the least bit of criticism but with the kindest purpose, you shrink and cry: 'Do not touch us! We are Americans; we criticize, curse, and abuse all the heathens of the world, but do not touch us, we are sensitive plants.' And whenever your missionaries criticize us, let them remember this: If all India stands up and takes all the mud that lies at the bottom of the Indian Ocean and throws it up against the Western countries, it will not be doing an infinitesimal part of what you are doing to us."

Referring to the part played by the missionaries in the colonial adventures of some of the European nations, Swami Vivekananda said:

"Such things tumble down; they are built upon sand; they cannot remain long. Everything that has selfishness for its basis, competition for its right hand, and enjoyment as its goal, must die sooner or later.

"If you want to live, go back to Christ. You are not Christians. No, as a nation you are not. Go back to Christ. Go back to him who had nowhere to lay his head. Yours is a religion preached in the name of luxury. What an irony of fate! Reverse this if you want to live; reverse this. You cannot serve God and Mammon at the same time. All this prosperity—all this from Christ! Christ would have denied all such heresies. If you can join these two, this wonderful prosperity with the ideal of Christ, well and good; but if you cannot, better go back to him and give up these vain pursuits. Better be ready to live in rags with Christ than to live in palaces without him."

Swami Vivekananda could not stomach one major doctrine of Christianity, namely the doctrine of sin. It was repulsive to the very basis of Vedanta, which calls all men and women "Children of Immortality." The swami called sins mistakes due to ignorance. Mountain-high sin is reduced to ashes the moment the fire of divine knowledge is lighted. No soul can ever be tied down to the earth. How can a so-called sinner, in whom also the light of God shines, though he may not be aware of it for the time being, be condemned forever to hell? Does not every sinner have a future, as every saint has a past?

When Swami Vivekananda's heart was at its most expansive he would say: "Buddhas and Christs are mere waves in the infinite Ocean of Existence that I am," or, "I do not want to Hinduize the world or to Christianize it: but I want to My-ize the world, that's all."

How did America respond to Swami Vivekananda and his teachings? Hundreds of meetings that he addressed were attended by, among others, professors from universities, ladies of good families, seekers of truth, and devotees of God with childlike faith. But mixed with these were curiosity-seekers, idlers, vagabonds, and charlatans. The American public, by and large, is receptive. That is why this country is a hotbed of various religious beliefs. The swami had to face all kinds of obstacles. The opposition of the Christian vested interests has already been mentioned. The leaders of many crankish, selfish, and fraudulent organizations tried to induce the swami to embrace their causes, first by promises of support, and then by threats of injury when he refused their offers. He was also challenged by many so-called free-thinkers, among whom were atheists, agnostics, rationalists, and materialists. But the swami was not to be intimidated—"the sickle had hit on a stone," as the Polish proverb says. To all opposition the swami's only answer was: "I stand for truth. Truth will never ally itself with falsehood. Even if the whole world should be against me, truth must prevail at the end."

Swami Vivekananda was a "cyclonic" lecturer. But he often got tired of people, excitement, and lectures. A born philosopher and lover of God, he wanted to train a few serious students in Vedanta, who would broadcast his ideas. He felt disgusted to bring himself down to suit anybody's or any audience's fad.

But the swami's personality was irresistible, whether one agreed with him or not. Those who came in contact with him could not forget him. Even today after over half a century one meets people who saw or heard him perhaps once or twice. They cherish that memory. How many people are moved today by merely reading his words! Romain Rolland said: "His words are like great music, phrases in the style of Beethoven, stirring rhythms like the march of Handel choruses. I cannot touch these sayings of his, scattered as they are through the pages of books at thirty years' distance, without receiving a thrill through my body like an electric shock. And what shocks, what transports, must have been produced when in burning words they issued from the lips of the hero."

Swami Vivekananda came to know many notables in the Western world: Max Müller, Paul Deussen, Robert Ingersoll, Nikola Tesla, William Thomson (afterwards Lord Kelvin), Sarah Bernhardt, Madame Emma Calvé. He was, however, deeply moved by the generous nature of the American people. A few of his devoted friends cheerfully assumed responsibility for his personal comfort. He was particularly impressed, as we shall see later on, by the warm affection of American women. Though he often admired the friendship and steady loyalty of the British, the artistic sensitivity of the French, the philosophical acumen of the Germans, and the various cultural monuments of Europe, yet his heart seemed to be devoted to America. In one of his letters written to an American woman devotee in May 1896, he said: "I love the Yankee land. I like to see new things. I do not care a fig to loaf about old ruins and mope a life out about old histories and keep sighing about the ancients. I have too much vigor in my blood for that. In America is the place, the people, the opportunity, for everything new. I have become horribly radical."

The full effect of Swami Vivekananda's teachings in America will be known only in years to come. Even now one can see a healthy beginning in the spread of Vedantic ideas. Vedanta societies in many of the major cities of America and retreats under the spiritual guidance of swamis of the Ramakrishna Order of monks are disseminating the truths of Hinduism. They are helping in the spiritual development of individuals. American monks and nuns have joined the Ramakrishna Order and taken the vows of poverty and chastity. Books about Hinduism are being published. The swamis are often invited to universities, colleges, churches, and other cultural organizations to discuss the ancient wisdom of India. Slowly Hindu ideas and ideals are entering into American minds. What the representatives of other faiths said at the Parliament of Religions has been practically forgotten. But the teachings of Vedanta are growing in volume and intensity.

Religion and the idealism inspired by it have played an important part in the creation of American culture and in its subsequent development. Certain spiritual concepts later presented by Swami Vivekananda had already begun to ferment underneath the robust, picturesque, gay, and dynamic surface of American life. The ideals of freedom, equality, and fellow feeling had always stirred American hearts. To these ideals, which Americans applied in politics and society for their material welfare, Swami Vivekananda gave a spiritual interpretation.

It is well known that the Pilgrim Fathers who crossed the Atlantic in the Mayflower and landed at Plymouth, Massachusetts, in the chilly November of 1620, were English people who had first left England and gone to Holland for freedom of worship. Later they were joined by other dissenters who could not submit to the restrictions placed upon their religious beliefs by the English rulers of the time. They were the forebears of the sturdy, religious-minded New Englanders who, two centuries later, were the leaders of the intellectual spiritual culture of America. Swami Vivekananda found among them some of his loyal and enthusiastic followers. Many of the Huguenots, too, who had left France in the seventeenth century, later went to America and found religious asylum there.

Both the Holy Bible and the philosophy of John Locke influenced the Bill of Rights and the American Constitution. Jefferson, imbued with the ideal of the Fatherhood of God and the brotherhood of men, and also agnostic Benjamin Franklin and atheistic Thomas Paine, penned the second paragraph of the Declaration of Independence, which clearly sets forth its political philosophy, namely, the equality of men before God, society, and the law, and waged an uncompromising war against tyranny. The same passion for social equality and justice was later to permeate the utterances of the great Lincoln, and the New Deal and the four Freedoms of Franklin D. Roosevelt. The very structure of the American federal government is opposed to the colonial system of the European powers. American society is free, in a remarkable degree, from the tyranny of the caste system of India or the class system of Europe. Here almost every citizen enjoys a minimum standard of social security, and no limitation is placed in the way of material success provided that the person is intelligent, ethical, and industrious.

During the first hundred years after gaining her independence, America produced a galaxy of great persons in various fields: politics and war, law and jurisprudence, science and technology, history and literature, business and practical affairs. With their aid and in the absence of foreign wars, America gained an unprecedented material prosperity. The country's vast hidden wealth was tapped. Towns grew into cities. Ambition stirred everywhere and the people's very manners changed with the new haste and energy that swept them on.

Material prosperity was accompanied by a new awakening of people's minds and consciousness. Jails were converted into penitentiary systems based upon humanitarian principles, and anti-slavery societies were inaugurated. During the five years between 1850 and 1855 were published some of the greatest books in American literature, such as *Leaves of Grass*, *The Scarlet Letter*, and *Moby Dick*, hardly surpassed in imaginative vitality. The crude frontier days were fast disappearing.

Meanwhile India entered into the rapidly growing thought-current of nineteenth-century America and contributed her share, however small. India and America had not been complete strangers. Everybody knows that Columbus set out to find a short route to India and stumbled upon America instead. What is not so well known is the fact that the chests of tea of the Boston Tea Party, which set off the War of Independence, came from India. Moreover, the victory of the English over the French during the eighteenth century in the war for the domination of India by the two great colonial powers made it easy for England to withdraw from America, and thus helped the American colonists in their struggle for freedom begun in 1775. Again, Commodore Perry made it possible, in 1853, for American merchant ships to trade with the Far East and then visit coastal towns on their long journeys.

On the cultural side, the Transcendental movement, of which Emerson was the leader, and Thoreau, Channing, Whittier, and Alcott, his associates, brought spiritual India into contact with the new continent. Emerson, a keen student of the Bhagavad Gita, was familiar with the Upanishadic doctrines, as evidenced by his beautiful poem "Brahma" and his essay "The Over-Soul." Thoreau, Emerson's neighbor for twenty-five years, read and discussed with him the Hindu religious classics. "I bathe my intellect," wrote Thoreau, "in the stupendous and cosmogonal philosophy of the Upanishads and the Bhagavad Gita, in comparison with which our modern world and literature seem to be puny and trivial." Alcott was instrumental in bringing out the American edition of Sir Edwin Arnold's *The Light of Asia*. The Transcendental Club, founded in Concord, near Boston, reached its height by 1840. The American Oriental Society was established in 1842. Walt Whitman, whom Swami Vivekananda once called "the sannyasin of America," wrote about the identity of living beings and seems to have come very near to Vedantic idealism. There is, however, no evidence to show that he was influenced by Hindu thought. A great religious individualist, he was free from all church conventions and creeds. To him religion consisted entirely of inner illumination, "the secret silent ecstasy." It should be noted, further, that the Unitarian religious movement of New England was encouraged by Raja Rammohan Roy of India.

Both Emerson and Thoreau dreamt about a marriage of East and West that would usher in a new culture, a new step in human progress. But for various reasons this marriage did not immediately take place. India came under the rule of the British crown in 1858. In America the Gold Rush of 1849 and the discovery of other fabulous resources underground, such as coal, oil, and iron, diverted people's attention to new directions. Then there was the Civil War, in which brother fought against brother and the passions of human minds were let loose. It preserved the Union but destroyed the aristocratic society of the South, especially in Virginia, which was once called the mother of American presidents. The slaves were emancipated and the Yankees of the North began to pour in to capture economic fields.

The publication of Darwin's *Origin of Species* in 1859 made a greater impression in America than in Europe. Intellectual people's religious convictions were profoundly disturbed. Technology developed more rapidly in the United States than on the Continent. All these waves, coming one after another, turned American thought into new channels. During the rude frontier days, when America was comparatively poor, she somehow preserved her spiritual sensitivity. But during and after the Civil War the idea of possessing "bigger and better" things cast its spell everywhere. Big utilities and corporations came into existence; the idealistic and romantic glow of the first century of American independence degenerated into the sordidness of competitive materialistic life; while the unceasing flow of immigrants from Europe made the stabilization of American culture difficult.

Emerson and Whitman were disillusioned by the aftermath of the Civil War. But the innate idealism and religious consciousness of the

Americans could not be destroyed either by the triumph of science or by material prosperity. Thoughtful Americans began to look for a philosophy which could harmonize the diverse claims of science, humanism, and mystical experience. The philosophy of Vedanta preached by Swami Vivekananda seemed to show the way, at least to some, to this reconciliation. Perhaps this accounts for the spontaneous welcome received by this representative of Hinduism in 1893 and afterwards.

Americans are by no means irreligious people. By and large they are God-fearing. They go to church and respect holiness. Even in a remote village there are two or more churches of different denominations. Though in America church and state are separate, the country is by no means a secular one. The American currency bears the inscription: "In God We Trust." Statesmen and public leaders often speak of America as a Christian country, in spite of the fact that a powerful section of her citizens is non-Christian. Congress, like the British Parliament, opens with a prayer from the official chaplain, and the presidents of the United States attend church services on Sundays. Most colleges and universities have chapel services in which the students and the faculty members join. At the inauguration of the president of the United States, divine blessings are invoked.

One must not judge the spiritual endeavor of the American people by the standard set up by a Buddha or a Ramakrishna, who are too lofty for most religious aspirants anywhere. Often students come to the Vedantist swamis in America with a sincere longing for inner illumination, and the present writer, for one, feels humble in their presence. No; Americans are by no means irreligious, though their religious ideals and disciplines are different from those of the Hindus.

Swami Vivekananda was not unaware of the materialistic aspect of Western society, which was especially encouraged by the rapid growth of science, technology, and industrialism. Similarly he was conscious of the evil elements in Hindu society and criticized them bitterly. He warned the West of imminent catastrophe, and his ominous prophecy that it was sitting on the crater of a smoldering volcano came true within fifty years of his death, with the two great world wars. In the following poem which he wrote on board a ship while passing through the Mediterranean Sea on his way back to India from his last visit to America, he hints of his mental distress caused by the sensate culture of the West and also of his nostalgic yearning for the peace of India.

On the Sea's Bosom

In blue sky floats a multitude of clouds—
White, black, of many shades and thicknesses;
An orange sun, about to say farewell,
Touches the massed cloud-shapes with streaks of red.

The wind blows as it lists, a hurricane
Now carving shapes, now breaking them apart:
Fancies, colors, forms, inert creations—
A myriad scenes, though real, yet fantastic.

There light clouds spread, heaping up spun cotton,
See next a huge snake, then a strong lion;
Again, behold a couple locked in love.
All vanish, at last, in the vapory sky.

Below, the sea sings a varied music,
But not grand, O India, nor ennobling:
Thy waters, widely praised, murmur serene
In soothing cadence, without a harsh roar.

Day in and day out Swami Vivekananda exhorted America and Europe to realize the unsubstantiality of the physical world, to give up greed and lust for power, to go back to God, and cultivate universal charity. *Azad*, or spiritual freedom, was the recurring topic of his lectures and discourses.

Most of the swami's years abroad were spent in America. There he worked incessantly, truly burning his candle at both ends. Often tired of the hectic life in the competitive American society, he longed for India. In 1897 he returned to his beloved Motherland. What impressions did he carry to India from his foreign experiences and how did he try to incorporate them into Indian life for its betterment?

The compelling purpose of his visit to America was not immediately fulfilled. He did not bring with him either money or knowledge of science and technology for the improvement of the condition of the Indian masses. India was still under the domination of an alien power. Political conditions were not favorable for foreign aid on a vast scale. But half a century after the swami's visit, when India became free, his dream showed signs of fulfillment. India has been sending thousands of students to the New World and Europe to acquire advanced knowledge of science and technology. American money is being spent to improve the material condition of the people. On the other hand, Americans have also welcomed with affection and respect swamis of the Ramakrishna Order to guide them in their spiritual life.

Swami Vivekananda carried with him many precious memories of America: the memory of sweet friendships, unflinching devotion, and warm appreciation; the memory of a society based on the ideals of equality, justice, and freedom, where a person—in sad contrast with India—was given every opportunity to develop his or her highest potentialities; the memory of the refinement attained by many people in intellectual knowledge, human relationships, and artistic taste; the memory of common people enjoying a high standard of living and their well-earned prosperity, unimaginable in any other part of the world; the memory of the American mind, alert, inquisitive, daring, and receptive. He saw in Americans sparks of spirituality which kindled at his magic words. He was impressed to see the generous confidence and richness of heart manifested through the pure and candid souls who gave themselves to him once they recognized him as a trustworthy and honorable man; who became slaves of his love and did not shrink from the highest sacrifice to help in the fulfillment of his mission.

America gave Swami Vivekananda his first recognition, and he was aware of it. She gave him this priceless asset to help him in his Herculean work in India—an authority which, it appears, he did not have before in the land of his birth. Though he came to America as a giver, he now, in a sense, returned to India as a gift from the New World. The wisdom of India which he planted in the heart of the English-speaking world, in New York and London, started the building of the spiritual bridge between East and West of which Swami Vivekananda dreamt.

The swami returned to India on January 15, 1897, and received a hero's welcome. He at once set himself to the task of planning for the country's regeneration. Till the hour of his death in 1902, he worked without respite, in spite of broken health, addressing numerous meetings from Colombo to Almora, organizing the Ramakrishna Mission and guiding its members in their spiritual practices, starting various relief activities, and giving instruction to many spiritual seekers. The awakening of the country from the slumber of ages became his most absorbing passion.

Swami Vivekananda once spoke of himself as a "condensed India." His adoration of India was not, however, the idolatry of geography. He loved India, where his ancestors had developed great ideas about the nature of the soul and God and followed the disciplines of renunciation and service. The soul of the mystical Orient, India was his "playground of childhood, pleasure garden of youth, and Varanasi of old age." His love of India was not confined merely to the glories of the past, but expressed itself equally through his warm sympathy for present-day Indians, oppressed and hungry. He regarded himself as brother to all Indians, including the illiterate, the untouchable and the poor.

With the clear vision of a prophet the swami realized that religion would play a vital part in the creation of a new India, and that it would be her mission to the world. An aggressive Hinduism, inspired by the Vedantic ideal of the divinity of the soul, would give Indians a renewed faith in themselves. By focusing the national energy on science, technology, and industrialization, in order to catch up with Europe and America, and neglecting her spiritual culture, India would be at best a poor imitation of the West. He did not condemn India's past; on the other hand he exhorted the Indians to build the superstructure of future progress on the solid foundation of past achievements. He knew very well that to see far into the future of one's country, one must look far into its past.

It is unrealistic to condemn a culture for three centuries of failure, forgetting its achievements of three thousand years. The Hindus have always shown respect to all faiths and allowed their devotees complete freedom in the practice of religious disciplines. India is a veritable Parliament of Religions. The bogey of Hinduism as a communal religion has no basis in fact. It is the most universal religion ever developed on earth. A good Hindu shows the same respect to other faiths as to his or her own. To be sure, one sees fanaticism here and there, as among the followers of any religion; but this is not at all the Hindu spirit. Its main cause is ignorance and also the instinct for self-preservation, developed by Hindu society during the period of ruthless foreign domination.

Swami Vivekananda asked the Hindus to familiarize themselves with the teachings of the Upanishads and the Bhagavad Gita, which would remove the contemporary superstition and the narrow outlook of bigoted Hindus. If Hinduism based upon the scriptures is taught in schools and colleges side by side with the sciences and humanities, what is incompatible with the progress of the country in the modern world will be discarded. A comparative study of religion will remove many erroneous ideas about other faiths and make real contributions to the promoting of mutual respect. Hinduism is not opposed to material

prosperity or rational knowledge. When India was spiritually creative and virile, she was also materially prosperous and achieved remarkable success in the physical sciences, art, literature, sculpture, and
philosophy.

India with her diverse communities can be integrated only on a spiritual foundation; economic, political, or social devices will help in
implementing this integration. The caustic critics of the Hindu caste system emphasize the evils of this grand social organization, whose real
purpose was the promotion of harmony among people of different tem-
peraments and aptitudes. It protected the weak from exploitation by the
rich and the powerful. Through the caste system Hindu philosophers
indicated the supremacy of spirituality and intellect over militarism,
wealth, and organized labor. The caste system, by its rigid rules, preserved Hindu society from total disintegration during the period of foreign domination. It is a law of the relative world that power always
corrupts, and the caste system was no exception. The Hindu ideal is to
raise all, by education and spiritual discipline, to the level of true brahmins. The present-day iniquities of the caste system must be removed
by appropriate laws, but modern India must not give up the ideal of the
leadership of society by persons of spirituality and intellect. Such leaders can be drawn from all levels of society. Swami Vivekananda, a few
hours before his passing away, made the significant remark: "India is
immortal if she persists in her search for God. But if she goes in for politics and social conflict, she will die."

As we have already stated, from the moment Swami Vivekananda
touched Indian soil on his return from the West, he devoted himself
to the task of the country's regeneration. He had studied America's economic system, industrial organization, educational institutions, muse-
ums and art galleries, her progress in science, technology, hygiene, and
social welfare work, and he called on his country to adopt them in keeping with India's spiritual ideals. Having a premonition of his fast

approaching death, he planted the ideas only in seminal form, leaving the details to others to work out. The two things uppermost in his mind were the masses and the women of India. He felt very sad when he contrasted their condition with what he had seen in America.

He was full of admiration for American women. In one letter he said in his usual enthusiastic way: "Nowhere in the world are women like those of this country. How pure, independent, self-reliant, and kind-hearted! It is the women who are the life and soul of this country. All learning and culture are centered in them." In another letter: "[Americans] look with veneration upon women, who play a most prominent part in their lives. Here this form of worship has attained its perfection—this is the long and short of it. I am almost at my wit's end to see the women of this country. They are Lakshmi, the goddess of fortune, in beauty, and Saraswati, the goddess of learning, in virtues—they are the Divine Mother incarnate. If I can raise a thousand such Madonnas—incarnations of the Divine Mother—in our country before I die, I shall die in peace. Then will our countrymen become worthy of their name." And in a third letter: "How many beautiful homes I have seen, how many mothers whose purity of character, whose unselfish love for their children, are beyond expression, how many daughters and pure maidens, 'pure as the icicle on Diana's temple'—and withal much culture, education, and spirituality in the highest sense!... There are good and bad everywhere, true—but a nation is not to be judged by its weaklings, called the wicked, for they are only the weeds which lag behind, but by the good, the noble, and the pure, who indicate the national life-current to be flowing clear and vigorous."

His heart bled at the sight and thought of the poverty of the Indian masses. "No religion on earth," he wrote angrily, "preaches the dignity of humanity in such a lofty strain as Hinduism, and no religion on earth treads upon the necks of the poor and the lowly in such a fashion as Hinduism. Religion is not at fault, but it is the Pharisees and the

Sadducees." When one day in New York he saw a millionaire lady sitting in a tram-car side by side with a woman with a wash-basket on her lap, he was impressed with the democratic spirit of the Americans. He wanted in India "an organization that will teach the Hindus mutual help and appreciation" after the pattern of Western democracies. He envisaged New India arising "out of the cottage of the peasant grasping the plough, out of the huts of the fishermen, the cobbler, and the sweeper. Let her spring from the grocer's shop, from beside the oven of the fritter-seller. Let her emanate from the factory, from marts and markets. Let her emerge from the groves and the forests, from hills and mountains." Swami Vivekananda had tremendous faith in the common people, who, through the oppression of hundreds of years, had developed great fortitude and vitality. If they had enough to eat, he thought, they would revolutionize the country. Though poverty generally destroys a people's virtues, yet they had stored up wonderful strength that came out of a pure and moral life which was not to be found anywhere else in the world. All that the people of India needed was good education and worldly security to manifest again the refinement in taste, intellect, and human relationship which is the pride of Western society.

Swami Vivekananda constantly exhorted the leaders to feel for the poor, to regard them as God, to work for them and pray for them. He asked them to take the vow to devote their whole lives to the cause of the three hundred million, going down and down every day. "So long," he wrote, "as the millions live in hunger and ignorance, I hold every man a traitor who, having been educated at their expense, pays not the least heed to them." Swami Vivekananda disliked the idea of pity for the poor. He asked the leaders to render service to them in a spirit of worship as taught by Sri Ramakrishna. It was he who coined the phrase *Daridra Narayana*, the Lord in the form of the poor.

The swami wanted *sannyasins* [Hindu monks] to devote themselves to improving the condition of the masses, instead of preaching religion to them all the time. He saw that thousands of men clothed in the garb of monks were floating like moss over the stagnant water of India's national life. How wonderful it would be if these world-renouncers went to the villages and taught them—side by side with religion—history, geography, hygiene, improved agriculture, and elementary sciences. He knew very well that religion does not take root in empty bellies. He made it a rule that the monks of the Ramakrishna Order, in addition to the traditional monastic vow of the liberation of the self, should take a second vow of dedicating themselves to the service of humanity.

America's opulence, achieved through hard work, moral discipline, and cooperative effort, impressed the swami. In a moment of apparent despair, surveying the Indian situation, he wrote to an American devotee that he would like to infuse some of the American spirit into India, "that awful mass of conservative jelly-fish, and then throw overboard all old associations and start a new thing, entirely new—simple, strong, new and fresh as the first-born baby—throw all of the past overboard and begin anew."

India must learn new things from the West, but not by sacrificing her own national heritage. The swami said: "You put the seed in the ground and give it plenty of earth and air and water to feed upon; when the seed grows into the plant, does it become the earth, does it become the air, or does it become the water? It becomes the mighty plant, the mighty tree, after its own nature, having absorbed everything that was given to it. Let that be your position." Swami Vivekananda was aware of India's need of foreign help. But he had his own idea about it. He said: "By preaching the profound secrets of Vedanta in the Western world, we shall attract the sympathy and regard of these mighty nations, maintaining for ourselves the position of their teachers in spiritual matters; let them remain our teachers in all material concerns. Nothing will come of crying day and night before them, 'Give me this' or 'Give me that.' When there grows a link of sympathy and regard between both nations by this give-and-take intercourse, there will be then no need for these noisy cries. They will do everything of their own accord. I believe that by this cultivation of religion and the wider diffusion of Vedanta, both our country and the West will gain enormously." If Indian students, scholars, and members of the diplomatic services present before the American and European public the true spirit of Hinduism, there will be created a tremendous fund of goodwill and respect for India. The Indians will no longer be stigmatized as "under-developed" people. It should be noted that Hinduism will be appreciated in America when India improves her material condition. Americans are practical people. They want to see how a religion functions in daily life. The Hindu dharma never supports poverty. Nonattachment is its ideal, and not poverty, except the voluntary poverty of genuine monks.

Swami Vivekananda firmly believed that Vedanta would help to resolve the conflict between religion and science. Modern science is the creation of the Western mind. The scientific era was inaugurated more than three hundred years ago by such eminent scientists as Copernicus, Galileo, and Newton, when they began their investigation of the laws controlling natural events. This tradition has been carried on up to the present time by many brilliant scientists. The one great implication of their research is that natural phenomena are explained by natural laws without the aid of any supernatural factors. This gave a severe blow to many of the religious beliefs which dominated Western minds before that time. The goal of modern science is to understand the nature of the universe and derive power from that knowledge for the betterment of the human condition. Science has delved into the structure of atoms as well as the vast space outside.

The theory of evolution propounded by Darwin is a great landmark in the scientific thinking of our age. Sailing in the *Beagle* in 1832, as the naturalist for a surveying expedition, he carried on his research in the

Galapagos Islands. He examined fossils, bones, and living animals, and found a gradual evolution of species through natural selection, adaptation, struggle for existence, and other means, without intervention from any supernatural agency. According to the evolution theory, as Sir Julian Huxley puts it, all aspects of reality are subject to evolution, from atoms and stars, to fish and flowers, from fish and flowers to human societies and values—indeed, all reality is a single process of evolution. The human being is the highest dominant type to be produced by billions of years of slow biological improvement effected by the automatic and blindly opportunistic workings of natural selection without any conscious effort on the human being's part. Matter has evolved into life and life into mind, though no scientist has yet been able to create in the laboratory life from non-life. The evolution theory has profoundly influenced all aspects of Western thinking: religious, philosophical, social, economic, and political. Physical science gives a purely mechanistic and materialistic interpretation of the human being and the universe.

The prestige of science rests mainly on the scientific method and the development of technology. By the former, a thing is explained not by any extraneous factor, but by reference to itself. It repudiates the outside authority employed by religion. Certainly the scientific method has revolutionized our thinking. The most tangible effect of technology, which has cast its spell upon the modern mind, is seen in the healing of many diseases, heretofore considered incurable, the general improvement of health and longevity, the preservation of physical vitality even in old age, the promotion of education and inter-communication, and the creation of many creature comforts never dreamt of before.

But some deep thinkers are realizing the limitations of science and the evil effect of the unbridled growth of technology. Science is not omnipotent or omniscient. The mere advancement of technology cannot be the panacea for all human evils. It can be truthfully said that though science has greatly helped us to understand the physical aspect of the human being and the universe, it has left out their essential elements, namely, the soul and God, or Universal Intelligence. The conclusions of science are not incorrect, but they are inadequate. The primal cause, or the Absolute, is outside the realm of science, which deals only with the manifestation. When science speaks of a cause, such as that of a comet or of rain, it means that science can forecast the appearance of a comet or control the rainfall. Certain deep values cherished by the human individual, such as aesthetic sensitivity, moral perfection, and self-transcendence in communion with the Infinite, are outside its jurisdiction.

Swami Vivekananda was fully aware of the implications of modern science and technology, both beneficial and harmful. Realizing their need in modern India, he wanted to turn the Belur Math[4] into a finished university where Western sciences and Hindu mysticism would be studied side by side. He asked Indians to go to the West for scientific knowledge. He also pointed out that certain of the important scientific truths were known to the ancient Indian thinkers, though presented in a form which may appear crude to the modern mind.

Swami Vivekananda knew well that India, the heart of the Orient, with all her lofty spiritual realizations, had not solved her national problems; nor had America, the leader of the progressive West, solved her problems in spite of great achievements in science and technology. Every problem is being realized today as a part of the world problem; no problem can be solved piecemeal. Therefore East and West should sit together in a spirit of humility and pool their efforts to solve the world problem, always bearing in mind the Vedantic ideal of the solidarity of all human

---

[4] Belur Math is the home and headquarters of the Ramakrishna Order, Calcutta, India, founded by Swami Vivekananda.

beings and the unity of existence. The fact that the world is one was realized long ago by Hindu philosophers and is now being hinted at by modern science. Science and religion must work in harmony to bring out the spiritual potentialities of every human being.

Swami Vivekananda, New York, 1895

2

The Ideal of a Universal Religion

The Way to the Realization of the Universal Religion
(Delivered at the Universalist Church, Pasadena, California,
January 28, 1900)

No search has been dearer to the human heart than that which brings to us light from God. No study has taken so much human energy, whether in times past or present, as the study of the soul, of God, and of human destiny. However deeply immersed we are in our daily occupations, in our ambitions, in our work, sometimes in the midst of the greatest of our struggles there comes a pause; the mind stops and wants to know something beyond this world. Sometimes it catches glimpses of a realm beyond the senses, and a struggle to get at it is the result. Thus it has been throughout the ages in all countries. Man has wanted to look beyond, wanted to expand himself; and all that we call progress, evolution, has always been measured by that one search, the search for human destiny, the search for God.

As our social struggles are represented, among different nations, by different social organizations, so man's spiritual struggles are represented by various religions. And as different social organizations are constantly quarrelling, are constantly at war with each other, so these spiritual

33

organizations have been constantly at war with each other, constantly quarrelling. Men belonging to a particular social organization claim that the
right to live belongs only to them, and so long as they can, they want to
exercise that right at the cost of the weak. We know that just now there is
a fierce struggle of that sort going on in South Africa.[1] Similarly each religious sect has claimed the exclusive right to live. And thus we find that
though nothing has brought man more blessings than religion, yet at the
same time there is nothing that has brought him more horror than religion. Nothing has made more for peace and love than religion; nothing
has engendered fiercer hatred than religion. Nothing has made the brotherhood of man more tangible than religion; nothing has bred more bitter enmity between man and man than religion. Nothing has built more
charitable institutions, more hospitals for men and even for animals, than
religion; nothing has deluged the world with more blood than religion.

We know, at the same time, that there has always been an opposing
undercurrent of thought; there have always been parties of men, philosophers, students of comparative religion, who have tried and are still trying to bring about harmony in the midst of all these jarring and
discordant sects. As regards certain countries these attempts have succeeded, but as regards the whole world they have failed. Then again,
there are some religions, which have come down to us from the remotest
antiquity, imbued with the idea that all sects should be allowed to live—
that every sect has a meaning, a great idea, imbedded in it, and therefore all sects are necessary for the good of the world and ought to be
helped. In modern times the same idea is prevalent, and attempts are
made from time to time to reduce it to practice. But these attempts do
not always come up to our expectations, up to the required efficiency.
Nay, to our great disappointment, we sometimes find that we are quarrelling all the more.

---

[1] A reference to the Boer War.

Now, leaving aside dogmatic study and taking a common-sense view of the thing, we find at the start that there is a tremendous life-power in all the great religions of the world. Some may say that they are unaware of this; but ignorance is no excuse. If a man says, "I do not know what is going on in the external world, therefore the things that are said to be going on there do not exist," that plea is inexcusable. Now, those of you who are watching the movement of religious thought all over the world are perfectly aware that not one of the great religions of the world has died. Not only so; each one of them is progressing. The Christians are multiplying, the Mohammedans are multiplying, and the Hindus are gaining ground; the Jews also are increasing in numbers, and as a result of their activities all over the world, the fold of Judaism is constantly expanding.

Only one religion of the world—an ancient, great religion—is dwindling away, and that is the religion of Zoroastrianism, the religion of the ancient Persians. After the Mohammedan conquest of Persia, about a hundred thousand of these people came to India and took shelter there, and some remained in Persia. Those who were in Persia, under the constant persecution of the Mohammedans, dwindled till there are at most only ten thousand. In India there are about eighty thousand of them, but they do not increase. Of course, there is an initial difficulty: they do not convert others to their religion. And then, this handful of persons living in India, with the pernicious custom of cousin-marriage, does not multiply. With this single exception, all the great religions are living, spreading, and increasing.

We must remember that all the great religions of the world are very ancient—not one has been formed at the present time—and that every religion of the world had its origin in the region between the Ganges and the Euphrates. Not one great religion has arisen in Europe; not one in America—not one. Every religion is of Asiatic origin and belongs to that part of the world. If what the modern scientists say is true, that the survival of the fittest is the test, these religions prove by

their still being alive that they are yet fit for some people. And there is
a reason why they should live: they bring good to many. Look at the
Mohammedans, how they are spreading in some places in southern
Asia, and spreading like wildfire in Africa. The Buddhists are spreading over central Asia all the time. The Hindus, like the Jews, do not convert others; still, gradually other races are coming within Hinduism and
adopting the manners and customs of the Hindus and falling into
line with them. Christianity, you all know, is spreading—though I am
not sure that the results are equal to the energy put forth. The Christians' attempt at propaganda has one tremendous defect, and that is the
defect of all Western institutions: the machine consumes ninety percent
of the energy; there is too much machinery. Preaching has always been
the business of the Asiatics. The Western people are grand in organization—social institutions, armies, governments, and so forth. But when
it comes to preaching religion, they cannot come near the Asiatics,
whose business it has been all the time—and they know it, and do
not use too much machinery.

This, then, is a fact in the present history of the human race: that all
these great religions exist and are spreading and multiplying. Now, there
is a meaning, certainly, to this; and had it been the will of an all-wise
and all-merciful creator that one of these religions should alone exist
and the rest die, it would have become a fact long, long ago. If it were
a fact that only one of these religions was true and all the rest were false,
by this time it would have covered the whole world. But this is not so;
not one has gained all the ground. All religions sometimes advance,
sometimes decline. Now, just think of this: in your own country there
are more than sixty millions of people, and only twenty-one millions
profess a religion of some sort. So it is not always progress. In every country, probably, if the statistics were taken, you would find that religions
sometimes progress and sometimes go back. Sects are multiplying all
the time. If the claim of any one religion that it has all the truth, and

that God has given it all that truth in a certain book, be true, why then are there so many sects? Not fifty years pass before there are twenty sects founded upon the same book. If God has put all the truth in certain books, he does not give us those books in order that we may quarrel over texts. That seems to be the fact. Why is this? Even if a book were given by God which contained all the truth about religion, it would not serve the purpose, because nobody could understand the book. Take the Bible, for instance, and all the sects that exist among the Christians. Each one puts its own interpretation upon the same text, and each says that it alone understands that text and all the rest are wrong. So with every religion. There are many sects among the Mohammedans and among the Buddhists, and hundreds among the Hindus.

Now, I place these facts before you in order to show you that any attempt to bring all humanity to one method of thinking in spiritual things has been a failure and always will be a failure. Every man who starts a theory, even at the present day, finds that if he goes twenty miles away from his followers they will make twenty sects. You see that happening all the time. You cannot make all conform to the same ideas: that is a fact, and I thank God that it is so. I am not against any sect. I am glad that sects exist, and I only wish they may go on multiplying more and more. Why? Simply because of this: If you and I and all who are present here were to think exactly the same thoughts, there would be no thoughts for us to think. We know that two or more forces must come into collision in order to produce motion. It is the clash of thought, the differentiation of thought, that awakes thought. Now, if we all thought alike, we should be like Egyptian mummies in a museum, looking vacantly at one another's faces—no more than that. Whirls and eddies occur only in a rushing, living stream. There are no whirlpools in stagnant, dead water.

When religions are dead, there will be no more sects; it will be the perfect peace and harmony of the grave. But so long as mankind thinks, there will be sects. Variation is the sign of life, and it must be there. I pray that sects may multiply so that at last there will be as many sects as human beings and each one will have his own method, his individual method of thought, in religion.

Such a situation, however, exists already. Each one of us is thinking in his own way. But this natural thinking has been obstructed all the time and is still being obstructed. If the sword is not used directly, other means are used. Just hear what one of the best preachers in New York says. He preaches that the Filipinos should be conquered because that is the only way to teach Christianity to them! They are already Catholics; but he wants to make them Presbyterians, and for this he is ready to lay all this terrible sin of bloodshed upon his race. How terrible! And this man is one of the greatest preachers of this country, one of the best-informed men. Think of the state of the world when a man like that is not ashamed to stand up and utter such arrant nonsense; and think of the state of the world when an audience cheers him. Is this civilization? It is the old bloodthirstiness of the tiger, the cannibal, the savage, coming out once more under new names in new circumstances. What else can it be? If such is the state of things now, think of the horrors through which the world passed in olden times, when every sect was trying, by every means in its power, to tear to pieces the other sects. History shows that the tiger in us is only asleep; it is not dead. When opportunities come it jumps up and, as of old, uses its claws and fangs. Apart from the sword, apart from material weapons, there are weapons still more terrible: contempt, social hatred, and social ostracism.

Now, these afflictions that are hurled against persons who do not think exactly in the same way we do are the most terrible of all afflictions. And why should everybody think just as we do? I do not see any reason. If I am a rational man, I should be glad that they do not think just as I do. I do not want to live in a grave-like land. I want to be a man in a world of men. Thinking beings must differ; difference is the first sign of thought. If I am a thoughtful man, certainly I ought to like to live among thoughtful persons, where there are differences of opinion.

Then arises the question: How can all this variety be true? If one thing is true, its negation is false. How can contradictory opinions be true at the same time? This is the question which I intend to answer. But I shall first ask you: Are all the religions of the world really contradictory? I do not mean the external forms in which great thoughts are clad. I do not mean the different buildings, languages, rituals, books, and so forth, employed in various religions, but I mean the internal soul of every religion. Every religion has a soul behind it, and that soul may differ from the soul of another religion; but are they contradictory? Do they contradict or supplement each other?—that is the question.

I took up this question when I was quite a boy, and have been studying it all my life. Thinking that my conclusion may be of some help to you, I place it before you. I believe that they are not contradictory; they are supplementary. Each religion, as it were, takes up one part of the great, universal truth and spends its whole force in embodying and typifying that part of the great truth. It is therefore addition, not exclusion. That is the idea. System after system arises, each one embodying a great ideal; ideals must be added to ideals. And this is how humanity marches on.

Man never progresses from error to truth, but from truth to truth— from lesser truth to higher truth, but never from error to truth. The child may develop more than the father; but was the father inane? The child is the father plus something else. If your present stage of knowledge is much higher than the stage you were in when you were a child, would you look down upon that earlier stage now? Will you look back and call it inanity? Your present stage is the knowledge of childhood plus something more.

Then again, we know that there may be almost contradictory points of view of a thing, but they all point to the same thing. Suppose a man is journeying towards the sun and as he advances he takes a photograph of the sun at every stage. When he comes back, he has many photographs of the sun, which he places before us. We see that no two are alike; and yet who will deny that all these are photographs of the same sun, from different standpoints? Take four photographs of this church from different corners. How different they would look. And yet they would all represent this church. In the same way, we are all looking at truth from different standpoints, which vary according to our birth, education, surroundings, and so on. We are viewing truth, getting as much of it as these circumstances will permit, coloring it with our own feelings, understanding it with our own intellects, and grasping it with our own minds. We can know only as much of truth as is related to us, as much of it as we are able to receive. This makes the difference between man and man and sometimes even occasions contradictory ideas. Yet we all belong to the same great, universal truth.

My idea, therefore, is that all these religions are different forces in the economy of God, working for the good of mankind, and that not one can become dead, not one can be killed. Just as you cannot kill any force in nature, so you cannot kill any one of these spiritual forces. You have seen that each religion is living. From time to time it may retrogress or go forward. At one time it may be shorn of a good many of its trappings; at another time it may be covered with all sorts of trappings. But all the same, the soul is ever there; it can never be lost. The ideal which every religion represents is never lost, and so every religion is intelligently on the march.

And that universal religion about which philosophers and others have dreamt in every country already exists. It is here. As the universal brotherhood of man already exists, so also does the universal religion. Which of you, that have traveled far and wide, have not found brothers and sisters in every nation? I have found them all over the world. Brotherhood already exists; only there are numbers of persons who fail to see this and upset it by crying for new brotherhoods. The universal religion, too, already exists. If the priests and other people who have taken upon themselves the task of preaching different religions simply cease preaching for a few moments, we shall see it is there. They are disturbing it all the time, because it is to their interest.

You see that the priests in every country are very conservative. Why is this so? There are very few priests who lead the people; most of them are led by the people and are their slaves and servants. If you say it is dry, they say it is dry; if you say it is black, they say it is black. If the people advance, the priests must advance. They cannot lag behind. So before blaming the priests—it is the fashion to blame the priests—you ought to blame yourselves. You get only what you deserve. What would be the fate of a priest who wanted to give you new and advanced ideas and lead you forward? His children would probably starve and he would be clad in rags. He is governed by the same worldly laws that you are governed by. If you move on, he says, "Let us march."

Of course, there are exceptional souls, not cowed by public opinion. They see the truth, and the truth alone they value. Truth has got hold of them, has got possession of them, as it were, and they cannot but march ahead. They never look backward. And they do not pay heed to people. God alone exists for them; he is the light before them and they are following that light.

I met a Mormon gentleman in this country who tried to convert me to his faith. I said: "I have great respect for your opinions, but in certain points we do not agree. I belong to a monastic order, and you believe in marrying many wives. But why don't you go to India to preach?" He was simply astonished. He said, "Why, you don't believe in any marriage at all, and we believe in polygamy, and yet you ask me to go to your country!" I said: "Yes. My countrymen will hear any religious thought, wherever it may come from. I wish you would go to India. First, because I am a great believer in sects. Secondly, there are many men in

India who are not at all satisfied with any of the existing sects, and on account of this dissatisfaction they will not have anything to do with religion; and possibly you might get some of them."

The greater the number of sects, the more chance of people's becoming religious. In a hotel, where there are all sorts of food, everyone has a chance to have his appetite satisfied. So I want sects to multiply in every country, that more people may have a chance to be spiritual.

Do not think that people do not like religion. I do not believe that. The preachers cannot give them what they need. The same man who may have been branded as an atheist, as a materialist, or what not, may meet a man who gives him the truth needed by him, and he may turn out the most spiritual man in the community. We can eat only in our own way. For instance, we Hindus eat with our fingers. Our fingers are suppler than yours; you cannot use your fingers the same way. Not only should the food be supplied; it should also be taken in your own particular way. Not only must you have the spiritual ideas; they must also come to you according to your own method. They must speak your own language, the language of your soul, and then alone will they satisfy you. When the man comes who speaks my language and gives me the truth in my language, I at once understand it and receive it forever. This is a great fact.

Now, from this we see that there are various grades and types of human minds—and what a task the religions take upon themselves! A man brings forth two or three doctrines and claims that his religion ought to satisfy all humanity. He goes out into the world, God's menagerie, with a little cage in hand, and says: "Man and the elephant and everybody have to fit into this. Even if we have to cut the elephant into pieces, he must go in." Again, there may be a sect with a few good ideas. It says, "All men must come in!" "But there is no room for them." "Never mind! Cut them to pieces; get them in anyhow; if they don't get in, why, they will be damned." No preacher, no sect, have I ever met that paused and asked, "Why is it that people do not listen to us?" Instead they curse them and say, "The people are wicked." They never ask: "How is it that people do not listen to my words? Why can I not make them see the truth? Why can I not speak in their language? Why can I not open their eyes?" Surely they ought to know better, and when they find that people do not listen to them, if they curse anybody it should be themselves. But it is always the people's fault! They never try to make their sect large enough to embrace every one.

Therefore we at once see why there has been so much narrow-mindedness, the part always claiming to be the whole, the little, finite unit always laying claim to the infinite. Think of little sects, born only a few hundred years ago, out of fallible human brains, making this arrogant claim of knowing the whole of God's infinite truth! Think of the arrogance of it! If it shows anything, it shows how vain human beings are. And it is no wonder that such claims have always failed, and by the mercy of the Lord are always destined to fail.

We are such babies! We always forget human nature. When we begin life we think that our fate will be something extraordinary, and nothing can make us disbelieve that. But when we grow old we think differently. So with religions. In their early stages, when they spread a little, they get the idea that they can change the minds of the whole human race in a few years, and they go on killing and massacring to make converts by force. Then they fail and begin to understand better. These religions did not succeed in what they started out to do, which was a great blessing. Just think! If one of those fanatical sects had succeeded all over the world, where would man be today? The Lord be blessed that they did not succeed! Yet each one represents a great truth; each religion represents a particular excellence, something which is its soul.

There is an old story which comes to my mind: There were some ogresses who used to kill people and do all sorts of mischief; but they themselves could not be killed until someone should find out that their souls were in certain birds and so long as the birds were alive nothing could destroy the ogresses. So each one of us has, as it were, such a bird, where his soul is—has an ideal, a mission to perform in life. Every human being is an embodiment of such an ideal, such a mission. Whatever else you may lose, so long as that ideal is not lost and that mission is not hurt, nothing can kill you. Wealth may come and go, misfortunes may be piled mountain high, but if you have kept the ideal pure, nothing can kill you. You may have grown old, even a hundred years old, but if that mission is fresh and young in your heart, what can kill you? But when that ideal is lost and that mission is forgotten, nothing can save you. All the wealth, all the power of the world will not save you.

And what are nations but multiplied individuals? So each nation has a mission of its own to perform in this harmony of races, and so long as a nation keeps to that ideal, nothing can kill that nation. But if the nation gives up its mission and goes after something else, its life becomes short and ultimately it vanishes.

And so with religions. The fact that all these old religions are living today proves that they must have kept that mission intact. In spite of all their mistakes, in spite of all difficulties, in spite of all quarrels, in spite of all the incrustation of forms and rituals, the heart of every one of them is sound—it is a throbbing, beating, living heart. They have not lost, any of them, the great mission they came for. And it is splendid to study that mission. Take Mohammedanism, for instance. As soon as a man becomes a Mohammedan, the whole nation of Islam receives him as a brother with open arms, without making any distinction, which no other religion does. If one of your American Indians became a Mohammedan, the Sultan of Turkey would have no objection to dining with him. If he has brains, no position would be barred to him. In this country I have never yet seen a church where the white man and the Negro can kneel side by side to pray. Just think of that: Islam makes its followers all equal. So that, you see, is the peculiar excellence of

Mohammedanism. In many places in the Koran you find very sensual ideas of life. Never mind. What Mohammedanism comes to preach to the world is this practical brotherhood of all belonging to their faith. That is the essential part of the Mohammedan religion; and all the other ideas, about heaven and of life and so forth, are not real Mohammedanism. They are accretions.

With the Hindus you will find one great idea: spirituality. In no other religion, in no other sacred books in the world, will you find so much energy spent in defining the idea of God. They tried to describe God in such a way that no earthly touch might mar him. The spirit must be divine; and spirit, as such, must not be identified with the physical world. The idea of unity, of the realization of God, the omnipresent, is preached throughout. They think it is nonsense to say that God lives in heaven, and all that. That is a mere human, anthropomorphic idea. All the heaven that ever existed is now and here. One moment in infinite time is quite as good as any other moment. If you believe in a God, you can see him even now. We Hindus think that religion begins when you have realized something. It is not believing in doctrines or giving intellectual assent or making declarations. If there is a God, have you seen him? If you say no, then what right have you to believe in him? If you are in doubt whether there is a God, why do you not struggle to see him? Why do you not renounce the world and spend the whole of your life for this one object? Renunciation and spirituality are the two great ideals of India, and it is because India clings to these ideals that all her mistakes count for so little.

With the Christians, the central idea that has been preached by them is the same: "Watch and pray, for the kingdom of heaven is at hand"— which means: Purify your minds and be ready. You recollect that the Christians, even in the darkest days, even in the most superstitious Christian countries, have always tried to prepare themselves for the coming of the Lord by trying to help others, building hospitals, and so on. So long as the Christians keep to that ideal, their religion lives.

Now, an ideal presents itself to my mind. It may be only a dream. I do not know whether it will ever be realized in this world; but sometimes it is better to dream a dream than to die on hard facts. Great truths, even in a dream, are good—better than bad facts. So let us dream a dream.

You know that there are various grades of mind. You may be a matter-of-fact, commonsense rationalist. You do not care for forms and ceremonies; you want intellectual, hard, ringing facts, and they alone will satisfy you. Then there are the Puritans and the Mohammedans, who will not allow a picture or a statue in their place of worship. Very well. But there is another man who is more artistic. He wants a great deal of art—beauty of lines and curves, colors, flowers, forms; he wants candles, lights, and all the insignia and paraphernalia of ritual, that he may see God. His mind grasps God in those forms, as yours grasps him through the intellect. Then there is the devotional man, whose soul is crying for God; he has no other idea but to worship God and to praise him. Then again, there is the philosopher, standing outside all these things, mocking at them. He thinks: "What nonsense they are! What ideas about God!"

They may laugh at each other, but each one has a place in this world. All these various minds, all these various types, are necessary. If there is ever going to be an ideal religion, it must be broad and large enough to supply food for all these minds. It must supply the strength of philosophy to the philosopher, the devotee's heart to the worshipper; to the ritualist it must give all that the most marvelous symbolism can convey; to the poet it must give as much of heart as he can absorb, and other things besides. To make such a broad religion, we shall have to go back to the very source and take them all in.

Our watchword, then, will be acceptance and not exclusion. Not only toleration; for so-called toleration is often blasphemy and I do not believe in it. I believe in acceptance. Why should I tolerate? Toleration means that I think that you are wrong and I am just allowing you to live. Is it not a blasphemy to think that you and I are allowing others to live? I accept all the religions that were in the past and worship with them all; I worship God with every one of them, in whatever form they worship him. I shall go to the mosque of the Mohammedan; I shall enter the Christian church and kneel before the Crucifix; I shall enter the Buddhist temple, where I shall take refuge in Buddha and his Law. I shall go into the forest and sit down in meditation with the Hindu, who is trying to see the light which enlightens the hearts of everyone.

Not only shall I do all this, but I shall keep my heart open for all the religions that may come in the future. Is God's Book finished? Or is revelation still going on? It is a marvelous Book—these spiritual revelations of the world. The Bible, the Vedas, the Koran, and all other sacred books are but so many pages, and an infinite number of pages remain yet to be unfolded. I shall leave my heart open for all of them. We stand in the present, but open ourselves to the infinite future. We take in all that has been in the past, enjoy the light of the present, and open every window of the heart for all that will come in the future. Salutation to all the prophets of the past, to all the great ones of the present, and to all that are to come in the future!

The Ideal of a Universal Religion
(Delivered at the Hardman Hall, New York, January 12, 1896)

Wheresoever our senses reach or whatsoever our minds imagine, we find therein the action and reaction of two forces, the one counteracting the other and thus causing the constant play of the mixed phenomena which we see around us or which we feel in our minds. In the external world, the action of these opposite forces expresses itself as attraction and repulsion, or as the centripetal and centrifugal forces; and in the internal, as love and hatred, good and evil. We repel some things, we attract others. We are attracted by one; we are repelled by another. Many times in our lives we find that without any reason whatsoever, we are, as it were, attracted towards certain persons; at other times, similarly, we are repelled by others. This is patent to all; and the higher the field of action, the more potent, the more remarkable, are the influences of these opposite forces.

Religion is the highest plane of human thought and life, and herein we find that the workings of these two forces have been most marked. The intensest love that humanity has ever known has come from religion, and the most diabolical hatred that humanity has known has also come from religion. The noblest words of peace that the world has ever heard have come from men on the religious plane, and the bitterest denunciation that the world has ever known has been uttered by religious men. The higher the goal of any religion and the finer its organization, the more remarkable are its activities. No other human motive has deluged the world with so much blood as religion; at the same time, nothing has brought into existence so many hospitals and asylums for the poor, no other human influence has taken such care, not only of humanity, but also of the lowest of animals, as religion. Nothing makes us so cruel as religion, and nothing makes us so tender as religion. This has been so in the past and will also, in all probability, be so in the future.

Yet out of the midst of this din and turmoil, this strife and struggle, this hatred and jealousy of religions and sects, there have arisen, from time to time, potent voices drowning all this noise—making themselves heard from pole to pole, as it were—proclaiming peace and harmony.

Will it ever come? Is it possible that there should ever reign unbroken harmony in this plane of mighty religious struggle? The world is exercised in the latter part of this century by the question of harmony. In society various plans are being proposed, and attempts are made to carry them into practice. But we know how difficult it is to do so. People find that it is almost impossible to mitigate the fury of the struggle of life, to tone down the tremendous nervous tension that is in man. Now, if it is so difficult to bring harmony and peace on the physical plane of life—the external and gross side of it—then it must be a thousand times more difficult to bring harmony and peace to rule over the internal nature of man.

I would ask you for the time being to come out of the network of words. We have all been hearing from childhood of such things as love, peace, charity, equality, and universal brotherhood; but they have become to us mere words without meaning, words which we repeat like parrots; and it has become quite natural for us to do so. We cannot help it. Great souls, who first felt these great ideas in their hearts, created these words; and at that time many understood their meaning. Later on, ignorant people took up those words to play with them, and they made religion a mere play with words and not a thing to be carried into practice. It has become "my father's religion," "our nation's religion," "our country's religion," and so forth. It has become part of patriotism to profess a certain religion; and patriotism is always partial.

To bring harmony into religion must always be difficult. Yet we shall consider this problem of the harmony of religions.

We see that in every religion there are three parts—I mean in every great and recognized religion. First, there is the philosophy, which presents the whole scope of that religion, setting forth its basic principles, its goal, and the means of reaching that goal. The second part is mythology, which is philosophy made concrete. It consists of legends relating to the lives of men or of supernatural beings, and so forth. It is abstract philosophy made concrete through the more or less imaginary lives of men and supernatural beings. The third part is ritual. This is still more concrete and is made up of forms and ceremonies, various physical attitudes, flowers and incense, and many other things that appeal to the senses.

You will find that all recognized religions have these three elements. Some lay more stress on one, some on another.

Let us now take into consideration the first part, philosophy. Is there one universal philosophy? Not yet. Each religion brings out its own doctrines and insists upon them as being the only true ones. And not only does it do that, but it thinks that he who does not believe in them must go to some horrible place. Some will even draw the sword to compel others to believe as they do. This is not through wickedness, but through a particular disease of the human brain, called fanaticism. They are very sincere, these fanatics, the most sincere of human beings; but they are quite as irresponsible as other lunatics in the world. This disease of fanaticism is one of the most dangerous of all diseases. All the wickedness of human nature is roused by it. Anger is stirred up, nerves are strung high, and human beings become like tigers.

Is there any mythological similarity, any mythological harmony, any universal mythology accepted by all religions? Certainly not. All religions have their own mythology; only each of them says, "My stories are not mere myths." Let us try to understand the matter through an illustration. I simply mean to illustrate; I do not mean to criticize any religion.

The Christian believes that God took the shape of a dove and came down to earth; to him this is history and not mythology. The Hindu believes that God is manifested in the cow. Christians say that to believe so is mere mythology, and not history; that it is superstition. The Jews think that if an image is made in the form of a box or a chest, with an angel on either side, then it may be placed in the Holy of Holies; it is sacred to Jehovah. But if the image is made in the form of a beautiful man or woman, they say, "This is a horrible idol; break it down!" This is our unity in mythology! Again, if a man stands up and says, "My prophet did such and such a wonderful thing," others will say, "That is only superstition." But at the same time they say that their own prophet did still more wonderful things, which they hold to be historical. Nobody in the world, as far as I have seen, is able to make out the fine distinction between history and mythology as it exists in the brains of these persons. All such stories, to whatever religion they may belong, are really mythological—mixed up occasionally, it may be, with a little history.

Next come the rituals. One sect has one particular form of rituals and thinks that they are holy whereas the rituals of another sect are simply arrant superstition. If one sect worships a peculiar sort of symbol, another sect says, "Oh, it is horrible." Take, for instance, a common Hindu symbol: the phallus. This is certainly a sex symbol; but gradually that aspect of it has been forgotten, and it stands now as a symbol of the creator. Those Hindus who use this as their symbol never connect it with sex; to them it is just a symbol, and there it ends. But a man from another race or creed sees in it nothing but the phallus, and condemns it; yet at the same time he may be doing something which to the so-called phallus-worshippers appears most horrible. Let me take two cases for illustration: the phallus symbol and the sacrament of the Christians. To the Christians the phallus is horrible, and to the Hindus the Christian sacrament is horrible. They say that the Christian sacrament, the killing of a man and the eating of his flesh and the drinking of his blood to get the good qualities of that man, is cannibalism. This is what some of the savage tribes do. If a man is brave, they kill him and eat his heart, because they think that it will give them the qualities of courage and bravery possessed by that man. Even such a devout Christian as Sir John Lubbock admits this and says that the origin of this Christian symbol is in this primitive idea. Most Christians, of course, do not admit this view of its origin, and what it originally implied never comes to their mind. It stands for a holy thing, and that is all they care about. So even in rituals there is no universal symbol which can command general recognition and acceptance.

Where, then, is there any universality in religion? How is it possible, then, to have a universal form of religion? I am convinced, however, that that form of religion already exists. Let us see what it is.

We all hear about universal brotherhood, and how societies spring up especially to preach it. I remember an old story. In India, wine drinking is considered very bad. There were two brothers who one night wished to drink wine secretly; and their uncle, who was a very orthodox man, was sleeping in a room quite close to theirs. So before they began to drink they said to each other, "We must be very quiet, or Uncle will wake up." When they were drinking they continued repeating to each other, "Silence! Uncle will wake up," each trying to shout the other down. And as the shouting increased, the uncle woke up, came into the room, and discovered the whole thing.

Now, we all shout like these drunken men: "Universal brotherhood! We are all equal; therefore let us make a sect." As soon as you make a sect you protest against equality, and equality is no more. Christians talk of universal brotherhood; but anyone who is not a Christian must go to that place where he will be eternally barbecued. And so we go on in this world in our search after universal brotherhood and equality.

When you hear such talk in the world, I would ask you to be a little reticent, to take care of yourselves, for behind all this talk is often the intensest selfishness. "In the winter sometimes a thunder-cloud comes up; it roars and roars, but it does not rain. But in the rainy season the clouds speak not, but deluge the world with water." So those who are real workers and who really feel at heart the universal brotherhood of man do not talk much, do not make little sects for universal brotherhood; but their acts, their movements, their whole life, show clearly that they in truth possess the feeling of brotherhood for mankind, that they have love and sympathy for all. They do not speak, they *do* and they *live*. This world is too full of blustering talk. We want a little more earnest work and less talk.

So far we see that it is hard to find any universal features in regard to religion; and yet we know that they exist. We are all human beings, but are we all equal? Certainly not. Who says we are equal? Only the lunatic. Are we all equal in our brains, in our powers, in our bodies? One man is stronger than another; one man has more brain-power than another. If we are all equal, why is there this inequality? Who made it? We ourselves. Because we have more or less powers, more or less brains, more or less physical strength, these must make a difference between us. Yet we know that the doctrine of equality appeals to our hearts. We are all human beings; but some are men, and some are women. Here is a black man, there is a white man; but all are men, all belong to one humanity. Various are our faces; I see no two alike; yet we are all human beings. Where is this one humanity? I find a man or a woman either dark or fair; and among all these faces, I know that there is an abstract humanity common to all. I may not find it when I try to grasp it, perceive it, and actualize it, yet I know for certain that it is there. If I am sure of anything, it is of this humanity which is common to us all. It is through this common entity that I see you as a man or a woman.

So it is with this universal religion which runs through all the various religions of the world in the form of God; it must and does exist through eternity. "I am the thread that runs through all these pearls," and each pearl is a religion or even a sect thereof. These are the different pearls, and the Lord is the thread that runs through all of them; only the majority of mankind are entirely unconscious of it.

Unity in variety is the plan of the universe. We are all men, and yet we are all distinct from one another. As a part of humanity I am one with you, and as Mr. So-and-so I am different from you. As a man you are separate from woman; as a human being you are one with woman. As a human being you are separate from the animals; but as living beings man, woman, and animal are all one. And as existence you are one with the whole universe. That universal existence is God, the ultimate unity in the universe. In him we are all one. At the same time, in manifestation these differences must always remain. In our work, in our energies as they are being manifested outside, these differences must always remain.

We find, then, that if by the idea of a universal religion it is meant that one set of doctrines should be believed in by all mankind, it is wholly impossible; it can never be. There can never be a time when all faces will be the same. Again, if we expect that there will be one universal mythology, that also is impossible; it cannot be. Neither can there be one universal ritual. Such a state of things can never come into existence. If it ever did, the world would be destroyed, because variety is the first principle of life.

What makes us beings endowed with forms? Differentiation. Perfect balance would be destruction. Take, for instance, the heat in this room, whose tendency is towards equal diffusion; suppose it gets that kind of diffusion; then for all practical purposes that heat will cease to be. What makes motion possible in this universe? Lost balance. Complete sameness can come only when this universe is destroyed; otherwise such a thing is impossible. Not only so; it would be dangerous to have it. We must not wish that all of us should think alike. There would then be no thought to think; we should all be alike, as the Egyptian mummies in a museum are, looking at each other without a thought to think. It is this difference, this differentiation, this losing of sameness between us, which is the very soul of our progress, the soul of all our thought. This must always be.

What, then, do I mean by the ideal of a universal religion? I do not mean any one universal philosophy or any one universal mythology or any one universal ritual held alike by all; for I know that this world must go on working, wheel within wheel, this intricate mass of machinery, most complex, most wonderful. What can we do then? We can make it run smoothly, we can lessen the friction, we can grease the wheels, as it were. How? By recognizing the natural necessity of variation. Just as we have recognized unity as our very nature, so we must also recognize variation. We must learn that truth may be expressed in a hundred thousand ways, and that each of these ways is true as far as it goes. We must learn that the same thing can be viewed from a hundred different standpoints and yet be the same thing. Take for instance the sun. Suppose a man standing on the earth looks at the sun when it rises in the morning; he sees a big ball. Suppose he starts on a journey towards the sun and takes a camera with him, taking photographs at every stage of his journey until he reaches the sun. The photographs of each stage will be seen to be different from those of the other stages; in fact, when he gets back, he brings with him so many photographs of so many different suns, as it would appear; and yet we know that the same sun was photographed by the man at the different stages of his progress.

Even so is it with the Lord. Through high philosophy or low, through the most exalted mythology or the grossest, through the most refined ritualism or arrant fetishism, every sect, every soul, every nation, every religion, consciously or unconsciously is struggling upward towards God; every vision of truth that man has is a vision of him and of none else. Suppose we all go with vessels in our hands to fetch water from a lake. One has a cup, another a jar, another a bucket, and so forth, and we all fill our vessels. The water in each case naturally takes the form of the vessel carried by each of us. He who brought the cup has the water in the form of a cup; he who brought the jar—his water takes the shape of a jar; and so forth. But in every case, water, and nothing but water, is in the vessel. So it is with religion. Our minds are like these vessels, and each one of us is trying to arrive at the realization of God. God is like that water filling these different vessels, and in each vessel the vision of God takes the form of the vessel. Yet he is one. He is God in every case. This is the only recognition of universality that we can get.

So far it is all right theoretically; but is there any way of practically working out this harmony in religions? We find that this recognition that all the various views of religion are true is very, very old. Hundreds of attempts have been made in India, in Alexandria, in Europe, in China, in Japan, in Tibet, and lastly in America, to formulate a harmonious religious creed to make all religions come together in love. They have all failed, because they did not adopt any practical plan. Many have admitted that all the religions of the world are right, but they show no practical way of bringing them together so as to enable each of them to maintain its own individuality in the conflux. That plan alone is practical which does not destroy the individuality of any man in religion and at the same time shows him a point of union with all others. But so far all the plans of religious harmony that have been tried, while proposing to take in all the various views of religion, have in practice tried to bind them all down to a few doctrines, and so have produced more new sects, fighting, struggling, and pushing against each other.

I have also my little plan. I do not know whether it will work or not; and I want to present it to you for discussion. What is my plan? In the first place I would ask mankind to recognize this maxim: "Do not destroy." Iconoclastic reformers do no good to the world. Break not, pull not anything down; but build. Help, if you can; if you cannot, fold your hands and stand by and see things go on. Do not injure if you cannot render help. Say not a word against any man's convictions so far as they are sincere. Secondly, take man where he stands, and from there give him a lift. If it is true that God is the center of all religions and that each of us is moving towards him along one of these radii, then it is certain that all of us must reach that center; and at the center, where all the radii meet, all our differences will cease. But until we reach it, differences there must be. All these radii converge upon the same center. One, according to his nature, travels along one of these lines, and another along another; and if we all push onward along our own lines, we shall surely come to the center, because "all roads lead to Rome."

Each of us is naturally growing and developing according to his own nature; each will in time come to know the highest truth; for after all, men must teach themselves. What can you and I do? Do you think you can teach even a child? You cannot. The child teaches himself. Your duty is to afford opportunities and to remove obstacles. A plant grows. Do you make the plant grow? Your duty is to put a hedge round it and see that no animal eats it up; and there your duty ends. The plant grows of itself. So is it in regard to the spiritual growth of every man. None can teach you; none can make a spiritual man of you. You have to teach yourself; your growth must come from inside. What can an external teacher do? He can remove the obstructions a little; and there his duty ends. Therefore help, if you can; but do not destroy. Give up all ideas that you can make men spiritual. It is impossible. There is no other teacher for you than your own soul. Recognize this.

What comes of it? In society we see so many different natures. There are thousands and thousands of varieties of minds and inclinations. A thorough generalization of them is impossible, but for our practical purpose it is sufficient to have them divided up into four classes. First, there is the active man, the worker; he wants to work, and there is tremendous energy in his muscles and his nerves. His aim is to work—to build hospitals, do charitable deeds, make streets, plan and organize. Then there is the emotional man, who loves the sublime and the beautiful to an excessive degree. He loves to think of the beautiful, to enjoy the aesthetic side of nature, to love and adore the God of love. He loves with his whole heart the great souls of all times, the prophets of religion, and the incarnations of God on earth. He does not care whether reason can or cannot prove that Christ or Buddha existed. He does not care for the exact date when the Sermon on the Mount was preached, or for the exact moment of Krishna's birth. What he cares for is their personalities, their lovable figures. Such is his ideal. This is the nature of the lover, the emotional man. Then there is the mystic, whose mind wants to analyze its own self, to understand the workings of the human mind—what the forces are that are working inside—and how to know, manipulate, and obtain control over them. This is the mystical mind. And finally there is the philosopher, who wants to weigh everything and use his intellect even beyond the possibilities of human thinking.

Now, a religion, to satisfy the largest portion of mankind, must be able to supply food for all these various types of minds; and where this capability is wanting, the existing sects all become one-sided. Suppose you go to a sect which preaches love and emotion. They sing and weep, and preach love. But as soon as you say: "My friend, that is all right, but I want something stronger than this, a little reason and philosophy; I want to understand things step by step and more rationally"—"Get out!" they say, and they not only ask you to get out but would send you to the other place if they could. The result is that that sect can only help people of an emotional turn of mind. They not only do not help others, but try to destroy them. And the most wicked part of the whole thing is that they not only will not help others, but do not believe in their sincerity. Again, there are philosophers who talk of the wisdom of India and the East and use big psychological terms, fifty syllables long; but if an ordinary man like me goes to them and says, "Can you tell me anything to make me spiritual?" the first thing they will do will be to smile and say: "Oh, you are too far below us in your reason. What can you understand about spirituality?" These are high-up philosophers. They simply show you the door. Then there are the mystical sects, who speak all sorts of things about different planes of existence, different states of mind, and what the power of the mind can do, and so on. If you are an ordinary man and say: "Show me something good that I can do. I am not much given to speculation; can you give me anything that will suit me?" they will smile, and say: "Listen to that fool! He knows nothing; his existence is for nothing." And this is going on everywhere in the world. I should like to get extreme exponents of all these different sects and shut them up in a room and photograph their beautiful derisive smiles! This is the existing condition of religion, the existing condition of things.

What I want to propagate is a religion that will be equally acceptable to all minds. It must be equally philosophic, equally emotional, equally mystical, and equally conducive to action. If professors from the colleges come—or scientific men and philosophers—they will court reason. Let them have it as much as they want. There will be a point beyond which they will discover they cannot go without breaking with reason. If they say, "These ideas of God and salvation are superstitions; give them up," I shall reply, "Mr. Philosopher, this body of yours is a bigger superstition. Give it up. Don't go home to dinner or to your philosophic chair. Give up the body, and if you cannot, cry quarter and sit down." Religion must be able to show how to realize the knowledge that teaches that this world is one, that there is but one existence in the universe. Similarly, if the mystic comes, we must welcome him, be ready to teach him the science of mental analysis, and practically demonstrate it before him. If emotional people come, we must sit with them and laugh and weep in the name of the Lord; we must "drink the cup of love and become mad." And if the energetic worker comes, we must work with him with all the energy that we have. And this combination will be the ideal, the nearest approach to a universal religion.

Would to God that all men were so constituted that in their minds all these elements—of philosophy, mysticism, emotion, and work— were equally present in full. That is the ideal, my ideal of a perfect man. Everyone who has only one or two of these elements I consider partial and one-sided. This world is almost full of such one-sided men, who possess knowledge of that one road only in which they move, and to whom anything else is dangerous and horrible. To become harmoniously balanced in all these four directions is my ideal of religion. And this ideal is attained by what we in India call yoga—union. To the worker, it is union between himself and the whole of humanity; to the mystic, the union between his lower self and higher Self; to the lover, union between himself and the God of love; and to the philosopher, the unity of all existence. That is what is meant by yoga. This is a Sanskrit term, and these four divisions of yoga have, in Sanskrit, different names. The man who seeks after this kind of union is called a yogi. The worker is called the karma-yogi. He who seeks union through love is called a bhakti-yogi. He who seeks it through mysticism is called a raja-yogi. And he who seeks it through philosophy is called a jnana-yogi. So this word *yogi* comprises them all.

Now, first of all let me take up raja-yoga. What is this raja-yoga, this controlling of the mind? In this country you associate all sorts of hob-goblins with the word yoga. I am afraid, therefore, I must start by telling you that it has nothing to do with such things. Not one of these yogas gives up reason; not one of them asks you to be hoodwinked or to deliver your reason into the hands of priests of any type whatsoever. Not one of them asks that you should give your allegiance to any superhuman messenger. Each one of them tells you to cling to your reason, to hold fast to it.

We find in all living beings three instruments of knowledge. The first is instinct, which you find most highly developed in animals; this is the lowest instrument of knowledge. What is the second instrument of knowledge? Reasoning. You find that most highly developed in man. Now in the first place, instinct is an inadequate instrument; to animals the sphere of action is very limited, and within that limit instinct acts. When you come to man, you see instinct largely developed into reason. The sphere of action also has here become enlarged. Yet even reason is insufficient. Reason can go only a little way and then it stops. It cannot go any farther; and if you try to push it, the result is helpless confusion; reason itself becomes unreasonable. Logic becomes argument in a circle. Take, for instance, the very bases of our perception: matter and force. What is matter? That which is acted upon by force. And force? That which acts upon matter. You see the complication, what the logicians call a "see-saw," one idea depending on the other, and this again depending on that. Thus you find a mighty barrier before reason, beyond which reasoning cannot go. Yet it always feels impatient to get into the region of the infinite beyond. This world, this universe, which our senses feel or our mind thinks about, is but one atom, so to say, of the infinite, projected onto the plane of consciousness. Within that narrow limit defined by the network of consciousness works our reason, and not beyond. Therefore there must be some other instrument to take us beyond; and that instrument is called inspiration.

So instinct, reason, and inspiration are the three instruments of knowledge. Instinct belongs to animals, reason to man, and inspiration to Godmen. But in all human beings are to be found in a more or less developed condition the germs of all these three instruments of knowledge. To have these mental instruments evolve, the germs must be there. And this must also be remembered: one instrument is a development of another and therefore does not contradict it. It is reason that develops into inspiration; and therefore inspiration does not contradict reason, but fulfils it. Things which reason cannot get at are brought to light by inspiration, and they do not contradict reason. The old man does not contradict the child, but fulfils the child.

Therefore you must always bear in mind that the great danger lies in mistaking the lower form of instrument for the higher. Many times instinct is presented before the world as inspiration, and then come all the spurious claims to the gift of prophecy. A fool or a semi-lunatic thinks that the confusion going on in his brain is inspiration, and he wants men to follow him. The most contradictory, irrational nonsense that has been preached in the world is simply the instinctive jargon of confused lunatic brains trying to pass for the language of inspiration. The first test of true instruction is that it does not contradict reason.

You can see that this is the basis of all these yogas. Take, for instance, raja-yoga, the psychological yoga, the psychological way to union. It is a vast subject, and I can only point out to you now the central idea of this yoga. We have but one method of acquiring knowledge. From the lowest man to the highest yogi, all have to use the same method; and that method is what is called concentration. The chemist who works in his laboratory concentrates all the powers of his mind, brings them into one focus, and throws them on the elements, and the elements stand analyzed; and thus his knowledge comes. The astronomer also concentrates the powers of his mind and brings them into one focus; he throws them on objects through his telescope, and stars and various heavenly systems roll forward and yield their secrets. So it is in every case—with the professor in his chair, the student with his book, with every man who is working to know. You are hearing me, and if my words interest you, your mind will become concentrated on them. Then suppose a clock strikes; you will not hear it, on account of this concentration. And the more you are able to concentrate your mind, the better you will understand me; and the more I concentrate my love and powers, the better I shall be able to give expression to what I want to convey to you.

The more there is of this power of concentration, the more knowledge is acquired, because this is the one and only method of acquiring knowledge. Even the lowest shoeblack, if he gives more concentration, will black shoes better; the cook with concentration will cook a meal all the better. In making money or in worshipping God or in doing anything, the stronger is the power of concentration, the better will that thing be done. This is the one call, the one knock, which opens the gates of nature and lets out floods of light. This, the power of concentration, is the only key to the treasure house of knowledge.

The system of raja-yoga deals almost exclusively with this concentration. In the present state of our body and mind we are much distracted; the mind is frittering away its energies upon a hundred sorts of things. As soon as I try to calm my thoughts and concentrate my mind upon any one object of knowledge, thousands of undesired impulses rush into the brain, thousands of thoughts rush into the mind and disturb it. How to check them and bring the mind under control is the whole subject of study in raja-yoga.

Now take karma-yoga, the attainment of God through work. It is evident that in society there are many persons who seem to be born for some sort of activity or other, whose minds cannot be concentrated on the plane of thought alone, and whose principal idea is to express themselves through work visible and tangible. There must be a science for this kind of mind too. Each one of us is engaged in some work or other, but the majority of us fritter away a great portion of our energy because we do not know the secret of work. Karma-yoga explains this secret and teaches where and how to work, how to employ to the greatest advantage the largest part of our energies in the work that is before us.

But with this secret we must take into consideration the great objection against work, namely, that it causes pain. All misery and pain come from attachment. I want to do work, I want to do good to a human being; and it is ninety to one that that human being whom I have helped will prove ungrateful and go against me. And the result to me is pain. Such things deter mankind from working; and fear of pain and misery wastes a good portion of the work and energy of mankind. Karma-yoga teaches us how to work for work's sake, unattached, without caring who is helped and why. The karma-yogi works because it is his nature to work, because he feels that it is good for him to do so; and he has no object beyond that. His position in this world is that of a giver; he never cares to receive anything. He knows that he is giving, and does not ask for anything in return, and there he eludes the grasp of misery. Pain, whenever it comes, is the result of attachment.

Then there is bhakti-yoga for the man of emotional nature, the lover. He wants to love God; he relies upon and uses all sorts of rituals, flowers,

incense, beautiful buildings, forms, and all such things. Do you mean
to say that these are wrong? One fact I must tell you. It is good for you
to remember, in this country especially, that the world's great spiritual
giants have all been produced by religious sects which have been in possession of very rich mythology and ritual. All sects that have attempted
to worship God without any form or ceremony have crushed without
mercy everything that is beautiful and sublime in religion. Their religion is fanaticism—at best a dry thing. The history of the world is a
standing witness to this fact. Therefore do not decry these rituals and
mythologies. Let people have them; let those who so desire have them.
Do not exhibit that unworthy derisive smile and say, "They are fools; let
them have it." For it is not so. The greatest men I have seen in my life,
the most wonderfully developed in spirituality, have all come through
the discipline of these rituals. I do not hold myself worthy to sit at their
feet; it would be shameful for me to criticize them. How do I know how
these ideas act upon the human mind, which of them I am to accept
and which to reject? We are apt to criticize everything in the world without sufficient warrant. Let people have all the mythology they want, with
its beautiful inspirations; for you must always bear in mind that emotional natures do not care for abstract definitions of the truth. God to
them is something tangible, the only thing that is real. They feel, hear,
and see him, and love him. Let them have their God. Your rationalist
seems to them to be like the fool who, when he sees a beautiful statue,
wants to break it to find out what material it is made of.

Bhakti-yoga teaches them how to love without any ulterior motives,
loving God and loving the good because it is good to do so—not in
order to go to heaven or to get children, wealth, or anything else. It
teaches them that love itself is the highest recompense of love—that
God himself is love. It teaches them to pay all kinds of tribute to God
as the creator, the omnipresent, omniscient, almighty ruler, the father
and mother.

The best phrase that can express him, the highest idea that the human mind can conceive about him, is that he is the God of love. Wherever there is love, it is he. "Wherever there is any love, it is he; the Lord is present there." Where the husband kisses the wife, he is there in the kiss; where the mother kisses the child, he is there in the kiss; where friends clasp hands, he, the Lord, is present as the God of love. When a great man loves and wishes to help mankind, he is there giving freely of his bounty out of his love for mankind. Wherever the heart expands, he is there manifested. This is what the bhakti-yoga teaches.

We lastly come to the jnana-yogi, the philosopher, the thinker, he who wants to go beyond the visible. He is the man who is not satisfied with the little things of this world. His idea is to go beyond the daily routine of eating, drinking, and so on. Not even the teachings of thousands of books will satisfy him. Not even all the sciences will satisfy him. At best they only explain this little world to him. What else, then, will give him satisfaction? Not even myriads of systems of worlds will satisfy him; they are to him but drops in the ocean of existence. His soul wants to go beyond all that into the very heart of Being, by seeing reality as it is—by realizing it, by being it, by becoming one with that universal Being. That is the philosopher. To say that God is the father or mother, the creator of this universe, its protector and guide, is to him quite inadequate to express him. To him, God is the life of his life, the soul of his soul. God is his own Self. Nothing else exists which is other than God. All the mortal parts of him become pulverized by the weighty strokes of philosophy and are brushed away. What at last truly remains is God himself.

Upon the same tree there are two birds, one on the top, the other below. The one on the top is calm, silent, and majestic, immersed in his own glory; the other on the lower branches, eating sweet and bitter fruits by turns, hopping from branch to branch, becomes happy and miserable by turns. After a time the lower bird eats a very bitter fruit and becomes disgusted. Then he looks up and sees the other bird, that wondrous one of golden plumage, who eats neither sweet nor bitter fruit, who is neither happy nor miserable, but is calm, Self-centered, and sees nothing beyond his Self. The lower bird longs for this condition, but soon forgets it and again begins to eat the fruit. In a little while he eats another exceptionally bitter fruit, which makes him feel miserable, and again he looks up and tries to get nearer to the upper bird. Once more he forgets, and after a time looks up; and so on he goes, again and again, until he comes very near to the beautiful bird and sees the reflection of light from his plumage playing around his own body, and he feels a change and seems to melt away. Still nearer he comes, and everything about him melts away, and at last he understands this wonderful phenomenon. The lower bird was, as it were, only a substantial-looking shadow, a reflection of the higher; he himself was in essence the upper bird all the time. This eating of fruits, sweet and bitter, and this lower little bird, weeping and happy by turns, were a vain chimera, a dream; all along, the real bird was there above, calm and silent, glorious and majestic, beyond grief, beyond sorrow.

The upper bird is God, the Lord of this universe; and the lower bird is the human soul, eating the sweet and bitter fruits of this world. Now and then comes a heavy blow to the soul. For a time he stops eating and goes towards the unknown God, and a flood of light comes. He thinks that this world is a vain show. Yet again the senses drag him down, and he begins as before to eat the sweet and bitter fruits of the world. Again an exceptionally hard blow comes. His heart becomes open again to divine light. Thus gradually he approaches God; and as he gets nearer and nearer he finds his old self melting away. When he has come near enough he sees that he is none other than God himself, and he exclaims: "He whom I have described to you as the life of this universe, present in the atom and in suns and moons—he is the basis of our own life, the soul of our soul. Nay, thou art that."

This is what jnana-yoga teaches. It tells man that he is essentially divine. It shows mankind the real unity of Being: that each one of us is the Lord God himself manifested on earth. All of us, from the lowest worm that crawls under our feet to the highest being to whom we look up with wonder and awe, all are manifestations of the same Lord.

Lastly, it is imperative that all these various yogas should be carried out in practice. Mere theories about them will not do any good. First we have to hear about them; then we have to think about them. We have to reason the thoughts out, impress them on our minds, and meditate on them, realize them, until at last they become our whole life. No longer will religion remain a bundle of ideas or theories, or an intellectual assent; it will enter into our very self. By means of intellectual assent we may subscribe today to many foolish things, and change our minds altogether tomorrow. But true religion never changes. Religion is realization—not talk or doctrines or theories, however beautiful they may be. It is being and becoming—not hearing or acknowledging. It is the whole soul's becoming changed into what it believes. That is religion.

From *Soul, God, and Religion*
(Delivered at the Unity Hall, Hartford, Connecticut,
March 8, 1895)

Religion does not consist in doctrines or dogmas. It is not what you read, nor what dogmas you believe that is of importance, but what you realize. "Blessed are the pure in heart, for they shall see God," yea, in this life. And that is salvation. There are those who teach that this can be gained by the mumbling of words. But no great Master ever taught that external forms were necessary for salvation. The power of attaining it is within ourselves. We live and move in God. Creeds and sects have their parts to play, but they are for children, they last but temporarily. Books never make religions, but religions make books. We must not forget that.

No book ever created God, but God inspired all the great books. And no book ever created a soul. We must never forget that.

The end of all religions is the realizing of God in the soul. That is the one universal religion. If there is one universal truth in all religions, I place it here—in realizing God. Ideals and methods may differ, but that is the central point. There may be a thousand different radii, but they all converge to the one center, and that is the realization of God: something behind this world of sense, this world of eternal eating and drinking and talking nonsense, this world of false shadows and self-ishness. There is that beyond all books, beyond all creeds, beyond the vanities of this world, and it is the realization of God within yourself.

A man may believe in all the churches in the world, he may carry in his head all the sacred books ever written, he may baptize himself in all the rivers of the earth, still, if he has no perception of God, I would class him with the rankest atheist. And a man may have never entered a church or a mosque, nor performed any ceremony, but if he feels God within himself and is thereby lifted above the vanities of the world, that man is a holy man, a saint, call him what you will.

As soon as a man stands up and says he is right or his church is right, and all others are wrong, he is himself all wrong. He does not know that upon the proof of all the others depends the proof of his own. Love and charity for the whole human race, that is the test of true religiousness. I do not mean the sentimental statement that all men are brothers, but that one must feel the oneness of human life. So far as they are not exclu-sive, I see that the sects and creeds are all mine; they are all grand. They are all helping men towards the real religion. I will add, it is good to be born in a church, but it is bad to die there. It is good to be born a child, but bad to remain a child. Churches, ceremonies, and symbols are good for children, but when the child is grown, he must burst the church or himself. We must not remain children forever. It is like trying to fit one coat to all sizes and growths. I do not deprecate the existence of sects in the world. Would to God there were twenty millions more, for the more there are, there will be a greater field for selection. What I do object to is trying to fit one religion to every case. Though all religions are essentially the same, they must have the varieties of form produced by dissimilar circumstances among different nations. We must each have our own individual religion, individual so far as the externals of it go.

Addresses Delivered at the Chicago World's Parliament of Religions

Response to Welcome
(Delivered September 11, 1893)

Sisters and Brothers of America:

It fills my heart with joy unspeakable to rise in response to the warm and cordial welcome which you have given us. I thank you in the name of the most ancient order of monks in the world. I thank you in the name of the mother of religions. And I thank you in the name of the millions and millions of Hindu people of all classes and sects.

My thanks, also, to some of the speakers on this platform, who, referring to the delegates from the Orient, have told you that these men from far-off nations may well claim the honor of bearing to different lands the idea of toleration.

I am proud to belong to a religion which has taught the world both tolerance and universal acceptance. We not only believe in universal toleration, but we accept all religions as true. I am proud to belong to a nation which has sheltered the persecuted and the refugees of all religions and all nations of the earth. I am proud to tell you that we have gathered in our bosom the purest remnant of the Israelites, who came to Southern India and took refuge with us in the very year in which their holy temple was shattered by Roman tyranny. I am proud to belong to the religion which has sheltered and is still fostering the remnant of the grand Zoroastrian nation.

I will quote to you, brethren, a few lines from a hymn that I remember to have repeated from my earliest boyhood, which is every day repeated by millions of human beings: "As the different streams, having their sources in different places, all mingle their water in the sea, so, O Lord, the different paths which men take through different tendencies, various though they appear, crooked or straight, all lead to Thee." The present convention, which is one of the most august assemblies ever held, is in itself a vindication, a declaration to the world, of the wonderful doctrine preached in the Gita: "Whosoever comes to me, through whatsoever form, I reach him. All men are struggling through paths which in the end lead to me."

Sectarianism, bigotry, and its horrible descendant, fanaticism, have long possessed this beautiful earth. They have filled the earth with violence, drenched it often and often with human blood, destroyed civilization, and sent whole nations to despair. Had it not been for these horrible demons, human society would be far more advanced than it is now. But their time is come; and I fervently hope that the bell that tolled this morning in honor of this convention may be the death-knell of all fanaticism, of all persecutions with the sword or with the pen, and of all uncharitable feelings between persons wending their way to the same goal.

From *Hinduism*
(Paper read on September 19, 1893)

If there is ever to be a universal religion, it must be one which will have no location in place or time; which will be infinite, like the God it will preach, and whose sun will shine upon the followers of Krishna and of Christ, on saints and sinners, alike; which will not be Brahminical or Buddhist, Christian or Mohammedan, but the sum total of all of these, and still have infinite space for development; which in its catholicity will embrace in its infinite arms, and find a place for, every human being, from the lowest groveling savage, not far removed from the brute, to the highest man, towering by the virtues of his head and heart almost above humanity, making society stand in awe of him and doubt his human nature. It will be a religion which will have no place for persecution or intolerance in its polity, which will recognize divinity in every man and woman, and whose whole scope, whose whole force, will be centered in aiding humanity to realize its own true, divine nature.

Offer such a religion and all the nations will follow you. Ashoka's council was a council of the Buddhist faith. Akbar's, though more to the purpose, was only a parlor meeting.[2] It was reserved for America to proclaim to all quarters of the globe that the Lord is in every religion.

May He who is the Brahman of the Hindus, the Ahura-Mazda of the Zoroastrians, the Buddha of the Buddhists, the Jehovah of the Jews, the Father in heaven of the Christians, give strength to you to carry out your noble idea! The star arose in the East; it traveled steadily towards the West, sometimes dimmed and sometimes effulgent, till it made a circuit of the world; and now it is again rising on the very horizon of the East, the borders of the Sanpo,[3] a thousandfold more effulgent than it ever was before.

Hail, Columbia, motherland of liberty! It has been given to thee, who never dipped thy hand in thy neighbor's blood, who never found out that the shortest way of becoming rich was by robbing one's neighbors—it has been given to thee to march at the vanguard of civilization with the flag of harmony.

---

[2] Both Ashoka, the great Buddhist emperor (c. 274–237 BCE), and Akbar, the great Moghul emperor (1556–1605 CE), were known for their liberal outlook in religious matters. They made serious efforts to establish harmony among different faiths.

[3] The Brahmaputra River, whose source is Lake Manasarovar in Tibet. The part of the river that flows through Tibet is called the Sanpo.

Swami Vivekananda, London, 1896

3

Worship of the Living God

What Is Religion?
(Delivered at the Vedanta Society, New York City, June 17, 1900)
A huge locomotive rushes down the tracks, and a small worm that has been creeping upon one of the rails saves its life by crawling out of the path of the locomotive. Yet this little worm, so insignificant that it can be crushed in a moment, is a living something, while the locomotive, so huge, so immense, is only an engine, a machine. You see, the one has life and the other is only dead matter, and all its power and strength and speed are only those of a dead machine, a mechanical contrivance. The poor little worm which moves upon the rail and which the least touch of the engine would surely deprive of its life is a majestic being compared to that huge locomotive. It is a small part of the Infinite and therefore it is greater than the powerful engine. Why should that be so? How do we know the living from the dead? The machine mechanically performs all the movements its maker made it to perform; its movements are not those of life. How can we make the distinction between the living and the dead, then? In the living there is freedom, there is intelligence; in the dead all is bound and no freedom is possible, because there is no intelligence. This freedom that distinguishes us from mere machines is what we are all striving for. To be more free is the goal of all our efforts; for only in perfect freedom can there be perfection.

This effort to attain freedom underlies all forms of worship, whether we know it or not.

If we were to examine the various sorts of worship all over the world, we would see that the crudest of mankind are worshipping ghosts, demons, and the spirits of their forefathers. Serpent-worship, worship of tribal gods, and worship of the departed ones—why do they practice all this? Because they feel that in some unknown way these beings are greater, more powerful, than themselves and so limit their freedom. They therefore seek to propitiate these beings in order to prevent them from molesting them—in other words, to get more freedom. They also seek to win favor from these superior beings, to get as a gift what ought to be earned by personal effort.

On the whole, this shows that the world is expecting a miracle. This expectation never leaves us, and however we may try, we are all running after the miraculous and extraordinary. What is mind but that ceaseless inquiry into the meaning and mystery of life? We may say that only uncultivated people are going after all these things; but the question still is there—why should it be so? The Jews were asking for a miracle. The whole world has been asking for the same thing these thousands of years.

There is, again, the universal dissatisfaction: we take up an ideal but we have rushed only half the way after it when we take up a new one. We struggle hard to attain a certain goal and then discover we do not want it. This dissatisfaction we are experiencing time after time; and what is there in life if there is to be only dissatisfaction? What is the meaning of this universal dissatisfaction? It indicates that freedom is every man's goal. He seeks it ever; his whole life is a struggle after it. The child rebels against law as soon as it is born. Its first utterance is a cry, a protest against the bondage in which it finds itself. This longing for freedom produces the idea of a being who is absolutely free. The concept of God is a fundamental element in the human constitution. Satchidananda, Existence-Knowledge-Bliss, is, in Vedanta, the highest concept of God possible to the mind. It is by its nature the essence of knowledge and the essence of bliss. We have been stifling that inner voice, seeking to follow law and suppress our true nature; but there is that human instinct to rebel against nature's laws.

We may not understand what all this means; but there is that unconscious struggle of the human with the spiritual, of the lower with the higher mind, and through this struggle we attempt to preserve our separate life, what we call our "individuality."

Even hell illustrates this miraculous fact that we are born rebels. Against the inevitable facts of life we rebel and cry out, "No law for us!" As long as we obey the laws we are like machines; and the universe goes on and we cannot change it. Laws become man's nature. The first inkling of life on its higher level is in seeing this struggle within us to break the bonds of nature and to be free. "Freedom, O freedom! Freedom, O freedom!" is the song of the soul. Bondage, alas—to be bound in nature—seems its fate.

Why should there be serpent-worship or ghost-worship or demon-worship and all the various creeds and forms for the obtaining of miracles? Why do we say that there is life, there is being, in anything? There must be a meaning in all this search, this endeavor to understand life, to explain being. It is not meaningless and vain. It is man's ceaseless endeavor to become free. The knowledge which we now call science has been struggling for thousands of years in its attempt to gain freedom, and people still ask for freedom. Yet there is no freedom in nature. It is all law. Still the struggle goes on. Nay, the whole of nature, from the very sun down to the atoms, is under law, and even for man there is no freedom. But we cannot believe it. We have been studying laws from the beginning and yet cannot—nay, will not—believe that man is under law. The soul cries ever, "Freedom, O freedom!"

With the conception of God as a perfectly free being, man cannot rest eternally in this bondage. Higher he must go, and were the struggle not for freedom he would think it too severe. Man says to himself: "I am a born slave, I am bound; nevertheless, there is a being who is not bound by nature. He is free and the master of nature." The conception of God, therefore, is as essential and as fundamental a part of the mind as is the idea of bondage. Both are the outcome of the idea of freedom. There cannot be life, even in the plant, without the idea of freedom. In the plant or in the worm, life has to rise to the concept of individuality; it is there, unconsciously working. The plant lives in order to preserve a principle; it is not simply nature. The idea of nature's controlling every step onward overrules the idea of freedom. Onward goes the material world, onward moves the idea of freedom. Still the fight goes on. We are hearing about all the quarrels of creeds and sects; yet creeds and sects are just and proper; they must be there. They no doubt lengthen the chain, and naturally the struggle increases; but there will be no quarrels if we only know that we are all striving to reach the same goal.

The embodiment of freedom, the master of nature, is what we call God. You cannot deny him. No, because you cannot move or live without the idea of freedom. Would you come here if you did not believe you were free? It is quite possible that the biologist can and will give some explanation of the perpetual effort to be free. Taking all that for granted, still the idea of freedom is there. It is a fact, as much so as the other fact that you cannot apparently get over, the fact of being under nature.

Bondage and liberty, light and shadow, good and evil, must be there; but the very fact of the bondage shows also this freedom hidden there. If one is a fact, the other is equally a fact. There must be this idea of freedom. While now we cannot see that this idea of bondage, in uncultivated man, is his struggle for freedom, yet the idea of freedom is there. The consciousness of the bondage of sin and impurity in the uncultivated savage is very slight; for his nature is only a little higher than that of the animal. What he struggles against is the bondage of physical nature, the lack of physical gratification; but out of this lower consciousness grows and broadens the higher conception of a mental or moral bondage and a longing for spiritual freedom. Here we see the divine dimly shining through the veil of ignorance. The veil is very dense at first, and the light may be almost obscured, but it is there, ever pure and undimmed—the radiant light of freedom and perfection. Man personifies this as the ruler of the universe, the one free being. He does not yet know that the universe is all one, that the difference is only in the concept and not in things themselves.

The whole of nature is worship of God. Wherever there is life there is this search for freedom, and that freedom is the same as God. Necessarily freedom gives us mastery over all nature and is impossible without knowledge. The more we know, the more we become masters of nature. Mastery alone makes us strong; and if there be some being who is entirely free and a master of nature, that being must have a perfect knowledge of nature, must be omnipresent and omniscient. Freedom must go hand in hand with these; and only that being who has acquired these will be beyond nature.

Blessedness, eternal peace, arising from perfect freedom, is the highest concept of religion, underlying all the ideas of God in Vedanta: absolutely free existence, not bound by anything—no change, no nature, nothing that can produce a change in him. This same freedom is in you and in me and is the only real freedom.

God is always established upon his own majestic changeless Self. You and I try to be one with him, but find ourselves diverted by nature, by the trifles of daily life, by money, by fame, by human love, and all these changing forms which make for bondage. When nature shines, upon what depends its shining? Upon God, and not upon the sun or the moon or the stars. Wherever anything shines, whether it is the light in the sun or in our own consciousness, it is he. He shining, all shines after him.

Now, we have seen that this God is self-evident, impersonal, omniscient, the knower and master of nature, the Lord of all. He is behind all worship, and all worship is directed to Him whether we know it or not. I go one step farther: That which we call evil is his worship too. This too is a part of freedom. When you are doing evil, the impulse behind is that of freedom. It may be misguided and misled, but it is there, and there cannot be any life or any impulse unless that freedom is behind it. Freedom throbs in the heart of the universe. Such is the conception of the Lord in the Upanishads.

Sometimes it rises even higher, presenting to us an ideal before which at first we stand aghast: that we are in essence one with God. He who is the coloring in the wings of the butterfly and the blossoming of the rose-bud is the power that is in the plant and in the butterfly. He who gives us life is the power within us. Out of his power comes life, and the direst death is also his power. He whose shadow is death—his shadow is immortality also.

Take a still higher conception; see how we are flying like hunted hares from all that is terrible, and like them hiding our heads and thinking we are safe. See how the whole world is flying from everything terrible. Once when I was in Benares, I was passing through a place where there was a large reservoir of water on one side and a high wall on the other. There were many monkeys around that place. The monkeys of Benares are huge brutes and are sometimes surly. They now took it into their heads not to allow me to pass through their street; so they howled and shrieked and clutched at my feet as I passed. As they pressed closer, I began to run; but the faster I ran, the faster came the monkeys and they began to bite at me. It seemed impossible to escape. But just then I met a stranger, who called out to me, "Face the brutes." I turned and faced the monkeys and they fell back and finally fled. That is a lesson for all life: face the terrible, face it boldly. Like the monkeys, the hardships of life fall back when we cease to flee before them. If we are ever to gain freedom, it must be by conquering nature, never by running away. Cowards never win victories. We have to fight fear and troubles and ignorance if we expect them to flee before us.

What is death? What are terrors? Do you not see the Lord's face in them? Fly from evil and terror and misery and they will follow you. Face them and they will flee. The whole world worships ease and pleasure, and very few dare to worship what is painful. To rise above both is the ideal of freedom. Unless a man passes through pleasure and pain he is not free. We have to face them. We strive to worship the Lord, but the body comes between, nature comes between him and us and blinds our vision. We must learn how to worship and love him in the thunderbolt, in shame, in sorrow, in sin. All the world has ever been preaching the God of virtue. I preach a God of virtue and a God of sin in one. Take him if you dare. That is the one way to salvation. Then alone will come to us the truth ultimate which comes from the idea of oneness. Then will be lost the idea that one is greater than another. The nearer we approach the ideal of freedom, the more we shall come under the Lord and troubles will vanish. Then we shall not differentiate the door of hell from the gate of heaven, nor differentiate between men and say, "I am greater than any other being in the universe." Until we see nothing in the world but the Lord himself, all these evils will beset us and we shall make all these distinctions; for it is only in the Lord, in the spirit, that we are all one, and until we see God everywhere, this unity will not exist for us.

The man who is groping through sin, through misery, the man who is choosing the path through hell, will reach freedom, but it will take time. We cannot help him. Some hard knocks on his head will make him turn to the Lord. The path of virtue, purity, unselfishness, spirituality, he will know at last, and what he has been doing unconsciously he will do consciously. The idea is expressed by St. Paul: "Whom therefore ye ignorantly worship, him declare I unto you." This is the lesson for the whole world to learn. What have these philosophies and theories of nature to do, if not to help us to attain this one goal in life? Let us come to that consciousness of the identity of everything and let man see himself in everything. Let us be no more the worshippers of creeds or sects with small, limited notions of God, but see him in everything in the universe. If you are knowers of God, you will everywhere find the same worship as in your own heart.

Get rid, in the first place, of all these limited ideas and see God in every person—working through all hands, walking through all feet, and eating through every mouth. In every being he lives, through all minds he thinks. He is self-evident, nearer unto us than ourselves. To know this is religion, is faith. May it please the Lord to give us this faith! When we shall feel that oneness we shall be immortal. We are immortal even physically: one with the universe. So long as there is one that breathes throughout the universe, I live in that one. I am not this limited little being; I am the universal. I am the life of all the sons of God. I am the soul of Buddha, of Jesus, of Mohammed. I am the soul of all the teachers, and I am the soul of all the robbers that robbed and of all the murderers that were hanged. Stand up then! This is the highest worship. You are one with the universe. That alone is humility—not crawling upon all fours and calling yourself a sinner. That is the highest evolution when this veil of differentiation is torn off. The highest creed is oneness. I am So-and-so—is a limited idea, not true of the real "I." I am the universal; stand upon that and ever worship the highest through the highest form; for God is spirit and should be worshipped in spirit and in truth. Through lower forms of worship man's materialistic thoughts rise to spiritual worship, and the universal infinite one is at last worshipped in and through the spirit. That which is limited is material. The spirit alone is infinite. God is spirit, is infinite; man is spirit and therefore infinite; and the infinite alone can worship the infinite. We will worship the infinite; that is the highest spiritual worship. How grand these

ideas are, and how difficult to realize! I theorize, talk, philosophize, and
the next moment I come up against something and I unconsciously
become angry; I forget there is anything in the universe but this little
limited self. I forget to say, "I am the spirit, what is this trifle to me? I
am the spirit." I forget it is all myself playing. I forget God; I forget
freedom.

Sharp as the blade of a razor, long and difficult and hard to cross,
is the way to freedom. The sages have declared this again and again. Yet
do not let these weaknesses and failures deter you. The Upanishads have
declared: "Arise! Awake! and stop not until the goal is reached." We will
then certainly cross the path, sharp as it is, like the razor, and long and
distant and difficult though it be. Man becomes the master of gods and
demons. No one is to blame for our miseries but ourselves. Do you
think there is only a dark cup of poison if man goes to look for nectar? The nectar is there and is for every man who strives to reach it.
The Lord himself tells us: "Give up all these paths and struggles. Do thou
take refuge in me. I will take thee to the other shore; be not afraid."
We hear that from all the scriptures of the world that come to us.

The same voice teaches us to say, "Thy will be done on earth as it
is in heaven, for thine is the kingdom and the power and the glory." It
is difficult, all very difficult. I say to myself this moment: "I will take
refuge in thee, O Lord; unto thy love I will sacrifice all, and on thine
altar I will place all that is good and virtuous. My sins, my sorrows, my
actions, good and evil, I will offer unto thee; do thou take them and I
will never forget." One moment I say, "Thy will be done," and the next
moment something comes to try me and I spring up in a rage. The goal
of all religions is the same, but the language of the teachers differs.
The goal is to kill the false "I" so that the real "I," the Lord, will reign.
"I, the Lord, am a jealous God. Thou shalt have no other god but me,"
say the Hebrew scriptures. We must cherish God alone. We must say,
"Not I, but thou," and then we should give up everything but the Lord.

He, and he alone, should reign. Perhaps we struggle hard and yet the next moment our feet slip, and then we try to stretch out our hands to mother. We find we cannot stand alone. Life is infinite, one chapter of which is, "Thy will be done," and unless we realize all the chapters we cannot realize the whole.

"Thy will be done"—every moment the traitor mind rebels against it; yet it must be said again and again if we are to conquer the lower self. We cannot serve a traitor and yet be saved. There is salvation for all except the traitor, and we stand condemned as traitors—traitors against our own selves, against the majesty of God—when we refuse to obey the voice of our higher Self. Come what will, we must give our bodies and minds to the supreme will. Well has it been said by the Hindu philosopher, "If man says twice, 'Thy will be done,' he commits sin." "Thy will be done"—what more is needed? Why say it twice? What is good is good. No more shall we take it back. "Thy will be done on earth as it is in heaven, for thine is the kingdom and the power and the glory for evermore."

From *The Real Nature of Man*
(Delivered at the Royal Institute of Painters in Watercolors, London, June 21, 1896)

People are frightened when they are told that they are Universal Being, everywhere present. "Through everything you work, through every foot you move, through every lip you talk, through every heart you feel." People are frightened when they are told this. They will again and again ask you if they are not going to keep their individuality. What is individuality? I should like to see it. A baby has no mustache; when he grows to be a man, perhaps he has a mustache and beard. His individuality would be lost if it were in the body. If I lose one eye or if I lose one of my hands, my individuality would be lost if it were in the body. Then a drunkard should not give up drinking, because he would lose his individuality. A thief should not be a good man, because he would thereby lose his individuality. Indeed, no man ought to change his habits, for fear of this. Nor can individuality be in memory. Suppose, on account of a blow on the head, I forget all about my past; then I have lost all individuality, I am gone. I do not remember two or three years of my childhood, and if memory and existence are one, then whatever I forget is gone. That part of my life which I do not remember, I did not live. That is a very narrow idea of individuality.

There is no individuality except in the infinite. That is the only condition which does not change. Everything else is in a state of flux. We are not individuals yet. We are struggling towards individuality; and that is the infinite. That is the real nature of man. He alone lives whose life is in the whole universe; the more we concentrate our lives on limited things, the faster we go towards death. Those moments alone we live when our lives are in the universe, in others; and living this little life is death, simply death, and that is why the fear of death comes. The fear of death can be conquered only when man realizes that so long as there is one life in this universe, he is living. When he can say, "I am in everything, in everybody; I am in all lives; I am the universe," then alone comes the state of fearlessness. To talk of immortality in constantly changing things is absurd. Says an old Sanskrit philosopher: "It is only the spirit that is the individual, because it is infinite." Infinity cannot be divided; infinity cannot be broken into pieces. It is the same one undivided unit forever; and this is the individual man, the real man. The apparent man is merely a struggle to express, to manifest, this individuality which is beyond. Evolution is not in the spirit.

These changes which are going on—the wicked becoming good, the animal becoming man; take them in whatever way you like—are not in the spirit. They are evolution of nature and the manifestation of the spirit. Suppose there is a screen hiding you from me, in which there is a small hole through which I can see some of the faces before me, just a few faces. Now suppose the hole begins to grow larger and larger, and as it does so, more and more of the scene before me reveals itself; when at last the whole screen has disappeared, I stand face to face with you all. You did not change at all; it was the hole that was evolving, and you were gradually manifesting yourselves. So it is with the spirit. No perfection is going to be attained. You are already free and perfect.

What are these ideas of religion and God and searching for the hereafter? Why does man look for a God? Why does man, in every nation, in every state of society, want a perfect ideal somewhere, either in man, in God, or elsewhere? Because that idea is within you. It was your own heart beating and you did not know; you were mistaking it for something external. It is the God within your own self that is impelling you to seek him, to realize him. After long searches here and there, in temples and in churches, on earth and in heaven, at last you come back to your own soul, completing the circle from where you started, and find that he whom you have been seeking all over the world, for whom you have been weeping and praying in churches and temples, on whom you were looking as the mystery of all mysteries, shrouded in the clouds, is the nearest of the near, is your own Self, the reality of your life, body, and soul.

That Self is your own nature. Assert it, manifest it. You are not to become pure; you are pure already. You are not to become perfect; you are that already. Nature is like a screen which is hiding the reality beyond. Every good thought that you think or act upon simply tears the veil, as it were, and the purity, the infinity, the God behind, is manifested more and more. This is the whole history of man. Finer and finer becomes the veil, more and more of the light behind shines forth; for it is its nature to shine.

The Self cannot be known; in vain we try to know it. Were it knowable, it would not be what it is; for it is the eternal subject. Knowledge is a limitation; knowledge is an objectification. It is the eternal subject of everything, the eternal witness of this universe—your own Self.

Knowledge is, as it were, a lower step, a degeneration. We are that eternal subject already; how can we know it?

The infinite Self is the real nature of every man, and he is struggling to express it in various ways. Otherwise, why are there so many ethical codes? Where is the explanation of all ethics? One idea stands out as the center of all ethical systems, expressed in various forms—namely, doing good to others. The guiding motive of mankind should be charity towards men, charity towards all animals. But these are all various expressions of that eternal truth that "I am the universe; this universe is one." Or else, where is the explanation? Why should I do good to my fellow men? Why should I do good to others? What compels me? It is sympathy, the feeling of sameness everywhere. The hardest hearts sometimes feel sympathy for other beings. Even the man who gets frightened if he is told that this assumed individuality is really a delusion, that it is ignoble to try to cling to this apparent individuality—that very man will tell you that extreme self-abnegation is the center of all morality. And what is perfect self-abnegation? It means the abnegation of this apparent self, the abnegation of all selfishness.

This idea of "me" and "mine"—*ahamkara* and *mamata*—is the result of past superstition, and the more this present self passes away, the more the real Self becomes manifest. This is true self-abnegation, the center, the basis, the gist of all moral teaching, and whether man knows it or not, the whole world is slowly going towards it, practicing it more or less. Only, the vast majority of mankind are doing it unconsciously. Let them do it consciously. Let them make the sacrifice, knowing that this "me" and "mine" is not the real Self, but only a limitation. But one glimpse of that infinite reality which is behind, but one spark of that infinite fire that is the All, represents the present man. The infinite is his true nature.

What is the utility, the effect, the result of this knowledge? In these days we have to measure everything by utility—by how many pounds, shillings, and pence it represents. What right has a person to ask that truth should be judged by the standard of utility or money? Suppose there is no utility, will it be less true? Utility is not the test of truth. Nevertheless, there is the highest utility in this. Happiness, we see, is what everyone is seeking for; but the majority seeks it in things which are evanescent and not real. No happiness was ever found in the senses. There never was a person who found happiness in the senses or in enjoyment of the senses. Happiness is only found in the spirit. Therefore the highest utility for mankind is to find this happiness in the spirit.

The next point is that ignorance is the great mother of all misery, and the fundamental ignorance is to think that the infinite weeps and cries, that it is finite. This is the basis of all ignorance—that we, the immortal, the ever pure, the perfect spirit, think we are little minds, we are little bodies. It is the mother of all selfishness. As soon as I think I am a little body, I want to preserve it, to protect it, to keep it nice, at the expense of other bodies. Then you and I become separate. As soon as this idea of separation comes, it opens the door to all mischief and leads to all misery. This, then, is the utility of this knowledge—that if a small fractional part of human beings living today can put aside the idea of selfishness, narrowness, and littleness, this earth will become a paradise tomorrow. But with machines and improvements of material knowledge only, it will never be so. These only increase misery, as oil poured on fire increases the flame all the more. Without the knowledge of the spirit, all material knowledge is only adding fuel to fire, only giving into the hands of selfish man one more instrument to take what belongs to others, to live upon the life of others instead of giving up his life for them.

Is it practical?—is another question. Can it be practiced in modern society? Truth does not pay homage to any society, ancient or modern. Society has to pay homage to truth or die. Societies should be molded upon truth; truth has not to adjust itself to society. If such a noble truth as unselfishness cannot be practiced in society, it is better for man to give up society and go into the forest. That is the daring man.

There are two sorts of courage. One is the courage of facing the cannon; and the other is the courage of spiritual conviction. An emperor who invaded India was told by his teacher to go and see some of the sages there. After a long search for one, he found a very old man sitting on a block of stone. The emperor talked with him a little and became very much impressed by his wisdom. He asked the sage to go to his country with him. "No," said the sage, "I am quite satisfied with my forest here." Said the emperor: "I will give you money, position, wealth. I am the emperor of the world." "No," replied the man, "I don't care for those things." The emperor replied, "If you do not go, I will kill you." The man smiled serenely and said: "That is the most foolish thing you ever said, Emperor. You cannot kill me. Me the sun cannot dry, fire cannot burn, sword cannot kill; for I am the birthless, the deathless, the ever living omnipotent, omnipresent spirit." This is spiritual boldness, while the other is the courage of a lion or a tiger.

During the Mutiny of 1857, there was a swami, a very great soul, whom a Mohammedan mutineer stabbed severely. The Hindu mutineers caught and brought the man to the swami, offering to kill him. But the swami looked up calmly and said, "My brother, thou art He, thou art He!" and expired. This is another instance.

What good is it to talk of the strength of your muscles, of the superiority of your Western institutions, if you cannot make truth square with your society, if you cannot build up a society into which the highest truth will fit? What is the good of this boastful talk about your grandeur and greatness if you stand up and say, "This courage is not practical"? Is nothing practical but pounds, shillings, and pence? If so, why boast of your society? That society is the greatest where the highest truths become practical. That is my opinion. And if society is not fit for the highest truths, make it so—and the sooner, the better.

Stand up, men and women, in this spirit, dare to believe in the truth, dare to practice the truth! The world requires a few hundred bold men and women. Practice that boldness which dares know the truth, which dares show the truth in life, which does not quake before death, nay, welcomes death, makes a man know that he is the spirit, that in the whole universe nothing can kill him. Then you will be free. Then you will know your real soul.

"This Atman [Self or soul] is first to be heard of, then thought about, and then meditated upon." There is a great tendency in modern times to talk too much of work and decry thought. Doing is very good, but that comes from thinking. Little manifestations of energy through the muscles are called work. But where there is no thought, there will be no work. Fill the brain, therefore, with high thoughts, with the highest ideals; place them day and night before you, and out of that will come great work. Talk not about impurity, but say that we are pure. We have hypnotized ourselves into this thought that we are little, that we are born and that we are going to die, and into a constant state of fear.

There is a story about a lioness who was big with young. Going about in search of prey, and seeing a flock of sheep, she jumped upon them. She died in the effort and a little baby lion was born, motherless. It was taken care of by the sheep and they brought it up. It grew up with them, ate grass, and bleated like the sheep. And although in time it became a full-grown lion, it thought it was a sheep. One day another lion came in search of prey and was astonished to find that in the midst of this flock of sheep was a lion, fleeing like the sheep at the approach of danger. He tried to get near the sheep-lion to tell it that it was not a sheep but a lion, but the poor animal fled at his approach. However, he watched his opportunity and one day found the sheep-lion sleeping. He approached it and said, "You are a lion." "I am a sheep," cried the other lion; it could not believe the contrary, but bleated. The lion dragged it towards a lake and said, "Look here: there is my reflection and there is yours." Then came the comparison. The sheep-lion looked at the lion and then at its own reflection, and in a moment came the idea that it was a lion. The lion roared; the bleating was gone.

You are lions; you are the soul, pure, infinite, and perfect. The might of the universe is within you. "Why weepest thou, my friend? There is neither birth nor death for thee. Why weepest thou? There is no disease or misery for thee. Thou art like the infinite sky: clouds of various colors come over it, play for a moment, then vanish; but the sky is ever the same eternal blue."

Why do we see wickedness? There was a stump of a tree, and in the dark a thief came that way and said, "That is a policeman." A young man waiting for his beloved saw it and thought that it was his sweetheart. A child who had been told ghost stories took it for a ghost and began to shriek. But all the time it was the stump of a tree. We see the world as we are. Suppose there is a baby in a room with a bag of gold on the table, and a thief comes and steals the gold. Would the baby know it was stolen? That which we have inside, we see outside. The baby has no thief inside and sees no thief outside. So with all knowledge.

Do not talk of the wickedness of the world and all its sins. Weep that you are bound to see wickedness yet. Weep that you are bound to see sin everywhere. If you want to help the world, do not condemn it. Do not weaken it more. For what is sin and what is misery—what are all these but the results of weakness? The world is made weaker and weaker every day by such teachings. Men are taught from childhood that they are weak and sinners. Teach them that they are all glorious children of immortality, even those who are the weakest in manifestation. Let positive, strong, helpful thoughts enter into their brains from very childhood. Lay yourselves open to these thoughts, and not to weakening and paralyzing ones. Say to your own minds, "I am He, I am He." Let it ring day and night in your minds like a song, and at the point of death declare "I am He." That is the truth. The infinite strength of the world is yours. Drive out the superstition that has covered your minds. Let us be brave. Know the truth and practice the truth. The goal may be distant, but awake, arise, and stop not till the goal is reached.

From *Practical Vedanta—Part II*
(Delivered in London, November 12, 1896)

The impersonal God is a living God, a principle. The difference between personal and impersonal God is this: the personal God is only a man, whereas the impersonal is angel, man, animal, and yet something more, which we cannot see, because impersonality includes all personalities, is the sum total of everything in the universe, and infinitely more besides. "As the one fire coming into the world manifests itself in so many forms, and yet is infinitely more besides"—even so is the impersonal.

We want to worship a living God. I have not seen anything but God all my life, nor have you. To see this chair you first see God and then the chair, in and through him. He is everywhere, as the "I am." The moment you feel "I am," you are conscious of existence. Where shall we find God if we cannot see him in our own hearts and in every living being? "Thou art the man, thou art the woman, thou art the girl, and thou art the boy; thou art the old man tottering with a stick, thou art the young man walking in the pride of his strength; thou art all that exists"—a wonderful, living God who is the only fact in the universe.

This seems to many to be a terrible contradiction of the traditional God, who lives behind a veil somewhere and whom nobody ever sees. The priests only give us an assurance that if we follow them, listen to their admonitions, and walk in the way they mark out for us, then, when we die, they will give us a passport to enable us to see the face of God! What are all these ideas of heaven but simply interventions of this nonsensical priestcraft?

Of course, the idea of the impersonal is very destructive: it takes away all trade from the priests, churches, and temples. In India there is a famine now, but there are temples in each one of which there are jewels worth a king's ransom. If the priests taught this idea of the impersonal to the people, their occupation would be gone. Yet we have to teach it unselfishly, without priestcraft. You are God and so am I. Who obeys whom? Who worships whom? You are the highest temple of God; I would rather worship you than any temple, image, or Bible. Why are some people's thoughts so full of contradictions? They say that they are hardheaded practical men. Very good. But what is more practical than worshipping you? I see you, feel you, and I know you are God. The Mohammedan says there is no God but Allah. Vedanta says that there is nothing that is not God. It may frighten many of you, but you will understand it by degrees. The living God is within you, and yet you are building churches and temples and believing all sorts of imaginary nonsense. The only God to worship is the human soul in the human body. Of course, all animals are temples too, but man is the highest, the greatest of all temples. If I cannot worship in that, no other temple will be of any advantage. The moment I have realized God sitting in the temple of every human body, the moment I stand in reverence before every human being and see God in him, that moment I am free from bondage, everything that binds vanishes, and I am free.

This is the most practical of all worship; it has nothing to do with theorizing and speculation. Yet it frightens many. They say it is not right. They go on theorizing about old ideas told them by their grandfathers, that a God somewhere in heaven had told someone that he was God. Since that time we have only theories. This is practicality according to them—and our ideas are impractical! No doubt, Vedanta says, each one must have his own path; but the path is not the goal. The worship of a God in heaven and all these things are not bad; but they are only steps towards the truth, and not the truth itself. They are good and beautiful, and some wonderful ideas are there, but Vedanta says at every point: "My friend, him whom you are worshipping as unknown—I worship him as you. He whom you are worshipping as unknown and seeking throughout the universe has been with you all the time. You are living through him and he is the eternal witness of the universe." He whom all the Vedas worship, nay, more, he who is always present in the eternal "I" —he existing, the whole universe exists. He is the light and life of the universe. If this "I" were not in you, you would not see the sun; everything would be a mass of darkness. He shining, you see the world.

One objection is generally raised, and it is this: that this may lead to a tremendous amount of difficulty. Every one of us will think, "I am God, and whatever I do or think must be good; for God can do no evil." In the first place, even taking this danger of misinterpretation for granted, can it be proved that on the other side the same danger does not exist? Men have been worshipping a God in heaven separate from them and of whom they are much afraid. They have been born shaking with fear, and all their life they will go on shaking. Has the world been made much better by this? Those who have understood and worshipped a personal God, and those who have understood and worshipped an impersonal God—which of these have been the great workers of the world? On which side have been the gigantic workers, gigantic moral powers? Certainly on the side of the impersonal. How can you expect morality to be developed through fear? It can never be. "When one sees another, when one hears another, that is *maya*.[1] When one does not see another, when one does not hear another, when everything has become Atman, who sees whom, who perceives whom?" It is all he and all I at the same time. The soul has become pure. Then and then alone do we understand what love is. Love cannot come through fear. Its basis is freedom. When we really begin to love the world, then we understand what is meant by the brotherhood or mankind, and not before.

---

[1] Cosmic illusion on account of which the One appears as many.

So it is not right to say that the idea of the impersonal will lead to a tremendous amount of evil in the world, as if the other doctrine never lent itself to works of evil; as if it did not lead to sectarianism, deluging the world with blood and causing men to tear each other to pieces. "My God is the greatest God; if anyone disagrees, let us decide it by a free fight"—that is the outcome of dualism all over the world. Come out into the broad, open light of day; come out from the little narrow paths. For how can the infinite soul rest content to live and die in small ruts? Come out into the universe of light. Everything in the universe is yours. Stretch out your arms and embrace it with love. If you ever felt you wanted to do that, you have felt God.

You remember that passage in the sermon of Buddha: how he sent a thought of love towards the south, the north, the east, and the west, above and below, until the whole universe was filled with this love, so grand, great, and infinite. When you have that feeling you have true personality; for the whole universe is one Person. Let little things go. Give up the small for the infinite; give up small enjoyments for infinite bliss. It is all yours, for the impersonal includes the personal. So God is personal and impersonal at the same time. And man—the infinite, impersonal man—is manifesting himself as a person. We, the infinite, have limited ourselves, as it were, into small parts.

Vedanta says that infinity is our true nature; it will never vanish; it will abide forever. But we limit ourselves by our karma, which like a chain round our necks has dragged us into this limitation. Break that chain and be free. Trample law under your feet. No law can bind man's true nature—no destiny, no fate. How can there be law in infinity? Freedom is its watchword. Freedom is its nature, its birthright. Be free and then have any number of personalities you like. Then we shall play like the actor who comes upon the stage and plays the part of a beggar. Contrast him with the actual beggar walking in the streets. The scene is perhaps the same in both cases; the words are perhaps the same; but yet what a difference! The one enjoys his beggary, while the other is suffering misery from it. And what makes this difference? The one is free and the other is bound. The actor knows that his beggary is not true, but that he has assumed it for the play, while the real beggar thinks that it is his own natural state and he has to bear it whether he will or not; for this is the law.

So long as we have no knowledge of our real nature, we are beggars, jostled about by every force in nature and made slaves of by everything in nature. We cry all over the world for help, but help never comes to us. We cry to imaginary beings and yet it never comes. But still we hope help will come; and thus in weeping, wailing, and hoping, this life is passed and the same play goes on and on.

Be free. Hope for nothing from anyone. I am sure if you look back upon your lives you will find that you were always vainly trying to get help from others which never came. All the help that ever came was from within yourselves. You had the fruits only of what you yourselves worked for, and yet you were strangely hoping all the time for help from others. A rich man's parlor is always full; but, if you notice, you do not find the same people there. The visitors are always hoping that they will get something from the wealthy man; but they never do. So are our lives spent in hoping, hoping, hoping, to which there is no end. Give up hope, says Vedanta. Why should you hope? You have everything, nay, you are everything. What are you hoping for? If a king goes mad and runs about trying to find the king of his country, he will never find him, because he is the king himself. He may go through every village and city in his own country, seeking in every house, weeping and wailing, but he will never find him, because he is the king himself. It is better that we know we are God and give up this fool's search after him. Knowing we are God, we become happy and contented.

Give up all these mad pursuits and then play your part in the universe as an actor on the stage. The whole scene will change, and instead of an eternal prison this world will appear a playground; instead of a land of competition it will be a land of bliss, where perpetual spring exists, flowers bloom, and butterflies flit about. This very world, which formerly was hell, will be a heaven. To the eyes of the bound it is a tremendous place of torment, but to the eyes of the free it is quite otherwise. This very life is the universal life. Heavens and all those places are here; all the gods are here, the so-called prototypes of man. The gods did not create man after their image, but man created the gods. And here are the prototypes; here is Indra, here is Varuna, and all the gods of the universe. We have been projecting our little doubles, and we are the originals of these gods; we are the real, the only gods to be worshipped.

This is the view of Vedanta, and this is its practicality. When we have become free, we need not go crazy and give up society and rush off to die in the forest or in a cave. We shall remain where we were, only we shall understand the whole thing. The same phenomena will remain, but with a new meaning.

We do not know the world yet; it is only through freedom that we shall see what it is and understand its nature. We shall see then that this so-called law, or fate, or destiny, touched only a small part of our nature. It was only one side, but on the other side there was freedom all the time. We did not know this, and that is why we tried to save ourselves from evil by hiding our faces in the ground, like hunted hares. Through delusion we tried to forget our nature, and yet we could not; it was always calling to us, and all our search after God or the gods or external freedom was a search after our real nature. We mistook the voice. We thought it came from the fire or from a god, or from the sun or moon or stars. But at last we have found that it is from within ourselves. Within ourselves is this eternal voice speaking of eternal freedom; its music is eternally going on. Part of this music of the soul has become the earth, the law, this universe; but it was always ours and always will be.

In one word, the ideal of Vedanta is to know man as he really is; and this is its message: If you cannot worship your brother man, the manifested God, how can you worship a God who is unmanifested? Do you not remember what the Bible says: "If you cannot love your brother whom you have seen, how can you love God whom you have not seen?" If you cannot see God in the human face, how can you see him in the clouds or in images made of dull, dead matter, or in the mere fictions of your brain? I shall call you religious from the day you begin to see God in men and women. Then you will understand what is meant by turning the left cheek to the man who strikes you on the right. When you see man as God, everything, even the tiger, will be welcome. Whatever comes to us is but the Lord, the eternal, the blessed one, appearing to us in various forms—as our father and mother and friend and child. They are our own soul playing with us.

As our human relationships can thus be made divine, so our relationship with God may take any of these forms, and we can look upon him as our father or mother or friend or beloved. Calling God mother is a higher ideal than calling God father, and to call him friend is still higher; but the highest is to regard him as the beloved. The culmination of all is to see no difference between lover and beloved. You may remember, perhaps, the old Persian story of how a lover came and knocked at the door of the beloved and was asked, "Who are you?" He answered, "It is I," and there was no response. A second time he came and exclaimed, "I am here," but the door was not opened. The third time he came, and the voice asked from inside, "Who is there?" He replied, "I am thyself, my beloved," and the door opened. So is the relation between God and ourselves. He is in everything; he is everything. Every man and woman is the palpable, blissful, living God. Who says God is unknown? Who says he is to be searched after? We have known God eternally. We have been living in him eternally. Everywhere he is eternally known, eternally worshipped.

Then comes another idea: that other forms of worship are not errors. This is one of the great points to be remembered: that those who worship God through ceremonials and forms, however crude we may think them, are not in error. It is the journey from truth to truth, from lower truth to higher truth. Darkness means less light; evil means less good; impurity means less purity. It must always be borne in mind that we should see others with eyes of love, with sympathy, knowing that they are going along the same path that we have trodden. If you are free, you must know that all will be so sooner or later; if you are free, how can you see anyone in bondage? If you are really pure, how do you see the impure? For what is within is without. We cannot see impurity without having it inside ourselves.

This is one of the practical sides of Vedanta, and I hope that we shall all try to carry it into our lives. Our whole life here is an opportunity to carry this into practice. But our greatest gain is that we shall work with satisfaction and contentment instead of with discontent and dissatisfaction; for we know that truth is within us, we have it as our birthright, and we have only to manifest it and make it tangible.

From *Vedanta and Privilege*
(Delivered in London, 1896)

There is a screen here, and some beautiful scenery outside. There is a small hole in the screen through which we can catch only a glimpse of it. Suppose this hole begins to increase; as it grows larger and larger, more and more of the scenery comes into view; and when the screen has vanished, we come face to face with the whole of the scenery. This scene outside is the soul, and the screen between us and the scenery is *maya*—time, space, and causation. There is a little hole somewhere, through which I can catch only a glimpse of the soul. As the hole grows bigger, I see more and more, and when the screen has vanished, I know that I am the soul.

So the changes in the universe are not in the Absolute, but in nature. Nature evolves more and more until the Absolute is fully manifest. In everyone it exists; in some it is manifested more than in others. The whole universe is really one. From the standpoint of the soul, to say that one is superior to another is meaningless. From the same standpoint, to say that man is superior to the animal or the plant is meaningless. In plants the obstacle to soul-manifestation is very great; in animals, a little less; in man, still less; in cultured, spiritual men, still less; and in perfect men it has vanished altogether. All our struggles, exercises, pains, pleasures, tears, and smiles—all that we do and think—tend towards that goal, the tearing up of the screen by making the hole bigger, the thinning of the layers that remain between the manifestation and the reality behind. Our work, therefore, is not to make the soul free, but to get rid of the bondage. The sun is covered by layers of clouds but remains unaffected by them. The work of the wind is to drive the clouds away, and the more the clouds disappear, the more the light of the sun appears. There is no change whatsoever in the soul—infinite, absolute, eternal knowledge, bliss, and existence.

Neither can there be birth or death for the soul. Dying and being born, reincarnation, and going to heaven cannot be for the soul. These are different appearances, different mirages, different dreams. If a man who is dreaming of this world now, dreams of wicked thoughts and wicked deeds, after a certain time the thought of that very dream will produce the next dream; he will dream that he is in a horrible place, being tortured. The man who is dreaming good thoughts and good deeds, after that period of dream is over will dream he is in a better place. And so on from dream to dream.

But the time will come when the whole of this dream will vanish. To every one of us there must come a time when the whole universe will be found to have been a dream, when we shall find that the soul is infinitely more real than its surroundings. In this struggle through what we call our environments, there will come a time when we shall find that these environments were almost zero in comparison with the power of the soul. It is only a question of time, and time is nothing compared to the infinite. It is a drop in the ocean. We can afford to wait and be calm.

Consciously or unconsciously, therefore, the whole universe is going towards that goal. The moon is struggling to get out of the sphere of attraction of other bodies, and will come out of it in the long run. But those who consciously strive to get free shorten the time. One practical benefit from this theory, we see, is that the idea of a real universal love is possible only from this point of view. All are our fellow travelers. All living things—plants, animals, and men; not only my brother man, but my brother brute, my brother plant; not only my brother the good man, but my brother the evil, my brother the spiritual man and my brother the wicked—they are all going to the same goal. All are in the same stream; each is hurrying towards that infinite freedom. We cannot stay the course; none can stay it, none can go back, however he may try; he will be driven forward and finally will attain to freedom. The cosmic process means the struggle to get back to freedom, the center of our being, from whence we have been thrown off, as it were. The very fact that we are here shows that we are going towards the center, and the manifestation of this attraction towards the center is what we call love.

The question is asked: From what does this universe come, in what does it remain, to what does it go back? And the answer is: From love it comes, in love it remains, back it goes unto love. Thus we are in a position to understand that, whether one likes it or not, there is no holding back for anyone. Everyone has to get to the center, however he may struggle to hold back. Yet if we struggle consciously, knowingly, it will smooth the passage; it will lessen the jar and quicken the time.

Another conclusion we naturally arrive at from this is that all knowledge and all power are within and not without. What we call nature is a reflecting glass; the only use of nature is to reflect, and all knowledge is this reflection of the internal on the glass of nature. What we call secrets of nature and powers are all within. In the external world is only a series of changes. There is no knowledge in nature; all knowledge comes from the human soul. Man manifests knowledge—discovers it within himself—which has existed through eternity. Everyone is the embodiment of knowledge, everyone is the embodiment of eternal bliss, and eternal existence.

The effect of this theory is the same, as we have seen elsewhere, with regard to equality. The idea of privilege is the bane of human life. Two forces, as it were, are constantly at work, the one making caste and the other breaking caste; in other words, the one making for privilege, and the other breaking down privilege. And whenever privilege is broken down, more and more light and progress come to a race. This struggle we see all around us. Of course there is first the brutal idea of privilege: that of the strong over the weak. There is the privilege of wealth: if a man has more money than another, he wants a little privilege over those who have less. There is the still subtler and more powerful privilege of intellect: because one man knows more than others he claims more privilege. And the last of all, and the worst, because the most tyrannical, is the privilege of spirituality: if some persons think they know more of spirituality, of God, they claim a privilege over everyone else; they say, "Come down and worship us, ye common herd; we are the messengers of God, and you have to worship us."

None can be Vedantists and at the same time sanction privilege for anyone, either mental, physical, or spiritual. There should be absolutely no privilege for anyone. The same power is in every man, one manifesting more, another less; the same potentiality is in all. Where then is the claim to privilege? All knowledge is in every soul, even in the most ignorant; he has not manifested it, but perhaps he has not had the opportunity; his environment was not, perhaps, suitable to him; when he gets the opportunity he will manifest it. The idea that one man is born superior to another has no meaning in Vedanta; that between two nations one is superior and the other inferior has no meaning whatsoever. Put them in the same circumstances and see whether the same intelligence comes out or not. Before that you have no right to say that one nation is superior to another.

And as to spirituality, no privilege should be claimed there. It is a privilege to serve mankind; for this is the worship of God. God is here in all these human souls. He is the soul of man; what privilege can men ask? There are no special messengers of God, never were, and never can be. All beings, great or small, are equally manifestations of God; the difference is only in the degree of manifestation. The same eternal message, which has been eternally given, comes to them all. The eternal message has been written in the heart of every being; it is there already, and all are struggling to express it. Some, in suitable circumstances, express it a little better than others; but as bearers of the message they are all one. What claim to superiority is there? The most ignorant man, the most ignorant child, is as great a messenger of God as any that ever existed and as great as any that is yet to come. For the infinite message is there imprinted once for all in the heart of every being. Wherever there is a being, that being contains the infinite message of the Most High. It is there.

The task of *Advaita* [philosophy of nondualism], therefore, is to break down all these privileges. It is the hardest work of all; and curious to say, in the land of its birth Advaita has been less active than anywhere else. If there is any land of privilege, it is the land which gave birth to this philosophy—privilege for the spiritual man as well as for the man of birth. In India there is not so much the privilege of money (that is one of the benefits, I think); but the privilege of birth and spirituality is everywhere.

Once a gigantic attempt was made in India to preach Vedantic ethics, which succeeded to a certain extent for several hundred years; and we know historically that those years were the best times for the country. I mean the Buddhist attempt to break down privilege. Some of the most beautiful epithets addressed to Buddha that I remember are: "Thou the breaker of castes, destroyer of privileges, preacher of equality to all beings." He preached this one idea of equality. Its power has been misunderstood to a certain extent in the brotherhood of Shramanas, where we find that hundreds of attempts have been made to form them into a church, with superiors and inferiors. You cannot make much of a church when you tell people that they are all gods. One of the good effects of Vedanta has been freedom of religious thought, which India has enjoyed throughout its history. It is something to glory in, that it is the land where there was never a religious persecution, where people are allowed perfect freedom in religion.

This practical side of Vedantic morality is necessary as much today as it ever was—more necessary, perhaps, than it ever was; for all this privilege-claiming has become tremendously intensified with the extension of knowledge. The idea of God and the Devil, or Ahura Mazda and Ahriman, has a good deal of poetry in it. The difference between God and the Devil is in nothing except in unselfishness and selfishness. The Devil knows as much as God, is as powerful as God, only he has no holiness: that makes him the Devil. Apply the same idea to the modern world: excess of knowledge and power, without holiness, makes human beings devils. Tremendous power is being acquired through machines and other appliances, and privilege is claimed today by those in power as it never has been claimed in the history of the world. That is why Vedanta wants to preach against it, to break down this tyrannizing over the souls of men.

Those of you who have studied the Gita will remember the memorable passages: "He who looks upon the learned Brahmin, upon the cow, the elephant, the dog, or the outcaste, with the same eye, he indeed is the sage and the wise man." "Even in this life he has conquered relative existence whose mind is firmly fixed on sameness; for the Lord is

one and the same to all, and the Lord is pure. Therefore those who
feel this sameness for all and are pure are said to be living in God." This
is the gist of Vedantic morality, this sameness for all. We have seen
that it is the subjective world that rules the objective. Change the subject, and the object is bound to change; purify yourself, and the world
is bound to be purified. This one thing requires to be taught now more
than ever before. We are becoming more and more busy about our
neighbors, and less and less about ourselves. The world will change if
we change; if we are pure the world will become pure. The question is
why I should see evil in others. I cannot see evil unless I am evil. I cannot be miserable unless I am weak. Things that used to make me miserable when I was a child do not do so now. The subject changed, and
so the object was bound to change—so says Vedanta. All these things
which we call causes of misery and evil, we shall laugh at when we arrive
at that wonderful state of equality, that sameness. This is what is called
in Vedanta attaining to freedom. The sign of approaching that freedom
is the realization of more and more of this sameness and equality. In
misery and happiness the same, in success and defeat the same—such
a mind is nearing the state of freedom.

But the mind cannot be easily conquered. Minds that rise into waves
at the approach of every little thing, at the slightest provocation or danger, in what a state they must be! How talk of greatness or spirituality
when these changes come over the mind? This unstable condition of
the mind must be changed. We must ask ourselves how far we can be
acted upon by the external world, and how far we can stand on our own
feet in spite of all the forces outside us. When we have succeeded in pre-
venting all the forces in the world from throwing us off our balance,
then alone have we attained to freedom, and not before. That is salvation. It is here and nowhere else, this very moment.

Out of this idea, out of this fountainhead, two beautiful streams
of thought have flowed upon the world, generally misunderstood in

their expression, apparently contradicting each other. We find hosts of brave and wonderfully spiritual souls, in every nation, taking to caves or forests for meditation, severing their connection with the external world. This is the one idea. And on the other hand, we find bright, illustrious beings coming into society, trying to raise their fellow men, the poor, the miserable. Apparently these two methods are contradictory. The man who lives in a cave, apart from his fellow beings, smiles contemptuously upon those who are working for the regeneration of their fellow men. "How foolish!" he says. "What work is there to do? The world of maya will always remain the world of maya; it cannot be changed."

If I ask one of our priests in India, "Do you believe in Vedanta?" he says: "That is my religion; I certainly do. That is my life." "Very well, do you admit the equality of all life, the sameness of everything?" "Certainly I do." The next moment, when a low-caste man approaches this priest, he jumps to one side of the street to avoid that man. "Why did you jump?" "Because his very touch would have polluted me." "But you were just saying we are all the same, and you admit there is no difference in souls." He says, "Oh, that does not apply to householders; when I become a monk, then I shall look upon everyone as the same." You ask one of your great men in England, of great birth and wealth, if he believes as a Christian in the brotherhood of mankind, since all came from God. He answers in the affirmative; but in five minutes he shouts something uncomplimentary about the common herd. Thus it has been only a theory for several thousand years, and has never come into practice. All understand it, declare it as the truth, but when you ask them to practice it, they say it will take millions of years.

There was a certain king who had a large number of courtiers, and each one of these courtiers declared that he was ready to sacrifice his life for his master and that he was the most sincere being ever born. In course of time, a sannyasin came to the king. The king said to him that there never was a king who had so many sincere courtiers as he had. The sannyasin smiled and said that he did not believe it. The king said that the sannyasin could test it if he liked. So the sannyasin declared that he would perform a great sacrifice by which the king's reign would be extended very long; as an accessory of the sacrifice, he wanted a small pond into which, in the dark of night, each one of his courtiers should pour a pitcher of milk. The king smiled and said, "Is this the test?" And he asked his courtiers to come to him and told them what was to be done. They all expressed their joyful assent to the proposal and returned. In the dead of night they came and emptied their pitchers into the tank. But in the morning it was found full of water only. The courtiers were assembled and questioned about the matter. Each one of them had thought there would be so many pitchers of milk that his water would not be detected. Unfortunately most of us have the same idea, and we do our share as did the courtiers in the story.

There is so much talk of equality, says the priest, that my little privilege will not be detected. So say our rich men; so say the tyrants of every country. There is more hope for the tyrannized over than for the tyrants. It will take a very long time for tyrants to arrive at freedom, but less time for the others. The cruelty of the fox is much more terrible than the cruelty of the lion. The lion strikes a blow and is quiet for some time afterwards; but the fox, persistently following his prey, never misses an opportunity to harass it. Priestcraft is in its nature cruel and heartless. That is why religion goes down where priestcraft arises. Vedanta says that we must give up the idea of privilege; then religion will come. Before that there is no religion at all.

Do you accept what Christ says? "Go and sell that thou hast, and give to the poor." Practical equality there—no trying to torture the texts, but taking the truth as it is. Do not try to torture texts. I have heard it said that that was preached only to the handful of Jews who listened to Jesus. The same argument will apply to other things also. Do not torture texts. Dare to face truth as it is. If we cannot reach it, let us confess our weakness, but let us not destroy the ideal. Let us hope that we shall attain to it sometime, and let us strive for it. There it is: "Sell that thou hast, and give to the poor, and follow me." Thus, trampling on every privilege and everything in us that works for privilege, let us work for that knowledge which will bring the feeling of sameness towards all mankind. You think that because you use a little more polished language you are superior to the man in the street. Remember that when you are thinking this, you are not going towards freedom, but are forging a fresh chain for your feet. And above all, if the pride of spirituality enters into you, woe unto you. It is the most awful bondage that ever existed. Neither can wealth nor any other bondage of the human heart bind the soul so much as this. "I am purer than others" is the most awful idea that can enter into the human heart. In what sense are you pure? The God in you is the God in all. If you have not known this, you have known nothing. How can there be difference? It is all one. Every being is the temple of the Most High; if you can see that, good; if not, spirituality has yet to come to you.

4

Great Spiritual Teachers of the World

The Great Teachers of the World
(Delivered at the Shakespeare Club, Pasadena, California, February 3, 1900)

The universe, according to a philosophical theory of the Hindus, is moving in cycles of wave form. It rises, reaches its zenith, and then falls and remains in the hollow, as it were, for some time, once more to rise, and so on in wave after wave. What is true of the universe is true of every part of it. The march of human affairs is like that; the history of nations is like that: they rise and they fall. After the rise comes a fall; again, out of the fall comes a rise, with greater power. This movement is always going on.

In the religious world the same movement exists. In every nation's spiritual life there is a fall as well as a rise. The nation goes down and everything seems to go to pieces. Then again it gains strength and rises. A huge wave comes—sometimes a tidal wave; and always on the crest of that tidal wave is a shining soul, a messenger. Creator and created by turns, he is the impetus that makes the wave rise, the nation rise; at the same time, he is created by the same forces which make the wave,

107

Swami Vivekananda, San Francisco, 1900

acting and interacting by turns. He puts forth his tremendous power upon society, and society makes him what he is. These are the great world thinkers; these are the prophets, the messengers, the incarnations of God.

Men have an idea that there can be only one religion, that there can be only one prophet, that there can be only one incarnation; but that idea is not true. By studying the lives of all these great messengers, we find that each was destined to play a part, as it were, and a part only; that the harmony consists in the sum total and not in one note. It is the same in the life of races: no race is born to alone enjoy the world. None dare say so. Each race has a part to play in this divine harmony of nations; each race has its mission to perform, its duty to fulfill. The sum total is the great harmony.

So not one of these prophets is born to rule the world forever. None has yet succeeded and none is going to succeed in the future. Each only contributes a part; and he will control the world and its destinies as far as that part is concerned.

Most of us are born believers in a personal God. We talk of principles, we think of theories, and that is all right; but every thought and every movement, every one of our actions, shows that we can only understand a principle when it comes to us through a person. We can only grasp an idea when it comes to us through a concrete ideal person. We can only understand the precept through the example. Would to God that all of us were so developed that we did not require any example, did not require any person. But that we are not; and naturally the vast majority of mankind have put their souls at the feet of these extraordinary personalities, the prophets, the incarnations of God—incarnations worshipped by the Christians, by the Buddhists, and by the Hindus. The Mohammedans from the beginning stood out against any such worship. They would have nothing to do with worshipping the prophets or the messengers, or paying any homage to them; but practically, instead of one prophet, thousands upon thousands of saints are being worshipped. We cannot go against facts. We are bound to worship personalities, and it is good. Remember the answer of your great prophet to the prayer, "Lord, show us the Father"—"He that hath seen me hath seen the Father." Which of us can have a better idea of God than that he is a man? We can see him only in and through humanity. The vibration of light is everywhere in this room; why cannot we see it everywhere? You can see it only in the lamp. God is an omnipresent principle—everywhere; but we are so constituted at present that we can see him, feel him, only in and through a human God.

When these great lights come, then man realizes God. And they come in a different way from the way we come. We come as beggars; they come as emperors. We come here like orphans, as people who have lost their way and do not know it. What are we to do? We do not know what is the meaning of our lives. We cannot realize it. Today we are doing one thing, tomorrow another. We are like little bits of straw drifting to and fro in water, like feathers blown about in a hurricane. But in the history of mankind you will find that these messengers come, and that from their very birth their mission is found and formed. The whole plan is there, laid down, and you see them swerving not one inch from it.

Because they come with a mission, they come with a message. They do not want to reason. Did you ever hear or read of these great teachers or prophets reasoning out what they taught? No; not one of them has done so. They speak direct. Why should they reason? They see the truth. And not only do they see it, but they show it. If you ask me, "Is there any God?" and I say "Yes," you immediately ask my grounds for saying so, and poor me has to exercise all his powers to provide you with some reason. If you had come to Christ and said, "Is there any God?" he would have said, "Yes"; and if you had asked, "Is there any proof?" he would have replied, "Behold the Lord!" And thus, you see, it is a direct perception, and not at all the ratiocination of logic. There is no groping in the dark; but there is the strength of direct vision. I see this table; no amount of reason can take that faith from me. It is a direct perception. Such is their faith—faith in their ideals, faith in their mission, above all else faith in themselves. The great shining ones believe in themselves as nobody else ever does.

The people say, "Do you believe in God? Do you believe in a future life? Do you believe in this doctrine or that dogma?" But here the base is wanting: this belief in oneself. Ay! the man who cannot believe in himself, how can they expect him to believe in anything else? I am not sure of my own existence. One moment I think that I am existing and nothing can destroy me; the next moment I am quaking in fear of death. One minute I think I am immortal; the next minute a spook appears, and then I don't know what I am or where I am. I don't know whether I am living or dead. One moment I think that I am spiritual, that I am moral; and the next moment a blow comes, and I am thrown flat on my back. And why? I have lost faith in myself; my moral backbone is broken.

But in these great teachers you will always find this sign: that they have intense faith in themselves. Such intense faith is unique and we cannot understand it. That is why we try to explain away in various ways what these teachers speak of themselves; and people invent twenty thousand theories to explain what they say about their realization. We do not think of ourselves in the same way, and naturally we cannot understand them.

Then again, when they speak the world is bound to listen. When they speak each word is direct; it bursts like a bombshell. What is in the word unless it has the power behind? What matters it what language you speak and how you arrange your language? What matters it whether or not you speak with correct grammar and fine rhetoric? What matters it whether your language is ornamental or not? The question is whether or not you have anything to give. It is a question of giving and taking, and not of listening. Have you anything to give?—that is the first question. If you have, then give. Words but convey the gift; they are but one of the many modes.

Sometimes they do not speak at all. There is an old Sanskrit verse which says: "I saw the teacher sitting under a tree. He was a young man of sixteen and the disciple was an old man of eighty. The preaching of the teacher was in silence, and the doubts of the doubter departed." Thus, though they do not speak at all, yet they can convey the truth from mind to mind. They come to give. They command—they, the messengers; you have to obey the command. Do you not remember in your own scriptures the authority with which Jesus speaks? "Go ye therefore, and teach all nations.... Teaching them to observe all things whatsoever I have commanded you." It runs through all his utterances, that tremendous faith in his own message. That you find in the life of all these great giants whom the world worships as its prophets.

These great teachers are the living Gods on this earth. Whom else should we worship? I try to get an idea of God in my mind, and I find what a false little thing I conceive; it would be a sin to worship that as God. I open my eyes and look at the actual life of these great ones of the earth. They are higher than any conception of God that I could ever form. For what idea of mercy could be formed by a man like me, who would go after a man if he steals anything from me and send him to jail? And what can be my highest idea of forgiveness? Nothing beyond myself. Which of you can jump out of his own body? Which of you can jump out of his own mind? Not one of you. What idea of divine love can you form except what you actually feel? What we have never experienced we can form no idea of. So all my best attempts at forming an idea of God will fail in every case. And here are plain facts and not ideas—actual facts of love, of mercy, of purity, of which I cannot even have any conception. What wonder that I should fall at the feet of these men and worship them as God? And what else can anyone do? I should like to see the man who can do anything else, however much he may talk. Talking is not actuality. Talking about God and the impersonal, and this and that, is all very good; but these man-Gods are the real Gods of all nations and all races. These divine men have been worshipped and will be worshipped so long as man is man. Therein is our faith, therein is our hope. Of what avail is a mere mystical principle?

The purpose and intent of what I have to say to you is this: that I have found it possible in my life to worship all of them and to be ready for all that are yet to come. A mother recognizes her son in any dress in which he may appear before her; and if she does not do so, I am sure that she is not the mother of that man. Now, as regards those of you who think you understand truth and divinity and God in only one prophet in the world, and not in any other, naturally, the conclusion which I draw is that you do not understand divinity in anybody; you have simply swallowed words and identified yourself with one sect, just as you would in party politics, as a matter of opinion. But that is no religion at all. There are some fools in this world who use brackish water although there is excellent sweet water nearby, because, they say, the brackish-water well was dug by their father. Now, in my little experience I have collected this knowledge: that for all the devilry that religion is blamed for, religion is not at all at fault. No religion ever persecuted men, no religion ever burnt witches, no religion ever did any of these things. What then incited people to do these things? Politics, but never religion; and if such politics takes the name of religion, whose fault is that?

So when each man stands and says, "My prophet is the only true prophet," he is not right; he knows not the A B C of religion. Religion is neither talk nor theory nor intellectual consent. It is realization in our heart of hearts; it is touching God; it is feeling, realizing that I am a spirit related to the universal spirit and all its great manifestations. If you have really entered the house of the Father, how can you have seen his children and not known them? And if you do not recognize them, you have not entered the house of the Father. The mother recognizes her child in any dress and knows him however disguised. Recognize all the great spiritual men and women in every age and country and see that they are not really at variance with one another. Wherever there has been actual religion—this touch of the divine, the soul coming in direct contact with the divine—there has always been a broadening of the mind which has enabled it to see the light everywhere.

Side by side with the modern theory of evolution there is another thing: atavism. There is a tendency in us to revert to old ideas in religion. Let us think something new, even if it be wrong. It is better to do that. Why should we not try to hit the mark? We become wiser through failures. Time is infinite. Look at the wall. Did the wall ever tell a lie? It is always the wall. Man tells a lie—and becomes a god, too. It is better to do something; never mind even if it proves to be wrong. It is better than doing nothing. The cow never tells a lie, but she remains a cow all the time. Do something. Think some thought; it doesn't matter whether you are right or wrong. But think something. Because my forefathers did not think this way, shall I sit down quietly and gradually lose my sense of feeling and my own thinking faculty? I may as well be dead. And what is life worth if we have no living ideas, no convictions of our own, about religion? There is some hope for the atheists, because though they differ from others, they think for themselves. The people who never think anything for themselves are not yet born into the world of religion; they have a mere jellyfish existence. They will not think; they do not care for religion. But the disbeliever, the atheist, cares and he is struggling. So think something. Struggle Godwards. Never mind if you fail, never mind if you get hold of a queer theory. If you are afraid to be called queer, keep it in your own mind; you need not go out and preach it to others. But do something. Struggle Godwards. Light must come. If a man feeds me every day of my life, in the long run I shall lose the use of my hands. Spiritual death is the result of following others as in a flock of sheep. Death is the result of inaction. Be active; and wherever there is activity there must be difference. Difference is the sauce of life; it is the beauty, it is the art, of everything: difference makes all beautiful here. It is variety that is the source of life, the sign of life. Why should we be afraid of it?

Now, we are coming into a position to understand about the prophets. We see that the historical evidence is—apart from the jellyfish acceptance of dogmas—that where there has been any real thinking, any real love of God, the soul has grown Godwards and has got, as it were, a glimpse now and then, has attained direct perception, even for a second, even once in its life. Immediately "all doubts vanish forever, all the crookedness of the heart is made straight, all bondage vanishes, and the results of past actions fly away; for he is seen who is the nearest of the near and the farthest of the far." That is religion; that is all of religion. The rest is mere theory, dogma, so many ways of going to that state of direct perception. Now we are fighting over the basket and the fruits have fallen into the ditch.

If two men quarrel about religion, just ask them the question: "Have you seen God? Have you seen spiritual things?" One man says that Christ is the only prophet. Well, has he seen Christ? "Has your father seen him?" "No, sir." "Has your grandfather seen him?" "No, sir." "Have you seen him?" "No, sir." "Then what are you quarrelling for? The fruits have fallen into the ditch and you are quarrelling over the basket!" Sensible men and women should be ashamed to go on quarrelling in that way.

These messengers and prophets were great and true. Why so? Because each one came to preach a great idea. Take the prophets of India, for instance. They are the oldest of the founders of religion. We take, first, Krishna. You who have read the Gita know that the one idea all through the book is nonattachment. Remain unattached. The heart's love is due to only one. To whom? To him who never changes. Who is that one? He is God. Do not make the mistake of giving the heart to anything that is changing, because that is misery. You may give it to a man; but if he dies, misery is the result. You may give it to a friend; but tomorrow he may become your enemy. If you give it to your husband, he may one day quarrel with you. You may give it to your wife, and she may die the day after tomorrow. Now, this is the way the world is going on. So says Krishna in the Gita. The Lord is the only one who never changes. His love never fails. Wherever we are and whatever we do, he is ever and ever the same merciful, the same loving spirit. He never changes, he is never angry, whatever we do.

How can God be angry with us? Your baby does many mischievous things: are you angry with that baby? Does not God know what we are going to be? He knows we are all going to be perfect sooner or later. He has patience, infinite patience. We must love him and, only in and through him, everyone that lives. This is the keynote. You must love your wife, but not for your wife's sake. "Never, O beloved, is the husband loved on account of the husband, but because the Lord is in the husband." The Vedanta philosophy says that even in the love of husband and wife, although the wife is thinking that she is loving the husband, the real attraction is the Lord, who is present there. He is the only attraction, there is no other. But the wife in most cases does not know that it is so; yet ignorantly she is doing the right thing, which is loving the Lord. Only, when one does it ignorantly it may bring pain. If one does it knowingly, that is salvation. This is what our scriptures say. Wherever there is love, wherever there is a spark of joy, know that to be a spark of his presence, because he is joy, blessedness, and love itself. Without him there cannot be any love.

This is the trend of Krishna's instruction all through. He has implanted that in his race; therefore, when a Hindu does anything, even when he drinks water, he says "If there is virtue in it, let it go to the Lord." The Buddhist says, if he does any good deed, "Let the merit of the good deed belong to the world; if there is any virtue in what I do, let it go to the world, and let the evils of the world come to me." The Hindu—he is a great believer in God—the Hindu says that God is omnipotent and that he is the soul of all souls everywhere. So he says, "If I give all my virtues unto him, that is the greatest sacrifice, and they will go to the whole universe."

Now, this is one message. And what is another message of Krishna? "Whosoever lives in the midst of the world, and works, giving up all the fruit of his action unto the Lord, is never touched by the evils of the world. The lotus, born under the water, rises up and blossoms above the water; even so is the man who is engaged in the activities of the world, giving up all the fruit of his activities unto the Lord."

Krishna strikes still another note as a teacher of intense activity. Work, work, day and night, says the Gita. You may ask: "Then where is peace? If all through life I am to work like a cart-horse and die in harness, what am I here for?" Krishna says: "Yes, you will find peace. Flying from work is never the way to find peace." Throw off your duties if you can and go to the top of a mountain; even there the mind keeps on going—whirling, whirling, whirling. Someone asked a sannyasin, "Sir, have you found a nice place? How many years have you been traveling in the Himalayas?" "For forty years," replied the sannyasin. "There are many beautiful spots to select from and to settle down in; why did you not do so?" "Because for these forty years my mind would not allow me to." We all say, "Let us find peace," but the mind will not allow us to do so.

You know the story of the man who caught a Tartar. A soldier was outside the town, and he cried out when he came near the barracks,

"I have caught a Tartar." A voice called out, "Bring him in." "He won't come in, sir." "Then you come in." "He won't let me come in, sir!" So, in this mind of ours, we have "caught a Tartar": neither can we quiet it down nor will it let us be quieted down. We have all "caught Tartars." We all say: Be quiet and peaceful and so forth. But every baby can say that and thinks he can do it. However, that is very difficult. I have tried. I threw overboard all my duties and fled to the tops of mountains; I lived in caves and deep forests; but all the same, I had "caught a Tartar," because I had my world with me all the time. The "Tartar" is what I have in my own mind; so we must not blame poor people outside. "These circumstances are good, and these are bad," so we say, while the "Tartar" is here within. If we can quiet him down, we shall be all right.

Therefore Krishna teaches us not to shirk our duties, but to take them up manfully and not think of the result. The servant has no right to question. The soldier has no right to reason. Go forward and do not pay too much attention to the nature of the work you have to do. Ask your mind if you are unselfish. If you are, never mind anything; nothing can resist you. Plunge in. Do the duty at hand. And when you have done this, by degrees you will realize the truth: "Whosoever in the midst of intense activity finds intense peace, whosoever in the midst of the greatest peace finds the greatest activity, he is a yogi, he is a great soul, he has arrived at perfection."

Now you can see that the result of this teaching is that all the duties of the world are sanctified. There is no duty in this world which we have any right to call menial; and each man's work is quite as good as that of the emperor on his throne.

Listen to Buddha's message—a tremendous message. It has a place in our heart. Says Buddha: Root out selfishness and everything that makes you selfish. Have neither wife, child, nor family. Be not of the world; become perfectly unselfish. A worldly man thinks he will be unselfish, but when he looks at the face of his wife it makes him self-ish. The mother thinks she will be perfectly unselfish, but she looks at her baby and immediately selfishness comes. So with everything in this world. As soon as selfish desires arise in a man, as soon as he follows some selfish pursuit, immediately the real man is gone; he becomes like a brute, he is a slave, he forgets his fellow men. No more does he say, "You first and me afterwards," but it is "Me first and let every one else look out for himself."

We find that Krishna's message has a place for us. Without that message we cannot move at all. We cannot conscientiously, and with peace, joy, and happiness, take up any duty of our lives without listening to the message of Krishna: "Be not afraid even if there is evil in your work, for there is no work which has no evil." "Leave it unto the Lord, and do not look for the results."

On the other hand, there is a corner in the heart for the other message: Time flies. This world is finite and all misery. With your good food, nice clothes, and your comfortable home, O sleeping man and woman, do you ever think of the millions that are starving and dying? Think of the great fact that it is all misery, misery, misery! Note the first utterance of the child: when it enters into the world, it weeps. That is the fact: the child weeps. This is a place for weeping. If we listen to Buddha, we shall not be selfish.

Behold another messenger, he of Nazareth. He teaches: "Be ready, for the kingdom of heaven is at hand." I have pondered over the message of Krishna, and am trying to work without attachment; but sometimes I forget. Then, suddenly, comes to me the message of Buddha: "Take care, for everything in the world is evanescent, and there is always misery in this life." I listen to that and I am uncertain which to accept. Then again comes, like a thunderbolt, the message: "Be ready, for the kingdom of heaven is at hand. Do not delay a moment. Leave nothing for tomorrow. Get ready for that final event, which may overtake you immediately, even now." That message, also, has a place, and we acknowledge it. We salute the Christ; we salute the Lord.

And then comes Mohammed, the messenger of equality. Mohammed was the prophet of equality, of the brotherhood of man, the brotherhood of all Mussulmans.

So we see that each prophet, each messenger, has a particular message. When you first listen to that message, and then look at his life, you see his whole life stand explained, radiant.

Now, ignorant fools start twenty thousand theories and put forward, according to their own mental development, explanations to suit their own ideas, and ascribe them to these great teachers. They take their teachings and put their misconstruction upon them. With every great prophet his life is the only commentary. Look at his life: what he did will bear out the texts. Read the Gita, and you will find that it is exactly borne out by the life of the teacher.

Mohammed by his life showed that amongst Mohammedans there should be perfect equality and brotherhood. There was no question of race, caste, creed, color, or sex. The sultan of Turkey may buy a Negro from the mart of Africa and bring him in chains to Turkey; but should he become a Mohammedan and have sufficient merit and abilities, he might even marry the daughter of the sultan. Compare this with the way in which the Negroes and the American Indians are treated in this country. And what do Hindus do? If one of your missionaries chanced to touch the food of an orthodox person, he would throw it away. Notwithstanding our grand philosophy, you note our weakness in practice; but there you see the greatness of Islam beyond other faiths, showing itself in equality, perfect equality, regardless of race or color.

Will other and greater prophets come? Certainly they will come in this world. But do not look forward to that. I should better like that each one of you become a prophet of this real New Testament, which is made up of all the Old Testaments. Take all the old messages, supplement them with your own realizations, and become a prophet unto others. Each one of these teachers has been great; each has left something for us. They have been our Gods. We salute them; we are their servants. And at the same we salute ourselves; for if they have been prophets and children of God, we are prophets also. They reached their perfection and we are going to attain ours now. Remember the words of Jesus: "The kingdom of heaven is at hand." This very moment let every one of us make a staunch resolution: "I will become a prophet, I will become a messenger of light, I will become a child of God, nay, I will become God himself."

Christ, the Messenger
(Delivered in Los Angeles, California, 1900)

A wave rises in the ocean, and then there is a hollow. Again another wave rises, perhaps bigger than the first, only to fall again, and again to rise, driving onward. Similarly, in the march of events, we may notice the same rise and fall, but we generally look towards the rise, forgetting the fall. Both are necessary and both are great. This is the nature of the universe. Whether in the world of our thoughts or in the world of our relations, in society or in our spiritual affairs, this same succession of movements, of rises and falls, is going on. Hence, in the march of events, liberal ideals move forward, afterwards to sink down in order to gather strength once more for a new rise and a greater one.

The history of nations, also, has been ever like this. The great soul, the messenger whom we are to study this afternoon, came at a period in the history of his race which we may well designate as a great fall. We catch but little glimpses here and there of the stray records that have been kept of his sayings and doings, for it has been well said that the sayings and doings of that great soul would have filled the world, could they all have been written down. And the three years of his ministry were like one compressed and concentrated age, which it has taken nineteen hundred years afterwards to unfold, and may yet take who knows how much longer. Little men like you and me are reservoirs of just a little energy. A few minutes, a few hours, a few years at best, are enough to spend it all, to stretch it out, as it were, to its fullest strength, and then we are gone forever. But mark this giant. Centuries and ages pass, yet the energy that he left upon the world is not yet stretched out, not yet expended to its full. It goes on gaining new vigor as the ages roll on.

Now what you see in the life of Christ is the life of all the past. The life of every man is, in a manner, the life of the past. It comes to him through heredity, through his surroundings, through education, through his own reincarnation—the past of the whole race. In a way the past of the earth, the past of the whole world, stands impressed upon every soul. What are we, in the present, but a result, an effect, of the infinite past of the world? What are we but floating wavelets in the eternal current of events, irresistibly moved forward and onward and incapable of rest? But you and I are only little things, bubbles. There are always some giant waves in the ocean of the world. In you and me the past life of the race may have been embodied only a little; but there are giants who embody, as it were, almost the whole of the past and stretch out their hands over the future also. They are the signposts, here and there, directing the march of humanity; they are verily giants, their shadows covering the earth; they stand undying, eternal. As was said by the same messenger: "No man hath seen God at any time, but through the Son." It is true. For where should we see God but in the Son? It is true that you and I, and the poorest and meanest of us, embody that God, even reflect that God. The vibration of light is everywhere, omnipresent; but we see it most vividly in a lamp. Likewise God is omnipresent; but he can be seen most vividly when he is reflected in some one of these giant lamps of the earth—the prophets, the man-Gods, the incarnations, the embodiments of God.

We all know that God exists, and yet we do not see him, we do not understand him. Take one of these great messengers of light, and compare his character with the highest ideal of God that you ever formed, and you will find that your ideal falls short of him, and that the character of the prophet exceeds your imagination. You cannot even imagine a higher ideal of God than what he actually embodied, practically realized, and set before us as an example. Is it wrong, therefore, to worship these as God? Is it a sin to fall at the feet of these man-Gods and worship them as the only divine beings in the world? If they are really, actually, higher than all our conceptions of God, what harm is there in worshipping them? Not only is there no harm, but it is the only possible and positive way of worship. However much you may try, by struggle, by abstraction, by whatsoever method you like, still so long as you are a man in the world of men, your world is human, your religion is human, and your God is human. And that must be so. Who is not practical enough to take up an actually existing thing and give up an idea which is only an abstraction that he cannot grasp, and which is difficult of approach except through a concrete medium? Therefore these incarnations of God have been worshipped in all ages and in all countries.

We are now going to study a little of the life of Christ, the incarnation of the Jews. When Christ was born, the Jews were in that state which I shall call a condition of fall between two waves: a state of conservatism, a state where the human mind is, as it were, tired for the time being of moving forward and is taking care only of what it has already won; a state when the attention is more bent upon particulars, upon details than upon the great and vital problems of life; a state of stagnation, rather than forging ahead; a state of suffering more than of achieving. Mark you, I do not blame this state of things; we have no right to criticize it. Because had it not been for this fall, the next rise, which was embodied in Jesus of Nazareth, would have been impossible. The Pharisees and Sadducees might have been insincere, they might have been doing things which they ought not to have done; they might even have been hypocrites; but whatever they were, these factors were the very cause of which the messenger was the effect. The Pharisees and Sadducees at one end were the very impetus which came out at the other end as the gigantic brain of Jesus of Nazareth.

The attention to forms, to formulas, to the everyday details of religion, and to rituals may sometimes be laughed at, but nevertheless within them is strength. Many times in our rushing forward we lose much vigor. It is a fact that the fanatic is stronger than the liberal man. Even the fanatic, therefore, has one great virtue: he conserves energy, a tremendous amount of it. As with the individual, so with the race, energy is gathered to be conserved. Hemmed in by external enemies, driven back upon its own center by the Roman might, by the Hellenic tendencies in the world of intellect, by waves of thought from Persia, India, and Alexandria—hemmed in physically, mentally, and morally—there stood the Jewish race, with an inherent, conservative, tremendous strength, which their descendants have not lost even today. That race was forced to concentrate and focus all its energies upon Jerusalem and Judaism; and, like all power when once gathered, it cannot remain collected; it must expand and expend itself. There is no power on earth which can be kept long confined within too narrow a limit. No power can be kept compressed very long without its expanding at a subsequent period.

It was the concentrated energy of the Jewish race which found expression, at the next period, in the rise of Christianity. The smallest streams formed into rivers. Gradually all the rivers joined together and became one vast, surging river. On the top of one of its mighty waves we see standing Jesus of Nazareth. In this way every prophet is the creation of his times; created by the past of his race, he himself is the creator of the future. The movement of today is the effect of the past and the cause of the future. In this position stands the messenger. In him is embodied all that is the best and greatest in his own race—the meaning, the life, for which that race has struggled for ages—and he himself is the impetus for the future, not only for his own race, but also for unnumbered other races of the world.

We must bear in mind another fact: that my view of the great prophet of Nazareth is necessarily from the standpoint of the Orient. Many times you forget that the Nazarene was an Oriental of Orientals. Notwithstanding all your attempts to paint him with blue eyes and yellow hair, the Nazarene is still an Oriental. All the similes, all the imagery, with which the Bible is filled—the scenes, the locations, the attitudes, the groups, the poetry and symbolism—speak to you of the Orient: of the bright sky, of the heat, of the sun, of the desert, of thirsty men and animals, of women coming with pitchers on their heads to fill them at the wells, of the flocks, of the ploughmen, of the cultivation that is going on all around, of the watermill and the wheel of the millpond, of the millstones. All these are to be seen today in Asia.

The voice of Asia is the voice of religion, and the voice of Europe is the voice of politics. Each is great in its own sphere. The voice of Europe is the voice of ancient Greece. To the mind of the Greek, his immediate society was all in all; beyond that lived barbarians. None but the Greek had the right to live. Whatever the Greek did was right and correct; whatever else might exist in the world was neither right nor correct, nor should it be allowed to live. Here was a mind intensely human in its sympathies, intensely natural, and therefore intensely artistic. The Greek lived entirely in this world. He did not care to dream. Even his poetry was practical. His gods and goddesses were not only human beings but intensely human, with almost the same human passions and feelings as we have. He loved what was beautiful, but mind you, it was always external nature. The beauty of the hills, of the snows, of the flowers; the beauty of forms and of figures; the beauty in the human face and, more often, in the human form—that is what the Greeks loved. And the Greeks being the teachers of all subsequent Europeans, the voice of Europe is Greek.

There is another type in Asia. Think of that vast continent, whose mountaintops rise beyond the clouds, almost touching the canopy of heaven's blue; whose deserts roll on for miles upon miles, where not a drop of water can be found, neither will a blade of grass grow; think of its interminable forests and its gigantic rivers rushing down to the sea. In the midst of such surroundings, the Oriental love of the beautiful and of the sublime developed in quite another direction. It looked within and not without. Here also there was the same thirst for nature, the same thirst for power, there was the same thirst for excellence—the common idea of the Greek and the Oriental. But here it extended over a wider circle. In Asia, even today, birth or color or language never alone makes a race. That which makes a race is its religion: we are all Christians; we are all Mohammedans; we are all Hindus or all Buddhists. No matter if the Buddhists be from China and from Persia, they will think of themselves as brothers, because of their professing the same religion. Religion is the supreme tie in the uniting of humanity. And then again, the Oriental, for the same reason, is a visionary, is a born dreamer. The ripples of waterfalls, the songs of birds, the beauties of the sun and moon and stars and the whole earth, are pleasant enough; but they are not sufficient for the Oriental. He wants to dream a dream of the beyond. He wants to go beyond the present. The present is, as it were, nothing to him.

The Orient has been the cradle of the human race for ages, and all the vicissitudes of fortune have been there: kingdoms succeeding kingdoms, empires succeeding empires; human power, glory, and wealth, all rolling on the ground—a Golgotha of power and learning. That is the Orient: a Golgotha of power, of kingdoms, of learning. No wonder the Oriental mind looks with contempt upon the things of this world and seeks to see something which changes not, something which dies not, something which in the midst of this world of misery and death is eternal, blissful, undying. An Oriental prophet never tires of insisting upon these ideals; and as for prophets, you may also remember that, without one exception, all of them were Orientals.

We see, therefore, in the life of this great messenger of light, the first watchword: "Not this life, but something higher." And like a true son of the Orient, he is practical in that. You people of the West are practical in your own department, in military affairs and in managing politics and other similar things. Perhaps the Oriental is not practical in those matters; but he is practical in his own field; he is practical in religion. If he preaches a philosophy, tomorrow there will be hundreds who will struggle their utmost to make it practical in their lives. If a man preaches that standing on one foot will lead to salvation, he will immediately get five hundred to stand on one foot. You may call it ludicrous; but mark you, beneath that is the secret of religion: intense practicality. In the West, plans of salvation mean intellectual gymnastics, plans which are never worked out, never brought into practical life. In the West, the preacher who talks the best is the greatest preacher.

So in the first place we find Jesus of Nazareth to be a true son of the Orient, intensely practical. He has no faith in this evanescent world and its various belongings. No need of text torturing, as is the fashion in the West in modern times, no need of stretching out texts until they will not stretch anymore. Texts are not india-rubber, and even that has its limits. Now, please do not make religion pander to the vanity of the present day! Let us all, mark you, be honest. If we cannot follow the ideal, let us confess our weakness, but let us not degrade it. Let us not try to pull it down. One gets sick at heart at the different accounts of the life of the Christ that Western people give. I do not know what he was or what he was not! One would make him a great politician; another, perhaps, would make of him a great military general; another, a great patriotic Jew, and so on. Is there any warrant in the Bible for all such assumptions? The best commentary on the life of a great teacher is his own life. "The foxes have holes, the birds of the air have nests, but the son of man hath not where to lay his head." That is what Christ says is the only way to salvation. He lays down no other way.

Let us confess in sackcloth and ashes that we cannot do that. We still have a fondness for "me" and "mine." We want property, power, wealth. Woe unto us! Let us confess and not put to shame that great teacher of humanity! He had no family ties. Do you think that that man had any physical ideas in him? Do you think that this mass of light, this God and not man, came down to earth to be a brother of animals? And yet people make him preach all sorts of things. He had no sex ideas. He was the soul—nothing but the soul, just working through a body for the good of men; and that was all his relation to the body. In the soul there is no sex. The disembodied soul has no relationship to the animal, no relationship to the body. The ideal may be far beyond us; but never mind; keep to the ideal. Let us confess that it is our ideal, but we cannot approach it yet.

He had no other idea of himself, no other except that he was spirit. He was disembodied, unfettered, unbound spirit. And not only so, but he, with his marvelous vision, had found that every man and woman, whether Jew or Gentile, whether rich or poor, whether saint or sinner, was the embodiment of the same undying spirit as himself. Therefore the one work of his whole life was calling upon them to realize their own spiritual nature. Give up, he says, these superstitious dreams that you are low and that you are poor. Think not that you are trampled upon and tyrannized over as if you were slaves; for within you is something that can never be tyrannized over, never be trampled upon, never be troubled, never be killed. You are all sons of God, immortal spirit. "Know ye," he declared, "the kingdom of heaven is within you." "I and my Father are one." Dare not only to stand up and say, "I am the son of God," but also to find in your heart of hearts: "I and my Father are one." That was what Jesus of Nazareth said. He never talks of this world and of this life. He has nothing to do with it, except that he wants to get hold of the world as it is, give it a push, and drive it forward and onward until the whole world has reached to the effulgent light of God, until everyone has realized his spiritual nature, until death is vanquished and misery banished.

We have read the different stories that have been written about him; we know the scholars and their writings, and the higher criticism; and we know all that has been achieved by study. We are not here to discuss how much of the New Testament is true; we are not here to discuss how much of that life is historical. It does not matter at all whether the New Testament was written within five hundred years of his birth; nor does it even matter how much of that life is true. But there is something behind it, something we want to imitate. To tell a lie, you have to imitate a truth, and that truth is a fact. You cannot imitate that which never existed. You cannot imitate that which you have never perceived. There must have been a nucleus through which has come down a tremendous power, a marvelous manifestation of spiritual power—and of that we are speaking. It stands there. Therefore we are not afraid of the criticisms of the scholars. If I, as an Oriental, am to worship Jesus of Nazareth, there is only one way left to me: that is to worship him as God and nothing else. Do you mean to say that we have we no right to worship him in that way? If we bring him down to our own level and simply pay him a little respect as a great man, why should we worship at all? Our scriptures say: "These great children of light, who manifest the light themselves, who are light themselves, they being worshipped, become one with us, and we become one with them."

For there are three ways in which man perceives God. First the undeveloped intellect of the uneducated man sees God as being far away, up in the heavens somewhere, sitting on a throne as a great judge. He looks upon him with fear, as a terror. Now, that is good; there is nothing bad in it. You must remember that humanity travels not from error to truth, but from truth to truth—it may be, if you like it better, from lower to higher truth; but never from error to truth. Suppose you start from here and travel towards the sun in a straight line. From here the sun looks small. Suppose you go forward a million miles; it will surely seem much larger. At every stage it will become bigger and bigger. Suppose that twenty thousand photographs are taken of the same sun, all from different standpoints; these twenty thousand photographs will all certainly differ from one another. But can you deny that each is a photograph of the same sun? So all forms of religion, high or low, are just different stages in the upward journey towards that eternal light, which is God himself. Some embody a lower view, some a higher, and that is all the difference. Therefore the religions of the unthinking masses all over the world teach, and have always taught, of a God who is outside the universe, who lives in heaven, who governs from that place, who is a punisher of the bad and a rewarder of the good, and so on. As man advances spiritually, he begins to feel that God is omnipresent, that he must be in him, that he must be everywhere, that he is not a distant God, but clearly the soul of all souls. As my soul moves my body, even so is God the mover of my soul—the soul within the soul. And a few individuals of pure heart and highly developed mind go still farther, and at last find God. As the New Testament says: "Blessed are the pure in heart, for they shall see God." And they find at last that they and the Father are one.

You will find that these three stages are taught by the great teacher in the New Testament. Note the common prayer he taught: "Our Father, which art in heaven, hallowed be thy name," and so on; a simple prayer, mark you, a child's prayer. It is indeed the "common prayer" because it is intended for the uneducated masses. To a higher circle, to those who had advanced a little more, he gave a more elevated teaching: "I am in my Father, and ye in me, and I in you." Do you remember that? And then, when the Jews asked him who he was, he declared that he and his Father were one; and the Jews thought that that was blasphemy. What did he mean by that? But the same thing had been taught by the Jewish prophets: "Ye are gods; and all of you are children of the Most High." Mark the same three stages. You will find that it is easier for you to begin with the first and end with the last.

The messenger came to show the path: that the spirit is not in forms; that it is not through all sorts of vexations and knotty problems of philosophy that you know the spirit. Better that you had had no learning; better that you had never read a book in your life. These are not at all necessary for salvation—neither wealth nor position nor power, not even learning. But what is necessary is that one thing, purity: "Blessed are the pure in heart," for the spirit in its own nature is pure. How can it be otherwise? It is of God; it has come from God. In the language of the Bible, "It is the breath of God." In the language of the Koran, "It is the soul of God." Do you mean to say that the spirit of God can ever be impure? But alas, it has been covered over, as it were, with the dust and dirt of ages, through our own actions, good and evil; various works which were not correct, which were not true, have covered the spirit with the dust and dirt of the ignorance of ages. It is only necessary to clear away the dust and dirt, and then the spirit shines immediately. "Blessed are the pure in heart, for they shall see God." "The kingdom of heaven is within you." Where goest thou to seek for the kingdom of God?— asks Jesus of Nazareth, when it is there within you? Cleanse your spirit and find it there. It is already yours. How can you get what is not yours? It is yours by right. You are the heirs of immortality, sons of the eternal Father.

This is the great lesson of the messenger; another lesson, forming the basis of all religions, is renunciation. How can you make your spirit pure? By renunciation. A rich young man asked Jesus, "Good master, what shall I do that I may inherit eternal life?" And Jesus said unto him, "One thing thou lackest: go thy way, sell whatsoever thou hast, and give to the poor, and thou shalt have treasure in heaven: and come, take up thy cross, and follow me." And the man was sad at that saying, and went away grieved; for he had great possessions. We are all more or less like that. The voice is ringing in our ears day and night. In the midst of our joys and pleasures, in the midst of worldly things, in the midst of the world's turmoil, we forget it; then comes a moment's pause, and the voice rings in our ears: "Give up all that thou hast and follow me. Whosoever will save his life shall lose it; and whosoever shall lose his life for my sake shall find it." For whoever gives up this life for his sake finds the life immortal. In the midst of all our weakness there is a moment of pause and the voice rings: "Give up all that thou hast; give it to the poor and follow me." This is the one ideal he preaches, and this has been the ideal preached by all the great prophets of the world: renunciation. What is meant by renunciation? Unselfishness. That is the only ideal in morality. The ideal is perfect unselfishness. When a man is struck on the right cheek, he is to turn the left also. When a man's coat is carried off, he is to give his cloak in addition.

We should work in the best way we can, without dragging the ideal down. Here is the ideal: When a man has no more of self in him, no possession, nothing to call "me" or "mine," has given himself up to God, destroyed himself, as it were—in that man God is manifest; for in him self-will is gone, crushed out, annihilated. That is the ideal man.

We cannot reach that state yet; nevertheless, let us worship the ideal and slowly struggle to reach the ideal, though it may be with faltering steps. It may be tomorrow, or it may be a thousand years hence, but that ideal has to be reached. For it is not only the end, but also the means. To be unselfish, perfectly selfless, is salvation itself; for the man within dies and God alone remains.

One more point. All the teachers of humanity are unselfish. Suppose Jesus of Nazareth was teaching, and a man came and told him: "What you teach is beautiful. I believe that it is the way to perfection and I am ready to follow it; but I do not care to worship you as the only-begotten son of God." What would be the answer of Jesus of Nazareth? "Very well, brother, follow the ideal and advance in your own way. I do not care whether you give me the credit for the teaching or not. I am not a shopkeeper; I do not trade in religion. I teach truth only and truth is nobody's property. Nobody can patent truth. Truth is God himself. Go forward." But what the disciples say nowadays is: "No matter whether you practice the teachings or not, do you give credit to the man? If you credit the master, you will be saved; if not, there is no salvation for you." And thus the whole teaching of the master has degenerated and all the struggle and fight is about the personality of the man. They do not know that in emphasizing that difference they are, in a manner, bringing shame to the very man they want to honor, the very man who would have shrunk with shame from such an idea. What did he care if there was one man in the world that remembered him or not? He had to deliver his message, and he gave it. And if he had twenty thousand lives, he would give them all up for the poorest man in the world. If he had to be tortured millions of times, for a million despised Samaritans, and if for each one of them the sacrifice of his own life would be the only condition of salvation, he would have given his life. And all this without wishing to have his name known even to a single person.

Quiet, unknown, silent, would he work, just as the Lord works. Now, what will the disciple say? He will tell you that you may be a perfect man, perfectly unselfish, but unless you give the credit to his teacher, to his saint, it is of no avail. Why? What is the origin of this superstition, this ignorance? The disciple thinks that the Lord can manifest himself only once: there lies the whole mistake. God manifests himself to you in man. But in nature, what happens once must have happened before and must happen in the future. There is nothing in nature which is not bound by law, and that means that whatever happened once must have been going on ever since.

In India they have the same idea of the incarnation of God. One of their great incarnations, Krishna, whose grand sermon, the Bhagavad Gita, some of you may have read, says: "Though I am unborn, of change-less nature, and Lord of beings, yet subjugating my *prakriti* [nature], I come into being by my own maya. Whenever virtue subsides and immorality prevails I body myself forth. For the protection of the good, for the destruction of the wicked, and for the establishment of dharma, I assume a body in every age." Whenever the world goes down, the Lord comes to help it forward; and so he comes from age to age, in place after place. In another passage he speaks to this effect: "Wherever thou find-est a great soul of immense power and purity struggling to raise human-ity, know that he is born of my splendor, that I am there working through him."

Let us, therefore, find God not only in Jesus of Nazareth, but in all the great ones who preceded him, in all who have come after him, and all who are yet to come. Our worship is unbounded and free. They are all manifestations of the same infinite God. They are all pure and unselfish; they suffer and give up their lives for us poor human beings. They each and all suffer vicarious atonement for every one of us, and also for all who are to come hereafter.

In a sense, you are all prophets; every one of you is a prophet, bearing the burden of the world on your own shoulders. Have you ever seen a man, have you ever seen a woman, who is not quietly, patiently, bearing his or her little burden of life? The great prophets were giants: they bore the whole world on their shoulders. Compared with them we are pygmies, no doubt; yet we are doing the same task. In our little circles, in our little homes, we are bearing our little crosses. There is no one so evil, no one so worthless, but he has to bear his own cross. But with all our mistakes, with all our evil thoughts and evil deeds, there is a bright spot somewhere, there is still somewhere the golden thread through which we are always in touch with the divine. For know for certain that the moment the touch of the divine was lost there would be annihilation; and because none can be annihilated, there is always somewhere in our heart of hearts, however low and degraded we may be, a little circle of light which is in constant touch with the divine.

Our salutations go to all the past prophets, whose teachings and lives we have inherited, whatever their race, clime, or creed. Our salutations go to all those God-like men and women who are working at present to help humanity, whatever their birth, color, or race. Our salutations go to those who are coming in the future—living Gods—to work unselfishly for our descendants.

Buddha's Message to the World
(Delivered in San Francisco, March 18, 1900)

Buddhism is historically the most important religion—historically, not philosophically—because it was the most tremendous religious movement that the world ever saw, the most gigantic spiritual wave ever to burst upon human society. There is no civilization on which its effect has not been felt in some way or other.

The followers of Buddha were most enthusiastic and very missionary in spirit. They were the first among the adherents of the various religions not to remain content with the limited sphere of their mother
church. They spread far and wide; they traveled east and west, north and
south. They reached into darkest Tibet; they went into Persia, Asia Minor;
they went into Russia, Poland, and many other countries of the Western world. They went into China, Korea, Japan; they went into Burma,
Siam, the East Indies, and beyond. When Alexander the Great, through
his military conquests, brought the Mediterranean world in contact with
India, the wisdom of India at once found a channel through which to
spread over vast portions of Asia and Europe. Buddhist priests went out
teaching among the different nations, and as they taught, superstition
and priestcraft began to vanish like mist before the sun.

To understand this movement properly you should know what conditions prevailed in India when Buddha was born, just as to understand
Christianity you have to grasp the state of Jewish society at the time of
Christ. It is necessary that you have an idea of Indian society six hundred years before the birth of Christ, by which time Indian civilization
had already completed its growth.

When you study the civilization of India you find that it has died
and revived several times; this is its peculiarity. Most races rise once and
then decline forever. There are two kinds of peoples: those who grow
continually and those whose growth comes to an end. The peaceful
nations, India and China, fall down, yet rise again. But the others, once
they go down, do not come up; they die. Blessed are the peacemakers,
for they shall enjoy the earth.

At the time Buddha was born, India was in need of a great spiritual leader, a prophet. There was already a most powerful body of priests.
You will understand the situation better if you remember the history of
the Jews—how they had two types of religious leaders: priests and

prophets, the priests keeping the people in ignorance and grinding superstitions into their minds. The methods of worship the priests prescribed were only a means by which they could dominate the people. All through the Old Testament you find the prophets challenging the superstitions of the priests. The outcome of this fight was the triumph of the prophets and the defeat of the priests.

Priests believe that there is a God, but that this God can be approached and known only through them. People can enter the holy of holies only with the permission of the priests. You must pay them, worship them, place everything in their hands. Throughout the history of the world this priestly desire for power has asserted itself; this tremendous thirst for power, this tiger-like thirst, seems a part of human nature. The priests dominate you, lay down a thousand rules for you. They describe simple truths in roundabout ways. They tell you stories to support their own superior position. If you want to thrive in this life or go to heaven after death, you have to pass through their hands. You have to perform all kinds of ceremonies and rituals. All this has made life so complicated and has so confused the brain that if I give you plain words you will go home unsatisfied. You have become thoroughly befuddled. The less you understand, the better you feel! The prophets have been giving warnings against the priests and their superstitions and machinations; but the vast mass of people have not yet learnt to heed these warnings; they must be educated about this.

Men must have education. They speak of democracy, of the equality of all men, these days. But how will a man know he is equal with all? He must have a strong brain, a clear mind free of nonsensical ideas; he must pierce through the mass of superstitions encrusting his mind to the pure truth that is in his inmost self. Then he will know that all perfections, all powers, are already within himself; that these have not to be given him by others. The moment he realizes this truth he becomes free, he achieves equality. He also realizes that everyone else is just as perfect as he, and that he does not have to exercise any power—physical, mental or moral—over his brother men. He abandons the idea that there was ever any man who was lower than himself. Then he can talk of equality—not until then.

Now, as I was telling you, among the Jews there was a continuous struggle between the priests and the prophets, and the priests sought to monopolize power and knowledge, till they themselves began to lose them and the chains they had put on the feet of the people were on their own feet. The masters always become slaves before long. The culmination of the struggle was the victory of Jesus of Nazareth. This triumph is the history of Christianity; Christ at last succeeded in overthrowing the mass of priestcraft. This great prophet killed the dragon of priestly selfishness, rescued from its clutches the jewel of truth, and gave it to all the world, so that whosoever desired to possess it would have absolute freedom to do so and would not have to wait on the pleasure of any priest or priests.

The priests in India, the brahmins, possessed great intellectual and psychic power. It was they who began the spiritual development of India, and they accomplished wonderful things. But the time came when the free spirit of development that had at first actuated the brahmins disappeared. They began to arrogate powers and privileges to themselves. If a brahmin killed a man he would not be punished. The brahmin, by his very birth, is the lord of the universe. Even the most wicked brahmin must be worshipped.

But while the priests were flourishing, there existed also the poet-prophets called sannyasins. All Hindus, whatever their caste may be, must, if they want to attain freedom, give up the world and prepare for death. No more is the world to be of any interest to them. They must go out and become sannyasins. The sannyasins have nothing to do with the two thousand ceremonies that the priests have invented—sanctifying them with certain words, ten syllables, twenty syllables long, and so on! All these things are nonsense.

So these poet-prophets of ancient India repudiated the ways of the priests and declared the pure truth. They tried to break the power of the priests and they succeeded a little. But in two generations their disciples went back to the superstitious, roundabout ways of the priests and became priests themselves: "You can get truth only through us." Truth became crystallized again, and again prophets came to break the encrustations and free the truth, and so it went on. Yes, there must always be prophets in the world; otherwise humanity will perish.

You wonder why there have to be all these roundabout methods of the priests. Why can you not come directly to the truth? Are you ashamed of God's truth, that you have to hide it behind all kinds of intricate ceremonies and formulas? Are you ashamed of God, that you cannot confess his truth before the world? Do you call that being religious and spiritual? The priests are the only people fit for the truth! The masses are not fit for it! It must be diluted! Water it down a little!

Take the Sermon on the Mount and the Gita: they are simplicity itself. Even the man in the street can understand them. How grand! In them you find the truth clearly and simply revealed. But no, the priests will not agree that truth can be found so directly. They speak of two thousand heavens and two thousand hells. If people follow their prescriptions they will go to heaven! If they do not obey the rules they will go to hell!

But people must know the truth. Some are afraid that if the full truth is given to all, it will hurt them. They should not be given the unqualified truth, they say. But the world is not much better off by compromising truth. How much worse can it be than it is already? Bring the truth out! If it is real, it will do good. When people protest and propose other methods, they only make apologies for priestcraft.

India was full of it in Buddha's day. Masses of people were debarred from all knowledge. If just a word of the Vedas entered the ears of a low-caste man, terrible punishment was visited upon him. The priests had made a secret of the Vedas—the Vedas, which contained the spiritual truths discovered by the ancient Hindus!

At last one man could bear it no more. He had the brain, the power, and the heart—a heart as infinite as the broad sky. He saw how the masses were being led by the priests and how the priests were glorying in their power, and he wanted to do something about it. He did not want any power over anyone, and he wanted to break the mental and spiritual bonds of men. His heart was large. The heart, many around us may have, and we also want to help others. But we do not have the brain; we do not know the ways and means by which help can be given. But this man had the brain to discover the means of breaking the bondages of souls. He learnt why men suffer and he found the way out of suffering. He was a man of accomplishment; he worked everything out. He taught one and all without distinction, and made them realize the peace of enlightenment. This was the man Buddha.

You know from Arnold's poem *The Light of Asia* how Buddha was born a prince and how the misery of the world struck him deeply; how, although brought up and living in the lap of luxury, he could not find comfort in his personal happiness and security; how he renounced the world, leaving his princess and new-born son behind; how he wandered searching for truth from teacher to teacher; and how he at last attained to enlightenment. You know about his long mission, his disciples, his organizations. You all know these things.

Buddha was the triumph in the struggle that had been going on between the priests and the prophets in India. One thing can be said for these Indian priests: they were not and never are intolerant of religion; they never have persecuted religion. Any man was allowed to preach against them—such was their catholicity. They never molested anyone for his religious views. But they suffered from the peculiar weaknesses of all priests: they sought power; they also promulgated rules and regulations and made religion unnecessarily complicated, and thereby undermined the strength of those who followed their religion.

Buddha cut through all these excrescences. He preached the most tremendous truths. He taught the very gist of the philosophy of the Vedas to one and all without distinction; he taught it to the world at large, because one of his great messages was the equality of man. Men are all equal. No concession there to anybody. Buddha was the great preacher of equality. Every man and woman has the same right to attain spirituality—that was his teaching. The difference between the priests and the other castes he abolished. Even the lowest were entitled to the highest attainments; he opened the door of nirvana to one and all. His teaching was bold even for India. No amount of preaching can ever shock the Indian soul; but it was hard for India to swallow Buddha's doctrine. How much harder it must be for you!

His doctrine was this: Why is there misery in our life? Because we are selfish. We desire things for ourselves—that is why there is misery. What is the way out? The giving up of the self. The self does not exist; the phenomenal world, all this that we perceive, is all that exists. There is nothing called soul underlying the cycle of life and death. There is the stream of thought, one thought following another in succession, each thought coming into existence and becoming non-existent at the same moment. That is all. There is no thinker of the thought, no soul. The body is changing all the time; so is mind, consciousness. The self therefore is a delusion. All selfishness comes of holding on to the self, to this illusory self. If we know the truth that there is no self, then we shall be happy and make others happy.

This was what Buddha taught. And he did not merely talk; he was ready to give up his own life for the world. He said, "If sacrificing an animal is good, sacrificing a man is better," and he offered himself as a sacrifice. He said: "This animal sacrifice is another superstition. God and soul are the two big superstitions. God is only a superstition invented by the priests. If there is a God, as these brahmins preach, why is there so much misery in the world? He is just like me, a slave to the law of causation. If he is not bound by the law of causation, then why does he create? Such a God is not at all satisfactory. If there is a ruler in heaven who rules the universe according to his sweet will and leaves us all here to die in misery—he never has the kindness to look at us for a moment. Our whole life is continuous suffering. But this is not sufficient punishment: after death we must go to places where we have other punishments. Yet we continually perform all kinds of rites and ceremonies to please this creator of the world!"

Buddha said: "These ceremonials are all wrong. There is but one ideal in the world. Destroy all delusions; what is true will remain. As soon as the clouds are gone, the sun will shine." How is one to kill the self? Be perfectly unselfish; be ready to give up your life even for an ant. Give up all superstition; work not to please God, to get any reward, but work because you are seeking your own release by killing your self. Worship and prayer and all that—these are all nonsense. You all say, "I thank God"—but where does he live? You do not know and yet you are all going crazy because of your belief in God.

The Hindus can give up everything except their God. To deny God is to cut the very ground from under the feet of devotion. Devotion and God the Hindus must cling to. They can never relinquish these. And here, in the teaching of Buddha, are no God and no soul—simply work. What for? Not for the self, for the self is a delusion. We shall be free when this delusion has vanished. Very few are there in the world that can rise to that height and work for work's sake.

Yet the religion of Buddha spread fast. It was because of the marvelous love which, for the first time in the history of humanity, overflowed a large heart and devoted itself to the service not only of all men but of all living things—a love which did not care for anything except to find a way of release from suffering for all beings.

Man was loving God and had forgot all about his brother man. The man who in the name of God could give up his life could also turn around and kill his brother man in the name of the same God. That was the state of the world. Men would sacrifice their sons for the glory of God, would rob nations for the glory of God, would kill thousands of beings for the glory of God, would drench the earth with blood for the glory of God. Buddha was the first to turn their minds to the other God—man. It was man that was to be loved. Buddha set in motion the first wave of intense love for all men, the first wave of true, unadulterated wisdom, which, starting from India, gradually inundated country after country—north, south, east, west.

This teacher wanted to make truth shine as truth. No softening, no compromise, no pandering to the priests and the powerful kings. No bowing before superstitious traditions, however hoary; no respect for forms and books just because they came down from the distant past. He rejected all scriptures, all forms of religious practice. Even the very language, Sanskrit, in which religion had been traditionally taught in India, he rejected, so that his followers would not have any chance to imbibe the superstitions which were associated with it.

There is another way of looking at the truth we have been discussing: the Hindu way. We claim that Buddha's great doctrine of selflessness can be better understood if it is looked at in our way. In the Upanishads there was already the great doctrine of Atman and Brahman. Atman, the Self, is the same as Brahman, the Lord. This Self is all that is; it is the only reality. Maya, delusion, makes us see it as differentiated. There is one Self, not many. That one Self shines in various forms. Man is man's brother because all men are one. A man is not only my brother, say the Vedas, but he is myself. Hurting any part of the universe, I only hurt myself. I am the universe. It is a delusion that I think I am Mr. So-and-so.

The more you approach your Self, the more quickly delusion vanishes. The more all differences and divisions disappear, the more you realize all as the one divinity. God exists, but he is not a man sitting upon a cloud. He is pure spirit. Where does he reside? Nearer to you than your very self. He is the soul. How can you perceive God as separate and different from yourself? When you think of him as someone separate from yourself, you do not know him. He is you yourself. That was the doctrine of the prophets of India.

It is selfishness to think that you are Mr. So-and-so and all the world is different from you. You believe that you are different from me. You do not take any thought of me. You go home and have your dinner and sleep. If I die you still eat, drink, and are merry. But you cannot really be happy when the rest of the world is suffering. We are all one. It is the delusion of separateness that is the root of misery. Nothing exists but the Self. There is nothing else.

Buddha's idea was that there was no God, but only man. He repudiated the mentality which underlay the prevalent ideas of God. He found they made men weak and superstitious. If God gives you everything you pray for, why then do you go out and work? God comes to those who work. God helps them that help themselves. An opposite idea of God weakens our nerves, softens our muscles, makes us dependent. Only the independent are happy; and the dependent are miserable. Man has infinite power within himself and he can realize it—he can realize himself as the one, infinite Self. It can be done; but you do not believe it. You pray to God and keep your powder dry all the time.

Buddha taught the opposite. Do not let men weep. Let them have none of this praying and all that. God is not keeping shop. With every breath you are praying to God. I am talking—that is a prayer. You are listening—that is a prayer. Is there ever any movement of yours, mental or physical, in which you do not make use of the infinite divine energy? It is all a constant prayer. If you call only a set of words prayer, you make prayer superficial. Such prayers are not much good; they can scarcely bear any real fruit.

Is prayer a magic formula by repeating which, even if you do not work hard, you gain miraculous results? No. All have to work hard; all have to reach the depths of that infinite energy. Behind the poor, behind the rich, there is the same infinite energy. It is not true that while one man works hard, another by repeating a few words achieves the same results. This universe is a constant prayer. If you take prayer in this sense, I am with you. Words are not necessary. Better is silent prayer.

The vast majority of people do not understand the meaning of this doctrine. In India any compromise regarding the Self means that we have given power into the hands of the priests and have forgotten the great teachings of the prophets. Buddha knew this; so he brushed aside all the priestly doctrines and practices and made man stand on his own feet. It was necessary for him to go against the accustomed ways of the people; he had to bring about revolutionary changes. As a result this sacrificial religion passed away from India forever and was never revived.

Buddhism apparently has passed away from India, but really it has not. There was an element of danger in the teaching of Buddha: it was a reforming religion. In order to bring about the tremendous spiritual change he did, he had to give many negative teachings. But if a religion emphasizes the negative side too much, it is in danger of eventual destruction. Never can a reforming sect survive if it is only reforming; the positive elements alone—the real impulse, that is, the principles—live on and on. After a reform has been brought about it is the positive side that should be emphasized; after the building is finished the scaffolding must be taken away.

It so happened in India that as time went on the followers of Buddha emphasized the negative aspect of his teachings too much and thereby caused the eventual downfall of their religion. The positive aspects of truth were suffocated by the forces of negation, and thus India repudiated the destructive tendencies that flourished in the name of Buddhism. That was the decree of the Indian national thought.

The negative ideas of Buddhism—there is no God and no soul—died out. I can say that God is the only being that exists; it is a very positive statement. He is the one reality. When Buddha says there is no soul, I say, "Man, thou art one with the universe; thou art all things." How positive! The reformative element died out, but the formative element has lived through all time. Buddha taught kindness towards lower beings, and since then there has not been a sect in India that has not taught charity to all beings, even to animals. This kindness, this mercy, this charity—greater than any doctrine—are what Buddhism left to us.

The life of Buddha has an especial appeal. All my life I have been very fond of Buddha, but not of his doctrine. I have more veneration for that character than for any other—that boldness, that fearlessness, and that tremendous love. He was born for the good of men. Others may seek God, others may seek truth for themselves; he did not even care to know truth for himself. He sought truth because people were in misery. How to help them—that was his only concern. Throughout his life he never had a thought for himself. How can we ignorant, selfish, narrow-minded human beings ever understand the greatness of this man?

And consider his marvelous brain. No emotionalism. That giant brain never was superstitious. "Believe not because an old manuscript has been produced, because it has been handed down to you from your forefathers, because your friends want you to—but think for yourself; search out truth for yourself; realize it yourself. Then if you find it beneficial to one and all, give it to people." Soft-brained men, weak-minded, chicken-hearted, cannot find the truth. One has to be free and as broad as the sky. One has to have a mind that is crystal clear; only then can truth shine in it. We are so full of superstitions! Even in your country, where you think you are highly educated, how full of narrownesses and superstitions you are! Just think, with all your claims to civilization in this country, on one occasion I was refused a chair to sit on, because I was a Hindu!

Six hundred years before the birth of Christ, at the time when Buddha lived, the people of India must have had wonderful education. Extremely free-minded they must have been. Great masses followed him. Kings gave up their thrones; queens gave up their thrones. People were able to appreciate and embrace his teaching—so revolutionary, so different from what they had been taught by the priests through the ages. Their minds must have been unusually free and broad.

And consider his death. If he was great in life, he was also great in death. He ate food offered to him by a member of a tribal race. Hindus do not touch these people because they eat indiscriminately. He told his disciples: "Do not eat this food, but I cannot refuse it. Go to the man and tell him he has done me one of the greatest services of my life: he has released me from the body." An old man came and sat near him—he had walked miles and miles to see the Master—and Buddha taught him. When he found a disciple weeping, he reproved him, saying, "What is this? Is this the result of all my teaching? Let there be no false bondage, no dependence on me, no false glorification of this passing personality. The Buddha is not a person; he is a state of realization. Work out your own salvation."

Even when dying he would not claim any distinction for himself. I worship him for that. What you call Buddhas and Christs are only the names of certain states of realization. Of all the teachers of the world, he was the one who taught us most to be self-reliant, who freed us not only from the bondage of our false selves but from dependence on

Sri Ramakrishna

the invisible being or beings called God or gods. He invited everyone to enter into that state of freedom which he called nirvana. All must attain to it one day, and that attainment is the complete fulfillment of man.

My Master (Sri Ramakrishna)
(Delivered in New York and England)

"Whenever virtue subsides and vice prevails, I come down to help mankind," declares Krishna in the Bhagavad Gita. Whenever this world of ours, on account of growth and of additional circumstances, requires a new adjustment, a wave of power comes; and as a man is acting on two planes, the spiritual and the material, the wave of adjustment comes on both planes. On the one side, on the material plane, Europe has mainly been the basis of the adjustment during modern times, and on the other side, on the spiritual plane, Asia has been the basis of the adjustment throughout the history of the world. Today man requires one more adjustment on the spiritual plane. Today, when material ideas are at the height of their glory and power, today, when man is likely to forget his divine nature through his growing dependence on matter, and is likely to be reduced to a mere money-making machine, an adjustment is necessary. And the voice has spoken; the power is coming to drive away the clouds of gathering materialism. The power has been set in motion which, at no distant date, will bring unto mankind once more the memory of its real nature, and again the place from which this power has started is Asia. This world of ours is built on the plan of the division of labor. It is vain to say that one nation shall possess everything. Yet how childish we are! The baby, in his childishness, thinks that his doll is the only possession that is to be coveted in this whole universe. So a nation which is great in the possession of material power thinks that this is all that is to be coveted, that this is all that is meant by progress, that this is all that is meant by civilization, and if there are other nations which do not care to possess, and do not possess this power, they are not fit to live, their whole existence is useless. On the other hand, another nation may think that mere material civilization is utterly useless. From the Orient came the voice which once told the world that if a man possessed everything that is under the sun or above it, and did not possess spirituality, it availed him nothing. This is the Oriental type; the other is the Occidental type.

Each of these types has its grandeur, each has its glory. The present adjustment will be the harmonizing, the blending, of these two ideals. To the Oriental, the world of the spirit is as real as to the Occidental is the world of the senses. In the spiritual, the Oriental finds everything he wants or hopes for; in it he finds all that makes life real to him. To the Occidental he is a dreamer. To the Oriental, the Occidental is a dreamer, playing with dolls that last only for five minutes, and he laughs to think that grownup men and women should make so much of a handful of matter which they will have to leave sooner or later. Each calls the other a dreamer. But the Oriental ideal is as necessary for the progress of the human race as the Occidental, and I think it is more necessary. Machines never made mankind happy, and never will. He who tries to make us believe this, claims that happiness is in the machine; but it is always in the mind. The man who is the lord of his mind alone can be happy, and none else.

But what, after all, is this power of the machine? Why should a man who can send a current of electricity through a wire be called a very great and a very intelligent man? Does not nature do a million times more than that every moment? Why not then fall down and worship nature? What matters it if you have power over the whole of the world, if you have mastered every atom in the universe? That will not make you happy unless you have the power of happiness in yourself, until you have conquered yourself. Man is born to conquer nature, it is true, but the Occidental means by "nature" only the physical or external nature. It is true that external nature is majestic, with its mountains and oceans and rivers, and with its infinite power and variety. Yet there is a more majestic, internal nature of man, higher than the sun, moon, and stars, higher than this earth of ours, higher than the physical universe, transcending these little lives of ours; and it affords another field of study. There the Orientals excel, just as the Occidentals excel in the other. Therefore it is fitting that, whenever there is a spiritual adjustment, it should come from the Orient. It is also fitting that when the Oriental wants to learn about machine making, he should sit at the feet of the Occidental and learn from him. When the Occident wants to learn about the spirit, about God, about the soul, about the meaning and the mystery of this universe, he must sit at the feet of the Orient.

I am going to present before you the life of a man who has put in motion a spiritual wave in India. But before going into the life of this man, I will try to present before you the secret of India, what India stands for. If those whose eyes have been blinded by the glamour of material things, whose whole life is dedicated to eating and drinking and enjoying, whose whole ideal of possession is lands and gold, whose whole ideal of pleasure is in the senses, whose God is money, and whose goal is a life of ease and comfort in this world and death after that, whose minds never look forward, and who rarely think of anything higher than the sense-objects in the midst of which they live—if such as these go to India, what do they see? Poverty, squalor, superstition, darkness, hideousness everywhere. Why? Because to their minds enlightenment means dress, education, social politeness. Whereas Occidental nations have used every effort to improve their material position, India has done differently. There lives the only race in the world who, in the whole history of humanity, never went beyond their frontiers to conquer anyone, who never coveted that which belonged to anyone else, and whose only fault was that their lands were so fertile, and their wits so keen, that they accumulated wealth by the hard labor of their hands and so tempted other nations to come and despoil them. They are content to be despoiled, and to be called barbarians, and in return they want to send to this world visions of the Supreme, to lay bare for the world the secrets of human nature, to rend the veil that conceals the real man, because they know that all this is a dream, because they know that behind matter lives the real, divine nature of man, which no sin can tarnish, no crime can spoil, no lust can kill; which fire cannot burn, nor water wet, which heat cannot dry, nor death kill; and to them this true nature of man is as real as is any material object to the senses of an Occidental.

Just as you are brave enough to jump into the mouth of a cannon with a hurrah, brave enough, in the name of patriotism, to stand up and give up your lives for your country, so they are brave in the name of God. There it is that when a man declares that this is a world of ideas, that it is all a dream, he casts off clothes and property to demonstrate that what he believes and thinks is true. There it is that a man sits on the bank of a river, when he has known that life is eternal, and is willing to give up his body as if it were nothing, just as you would give up a bit of straw. Therein lies his heroism; he is ready to face death as a brother because he is convinced that there is no death for the soul. Therein lies the strength that has made India invincible through hundreds of years of oppression and foreign invasion and foreign tyranny. The nation lives today, and in that nation, even in the days of the direst disaster, spiritual giants have never failed to arise. Asia produces giants in spirituality, just as the Occident produces giants in politics, giants in science.

In the beginning of the present century, when Western influence began to pour into India, when Western conquerors, swords in hand, came to demonstrate to the children of the sages that they were mere barbarians, a race of dreamers, that their religion was but mythology, and God and soul and everything they had been struggling for were mere words without meaning, that the thousands of years of struggle, the thousands of years of endless renunciation, had all been in vain—at that time certain questions began to agitate young men at the universities: whether their whole national existence up to then had been a failure, whether they must begin anew on the Occidental plan, tear up their old books, burn their philosophies, drive away their preachers, and break down their temples. Did not the Occidental conqueror, the man who demonstrated his religion with sword and gun, say that all the old ways were mere superstition and idolatry? Children brought up and educated in the new schools started on the Occidental plan drank in these ideas from their childhood, and it is not to be wondered at that doubts assailed their minds. But instead of throwing away superstition and making a real search after truth, they asked: "What does the West say?" This, for them, became the test of truth. The priests must go, the Vedas must be burned, because the West said so. Out of the feeling of unrest thus produced there arose a wave of so-called reform in India.

If you wish to be a true reformer, you must possess three things. The first is to feel. Do you really feel for your brothers? Do you really feel that there is so much misery in the world, so much ignorance and superstition? Do you really feel that all men are your brothers? Does this idea permeate your whole being? Does it run in your blood? Does it tingle in your veins? Does it course through every nerve and filament of your body? Are you full of that idea of sympathy? If you are, that is only the first step. Next you must ask yourself if you have found any remedy. The old ideas may be all superstition, but in and around these masses of superstition are nuggets of truth. Have you discovered means by which to keep that truth alone, without any of the dross? If you have done that, that is only the second step; one more thing is necessary. What is your motive? Are you sure that you are not actuated by greed for gold, by thirst for fame or power? Are you really sure that you can stand for your ideals and work on, even if the whole world wants to crush you down?

Are you sure that you know what you want and will perform your duty, and that alone, even if your life is at stake? Are you sure that you will persevere so long as life endures, so long as there is one pulsation left in the heart? Then you are a real reformer, you are a teacher, a master, a blessing to mankind. But man is so impatient, so shortsighted! He has not the patience to wait, he has not the power to see. He wants to rule, he wants results immediately. Why? He wants to reap the fruits himself and does not really care for others. Duty for duty's sake is not what he wants. "To work you have the right, but not to the fruits thereof," says Krishna. Why cling to results? Ours is to do our duties. Let the fruits take care of themselves. But man has no patience; he takes up any scheme that will produce quick results; and the majority of reformers all over the world can be classed under this heading.

As I have said, an intense desire for reform came to India, and it seemed as if the wave of materialism that had invaded her shores would sweep away the teachings of the sages. But the nation had borne the shocks of a thousand such waves of change. This one was mild in comparison. Wave after wave had flooded the land, breaking and crushing everything for hundreds of years; but these floods subsided, leaving the national ideals unchanged.

The Indian nation cannot be killed. Deathless it stands, and it will stand so long as that spirit shall remain as the background, so long as her people do not give up their spirituality. Beggars they may remain, poor and poverty-stricken; dirt and squalor may surround them perhaps throughout all time, but let them not give up their God, let them not forget that they are the children of the sages. Just as, in the West, even the man in the street wants to trace his descent from some robber-baron of the Middle Ages, so in India, even an emperor on the throne wants to trace his descent from some beggar-sage in the forest, from a man who wore the bark of a tree, lived upon the fruits of the forest, and communed with God. That is the type of heritage we want; and so long as holiness is thus supremely venerated, India cannot die.

Many of you, perhaps, have read the article by Prof. Max Müller in a recent issue of the *Nineteenth Century*, entitled "A Real Mahatman." The life of Sri Ramakrishna is deeply interesting; for it is a living illustration of the ideas that he preached. Perhaps it will seem a little romantic for you who live in the West, in an atmosphere entirely different from that of India; for the methods and manners in the busy rush of life in the West differ utterly from those of India. Yet perhaps it will be all the more interesting for that, because it will bring into a new light things about which many of you have heard.

It was while reforms of various kinds were being inaugurated in India that a child was born of poor brahmin parents on the eighteenth of February, 1836, in one of the remote villages of Bengal. The father and mother were very orthodox people. The life of an orthodox brahmin is one of continuous renunciation. Very few things can he do to earn a living, and beyond these the orthodox brahmin must not occupy himself with any secular business. At the same time he must not receive gifts from everybody. You may imagine how rigorous that life becomes. You have heard of the brahmins and their priestcraft many times, but very few of you have ever stopped to ask what makes this wonderful band of men the rulers of their fellows. They are the poorest of all the classes in the country, and the secret of their power lies in their renunciation. They never covet wealth. Theirs is the poorest priesthood in the world, and therefore the most powerful. Even in this poverty, a brahmin's wife will never allow a poor man to pass through the village without giving him something to eat. That is considered the highest duty of the mother in India; and because she is the mother it is her duty to be served last; she must see that everyone is served before her turn comes. That is why the mother is regarded as God in India. This particular woman, the mother of the child we are talking about, was an ideal Hindu mother.

The higher the caste, the greater the restrictions. The people of the lowest caste can eat and drink anything they like, but as men rise in the social scale, more and more restrictions come, and when they reach the highest caste, the brahmin, the hereditary priesthood of India, their lives, as I have said, are very much circumscribed. Judged by Western standards, their lives are of continuous asceticism. But they have great steadiness. When they get hold of an idea they carry it out to its very conclusion, and they keep hold of it generation after generation until they make something out of it. Once you have given them an idea, it is not easy to take it back again; but it is hard to make them grasp a new idea.

The orthodox Hindus, therefore, are very exclusive, living entirely within their own horizon of thought and feeling. Their lives are laid down in our old books in every little detail, and the least detail is grasped by them with almost adamantine firmness. They would starve rather than eat a meal cooked by the hands of a man not belonging to their own small sub-caste. But withal, they have intensity and tremendous earnestness. That force of intense faith and religious life is often found among the orthodox Hindus, because their very orthodoxy comes from a tremendous conviction that it is right. We may not all think that what they hold on to with such perseverance is right; but to them it is.

Now, as our books say, a man should always be charitable, even if it means extreme suffering. If a man starves to death in order to help another man, to save that man's life, it is all right; it is even held that a man ought to do that. And it is expected of a brahmin to carry this idea out to the very extreme. Those who are acquainted with the literature of India will remember a beautiful old story about this extreme charity, as related in the Mahabharata: how a whole family starved themselves to death and gave their last meal to a beggar. This is not an exaggeration, for such things still happen.

The character of the father and the mother of my Master was very much like that. Very poor they were, and yet many a time the mother would starve herself a whole day to help a poor man. Of them this child was born, and he was a peculiar child from his very babyhood. He remembered his past from his birth and knew for what purpose he had come into the world, and all his powers were devoted to the fulfillment of that purpose.

While he was quite young his father died and the boy was sent to school. A brahmin's boy must go to school; the caste restricts him to a learned profession only. The indigenous system of education in India, especially of the orthodox type, still prevalent in many parts of the country, was very different from the modern system. The students did not have to pay for their education. It was thought that knowledge is so sacred that no man ought to sell it. Knowledge must be given freely. The teachers used to take students without charge; and not only so, but most of them gave their students food and clothes. To support these teachers the wealthy families on certain occasions, such as a marriage festival or the ceremonies for the dead, made gifts to them. They were considered the first and foremost claimants to such gifts, and they in their turn had to maintain their students.

Now, this boy about whom I am speaking had an elder brother, a learned professor, who took him to Calcutta to study with him. After a short time the boy became convinced that the aim of all secular learning was mere material advancement, and he resolved to give up study and devote himself solely to the pursuit of spiritual knowledge. The father being dead, the family was very poor, and this boy had to make his own living. He went to a place near Calcutta and became a temple priest. To become a temple priest is thought very degrading to a brahmin. Our temples are not churches in your sense of the word; they are not places for public worship; for, properly speaking, there is no such thing as public worship in India. Temples are erected mostly by rich persons as a meritorious religious act.

If a man has much property he wants to build a temple. In that temple he puts a symbol of God or an image of an incarnation and dedicates it in the name of God. The worship is akin to that which is conducted in Roman Catholic churches, very much like the Mass, the priest reading certain sentences from the sacred books, waving a light before the image, and treating the image in every respect as we treat a great man. This is all that is done in the temple. The man who goes to a temple is not considered thereby a better man than he who never goes. Rather, the latter is considered the more religious, for in India religion is to each man his own private affair, and all his worship is conducted in the privacy of his own home.

It has been held from the most ancient times in our country that to be a temple priest is degrading. The idea is that temple priests, like schoolteachers, but in a far more intense sense, make merchandise of sacred things by taking fees for their work. So you may imagine the feelings of this boy when he was forced through poverty to take up the only occupation open to him, that of a temple priest.

There have been various poets in Bengal whose songs have passed down to the people and are sung in the streets of Calcutta and in every village. Most of these are religious songs, and their one central idea, which is perhaps peculiar to the religions of India, is the idea of realization. There is not a book in India on religion which does not breathe this idea. Man must realize God, feel God, see God, talk to God. That is religion. The Indian atmosphere is full of stories of saintly persons who have had visions of God. Such ideas form the basis of their religion; and all these ancient books and scriptures are the writings of persons who came into direct contact with spiritual facts. These books were not written to appeal to the intellect, nor can any reasoning understand them; they were written by men who saw the things of which they wrote, and they can be understood only by men who have raised themselves to the same height. They declare there is such a thing as realization even in this life, and it is open to everyone, and religion begins with the opening of this faculty—if I may call it so. This is the central idea in all religions. And this is why, in India, we find that one man, with the most finished oratorical powers or the most convincing logic, may preach the highest doctrines and yet is unable to get people to listen to him, while another, a poor man who scarcely can speak the language of his own motherland, is yet worshipped as God by half the nation in his own lifetime. When the idea somehow or other gets abroad that a man has raised himself to a high state of realization—that religion is no more a matter of conjecture to him, that he is no longer groping in the dark about such momentous questions of religion as the immortality of the soul and God—people come from all quarters to see him and gradually they begin to worship him.

In the temple was an image of the "Blissful Mother." The boy had to conduct the worship morning and evening, and by and by this one idea filled his mind: "Is there any reality behind this image? Is it true that there is a Blissful Mother of the universe? Is it true that she is living and guides this universe, or is it all a dream? Is there any reality in religion?" This kind of doubt comes to almost every Hindu aspirant—Is this that we are doing real? And theories will not satisfy us, although there are ready at hand almost all the theories that have ever been made with regard to God and the soul. Neither books nor dogmas can satisfy us; the one idea that gets hold of thousands of our people is this idea of realization. Is it true that there is a God? If it be true, can I see him? Can I realize the truth? The Western mind may think all this very unpractical, but to us it is intensely practical. For this idea men will give up their lives. For this idea thousands of Hindus every year give up their homes, and many of them die through the hardships they have to undergo. To the Western mind this must seem most visionary, and I can see the reason for this point of view. But after years of residence in the West, I still think this idea the most practical thing in life.

Life is but momentary, whether you are a toiler in the streets or an emperor ruling millions. Life is but momentary, whether you have the best of health or the worst. There is but one solution of life, says the Hindu, and that solution is what they call God and religion. If God and religion are real, then life becomes explained, life becomes bearable, becomes enjoyable. Otherwise life is but a useless burden. That is our idea. But no amount of reasoning can demonstrate religion; it can only make it probable, and there it rests. Facts are based only upon experience, and we have to experience religion to demonstrate it to ourselves. We have to see God to be convinced that there is a God. Nothing but our own realization can make religion real to us. That is the Hindu conception.

This idea of realization took possession of the boy, and his whole life became concentrated upon it. Day after day he would weep and say: "Mother, is it true that thou dost exist, or is it all poetry? Is the Blissful Mother an imagination of poets and misguided people, or is there such a reality?" We have seen already that of education in our sense of the word he had none; therefore so much the more natural, so much the more healthy, was his mind, so much the purer his thoughts, undiluted by drinking in of the thoughts of others. Because he never went to a university, he was able to think for himself. Well has Prof. Max Müller said, in the article I have just referred to, that he was a clean, original man, and that the secret of his originality was that he was not brought up within the precincts of a university.

Now this thought—whether God can be realized—which was uppermost in his mind gained in strength every day until he could think of nothing else. He could no longer conduct the worship properly, could no more attend to the various details in all their minuteness. Often he would forget to place the food offering before the image, sometimes he would forget to wave the light, at other times he would wave the light for hours, and forget everything else.

At last it became impossible for the boy to serve in the temple. He gave up the worship and spent most of his time in meditation in a wood nearby. About this part of his life he told me many times that he could not tell when the sun rose or set, or how he lived. He lost all thought of himself and forgot to eat. During this period he was lovingly watched over by a relative who put into his mouth food which he mechanically swallowed.

Days and nights thus passed with the boy. At the end of the day, towards evening, when the peals of bells and the singing in the temples would reach the wood, it would make him very sad, and he would cry: "Another day is gone in vain, Mother, and thou hast not come. One more day of this short life has gone and I have not known the truth." In the agony of his soul, sometimes he would rub his face against the ground and weep.

This is the tremendous thirst that seizes the devotees' heart. Later on, this very man said to me: "My child, suppose there is a bag of gold in one room, and a robber is in the next room. Do you think that robber can sleep? He cannot. His mind will be always thinking how to get into that room and obtain possession of the gold. Do you think, then, that a man firmly persuaded that there is a reality behind all these appearances, that there is a God, that there is one who never dies, one whose nature is infinite bliss, compared to which these pleasures of the senses are simply playthings—can rest contented without struggling to attain him? Can he cease his efforts for a moment? No. He will become mad with longing." This divine madness seized the boy. At that time he had no teacher, nobody to tell him anything, and everyone thought he was out of his mind. This is the ordinary condition of things: If a man throws aside the vanities of the world, we hear him called mad. But such men are the salt of the earth. Out of such madness have come the powers that have moved this world of ours, and out of such madness alone will come the powers of the future that are going to move the world.

So days, weeks, months passed in continuous struggle of his soul to arrive at truth. The boy began to see visions, to see wonderful things; the secrets of his nature were beginning to open up to him. Veil after veil was, as it were, being taken off. Mother herself became the teacher and initiated the boy into the truths he sought. At this time there came to the place a woman beautiful to look at, learned beyond compare. Later on this saint used to say about her that she was not learned, but was the embodiment of learning; she was learning itself in human form. There too you find the peculiarity of the Indian nation. In the midst of the ignorance in which the average Hindu woman lives, in the midst of what is called in Western countries her lack of freedom, there could arise a woman of supreme spirituality. She was a sannyasini; for women also give up the world, renounce their property, do not marry, and devote themselves to the worship of the Lord. She came, and when she heard of this boy's yearning she offered to go and see him; and hers was the first help he received. At once she recognized what his trouble was, and she said to him: "My son, blessed is the man upon whom such madness comes. All men in this world are mad: some are mad for wealth, some for pleasure, some for fame, some for a hundred other things. But blessed are they who are mad after God. Such men are very few." This woman remained near the boy for years, taught him various religious disciplines, and initiated him into the different practices of yoga.

Later, there came to the same temple a sannyasin, one of the begging friars of India, a learned man, a philosopher. He was an unusual man; he was an idealist. He did not believe that this world existed in reality, and to demonstrate that, he would never live under a roof; he would always live out of doors, in storm and sunshine alike. This man began to teach the boy the philosophy of the Vedas, and he found very soon, to his astonishment, that the pupil was in some respects wiser than the master. He spent several months with the boy, after which he initiated him into the order of sannyasins, and finally he departed.

Previously, when his extraordinary conduct as a temple priest had made people think him mad, his relatives had taken him home and married him to a girl of five, thinking that that would restore the balance of his mind. But he came back and only merged deeper in his madness. Sometimes, in our country, children are married by their parents without having any voice in the matter. Of course such a marriage is little more than a betrothal. When they are married they still continue to live with their parents, and the real marriage takes place when the wife grows older, at which time it is customary for the husband to bring his bride home. In this case, however, the husband, absorbed in worship, had entirely forgotten that he had a wife. In her far-off home the girl had heard that her husband had become a religious enthusiast and that he was even considered insane by many. She resolved to learn the truth for herself; so she set out and walked to the place where her husband was. When at last she stood in her husband's presence, he at once admitted her rights as his wife—although in India any person, man or woman, who embraces a monastic life is thereby freed from all worldly obligations. The young man said to her: "As for me, the Mother has shown me that she resides in every woman, and so I have learnt to look upon every woman as Mother. But if you wish to draw me into the world, since I have been married to you, I am at your service."

The maiden was a pure and noble soul and was able to understand her husband's aspirations and sympathize with them. She quickly told him that she had no wish to drag him down to a life of worldliness, but that all she desired was to remain near him, to serve him, and to learn from him. She became one of his most devoted disciples, always revering him as a divine being. Thus through his wife's consent the last barrier was removed and he was free to lead the life he had chosen.

The next desire that seized upon the soul of this man was to know the truth about the various religions. Up to that time he had not known any religion but his own. He wanted to understand what other religions were like. So he sought teachers of other religions. By a teacher you must always remember what we mean in India: not a bookworm, but a man of realization, one who knows truth at first hand and not through an intermediary. He found a Mohammedan saint and underwent the disciplines prescribed by him. To his astonishment he found that, when faithfully carried out, these devotional methods led him to the same goal he had already attained. He gathered a similar experience from following the religion of Jesus Christ. He went to all the sects he could find, and whatever he took up he went into with his whole heart. He did exactly as he was told, and in every instance he arrived at the same result. Thus from actual experience he came to know that the goal of every religion is the same, that each is trying to teach the same thing, the difference being largely in method and still more in language. At the core, all sects and all religions have the same aim; they only quarrel for their own selfish purposes.

He then set about to learn humility, because he had found that the common idea in all religions is "Not I, but thou," and the Lord fills the heart of him who says, "Not I." The less of this little "I," the more of God there is in him. This, he found, was taught by every religion in the world, and he set himself to realize it. As I have told you, whenever he wanted to do anything he never confined himself to theories, but would enter into the practice immediately. Now, there was a family of pariahs living near the temple. The pariahs number several millions in the whole of India, and are so low in society that some of our books say that if a brahmin, on coming out of his house, sees the face of a pariah, he has to fast that day and recite certain prayers before he becomes holy again. In the dead of night, when all were sleeping, my Master would enter the house of the pariahs and cleanse the dirty places there, saying, "O Mother, make me the servant of the pariah, make me feel that I am even lower than the pariah."

There were various other disciplines, which would take a long time to relate, and I want to give you just a sketch of his life.

Then came to him the conviction that to be perfect, the idea of sex must go, because the soul has no sex, the soul is neither male nor female. It is only in the body that sex exists, and the man who desires to reach the spirit cannot at the same time hold to sex distinctions. Having been born in a masculine body, this man wanted to bring the feminine idea into everything. He began to think that he was a woman: he dressed like a woman, spoke like a woman, behaved like a woman, and lived as a member of the household among the women of a good family, until, after months of this discipline, his mind became changed and he entirely forgot the idea of sex. Thus the whole view of life became changed.

We hear in the West about worshipping woman, but this is usually for her youth and beauty. This man meant by worshipping woman that to him every woman's face was that of the Blissful Mother, and nothing but that. I myself have seen him standing, bathed in tears, before those women whom society would not touch, and saying with utmost humility: "Mother, in one form thou art in the street, and in another form thou art the universe. I salute thee, Mother, I salute thee." Think of the blessedness of that life from which all carnality has vanished, which can look upon every woman with that love and reverence, to which every woman's face becomes transfigured and only the face of the Divine Mother, the blissful one, the protectress of the human race, shines instead! That is what we want. Do you mean to say that the divinity of woman can ever be cheated? It never was and never will be. It always asserts itself. Unfailingly it detects fraud, it detects hypocrisy; unerringly it feels the warmth of truth, the light of spirituality, the holiness of purity. Such purity is absolutely necessary if real spirituality is to be attained.

This rigorous, unsullied purity came into the life of my Master; all the struggles which we have in our lives were past for him. The hard-earned jewels of spirituality, for which he had given three-quarters of his life, were now ready to be given to humanity; and then began his work. His teaching and preaching were peculiar: he would never take the position of a teacher. In our country a teacher is a most highly venerated person; he is regarded as God himself. We have not even the same respect for our father and mother. Our father and mother give us our body, but the teacher shows us the way to salvation. We are his children; we are born in the spiritual line of the teacher. All Hindus come to pay respect to an extraordinary teacher; they crowd around him. And here was such a teacher. But the teacher had no thought whether he was to be respected or not; he had not the least idea that he was a great teacher; he thought that it was the Mother who was doing everything, and not he. He always said: "If any good comes from my lips, it is the Mother who speaks. What have I to do with it?" That was his one idea about his work, and to the day of his death he never gave it up. This man sought no one. His principle was: first form character, first earn spirituality, and results will come of themselves. His favorite illustration was: "When the lotus opens, the bees come of their own accord to seek the honey. So let the lotus of your character be full-blown, and the results will follow." This is a great lesson to learn. My Master taught me this lesson hundreds of times, yet I often forget it.

Few understand the power of thought. If a man goes into a cave, shuts himself in, and thinks one really great thought and dies, that thought will penetrate the walls of that cave, vibrate through space, and at last permeate the whole human race. Such is the power of thought.

Be in no hurry, therefore, to give your thoughts to others. First have something to give. He alone teaches who has something to give. For teaching is not talking, teaching is not imparting doctrines; it is communicating. Spirituality can be communicated just as directly as I can give you a flower. This is true in the most literal sense. This idea is very old in India and finds illustration in the West in the theory of apostolic succession. Therefore first form character: that is your highest duty. Know truth for yourself, and there will be many to whom you can teach it afterwards. They will all come.

This was the attitude of my Master. He criticized no one. For years I lived with that man, but never did I hear those lips utter one word of condemnation for any sect. He had the same sympathy for all sects; he had found the inner harmony of religions. A man may be intellectual or devotional or mystical or active: the various religions represent one or other of these types. Yet it is possible to combine all the four in one man, and this is what future humanity is going to do. That was his idea. He condemned no one, but saw the good in all.

People came by thousands to see and hear this wonderful man, who spoke in a patois every word of which was forceful and instinct with light. For it is not what is spoken, much less the language in which it is spoken, but the personality of the speaker, which dwells in everything he says, that carries weight. Every one of us feels this at times. We hear most splendid orations, most wonderfully reasoned-out discourses, and we go home and forget everything. At other times we hear a few words in the simplest language, and they remain with us all the rest of our lives, become part and parcel of ourselves and produce lasting results. The words of a man who can put his personality into them take effect; but he must have tremendous personality. All teaching means giving and taking: the teacher gives and the taught receives; but the one must have something to give, and the other must be open to receive.

This man lived near Calcutta, the capital of India, the most important university town in our country, which was sending out skeptics and materialists by the hundreds every year; yet great men from the colleges—many of them skeptics and agnostics—used to come and listen to him. I heard of this man, and I went to see him. He looked just like an ordinary man, with nothing remarkable about him. He used the most simple language, and I thought, "Can this man be a great teacher?" I crept near him and asked him the question I had been asking others all my life: "Do you believe in God, sir?" "Yes," he replied. "Can you prove it, sir?" "Yes." "How?" "Because I see him just as I see you here, only much more intensely."

That impressed me at once. For the first time I found a man who dared to say that he saw God, that religion was a reality—to be felt, to be sensed in an infinitely more intense way than we can sense the world. I began to go to that man day after day, and I actually saw that religion could be given. One touch, one glance, can change a whole life. I had read about Buddha and Christ and Mohammed, about all those different luminaries of ancient times, and how they would stand up and say, "Be thou whole," and men became whole. I now found it to be true; and when I myself saw this man, all skepticism was brushed aside. It could be done. As my Master used to say: "Religion can be given and taken more tangibly, more directly, than anything else in the world." Be therefore spiritual first; have something to give, and then stand before the world and give it.

Religion is not talk or doctrines or theories, nor is it sectarianism. Religion cannot live in sects and societies. It is the relation between the soul and God. How can it be fitted into a society? It would then degenerate into business, and wherever there are business and business principles in religion, spirituality dies. Religion does not consist in erecting temples or building churches or attending public worship. It is not to be found in books or in words or in lectures or in organizations. Religion consists in realization. We all know as a fact that nothing will satisfy us until we realize the truth for ourselves. However we may argue, however much we may hear, but one thing will satisfy us, and that is our own realization; and such an experience is possible for every one of us, if we will only try.

The first idea in this attempt to realize religion is that of renunciation. As far as we can, we must give up. Darkness and light, enjoyment of the world and enjoyment of God, will never go together. "Ye cannot serve God and Mammon."

The second idea that I learnt from my Master, which is perhaps the most vital, is the wonderful truth that the religions of the world are not contradictory or antagonistic; they are but various phases of one eternal religion. There never was my religion or yours, my national religion or your national religion. There never existed many religions; there is only one religion. One infinite religion has existed all through eternity and will ever exist, and this religion is expressing itself in various countries in various ways. Therefore we must respect all religions and we must try to accept them all as far as we can.

Religions manifest themselves not only according to race and geographical position, but according to individual powers. In one man, religion is manifesting itself as intense activity, as work; in another, it is manifesting itself as intense devotion; in yet another, as mysticism; in others, as philosophy, and so forth. It is wrong when we say to others, "Your methods are not right." To learn this central secret that the truth may be one and yet many at the same time, that we may have different visions of the same truth from different standpoints, is exactly what must be done. Then, instead of feeling antagonism towards anyone, we shall have infinite sympathy for all. Knowing that there are different natures born into this world and that they will require different applications of the same religious truths, we shall understand why we should bear with each other. Just as in nature there is unity in variety—an infinite variation in the phenomenal, and behind all these variations, the Unchangeable, the Absolute—so it is with every human being. The microcosm is but a miniature repetition of the macrocosm. In spite of all these variations, in and through them all runs this eternal harmony, and we have to recognize this. This idea, above all other ideas, I find to be the crying necessity of the day.

Born in a country which is a hotbed of religious sects—through good fortune or ill fortune, everyone who has a religious idea wants to send an advance-guard there—I have been acquainted from my childhood with the various sects of the world. Even the Mormons came to preach in India. Welcome to them all! That is the place to preach religion. There it takes deeper root than in any other country. If you teach politics to the Hindus they will not understand, but if you preach religion, however curious it may be, you will have hundreds and thousands of followers in no time, and you have every chance of becoming a living God in your lifetime. I am glad it is so; for it shows that one thing we prize in India is God.

The sects among the Hindus are various, almost innumerable, and some of them apparently hopelessly contradictory. Yet the Hindus will tell you that they are but different manifestations of one religion. "As different rivers, taking their start from different mountains, running crooked or straight, all finally mingle their waters in the ocean, so the different sects, with their different points of view, at last all come unto Thee." This is not a theory. This has to be recognized—but not in that patronizing way in which some people do, when they say: "Oh yes, there are some very good things in them." Some even have the most wonderfully liberal idea that while other religions are remnants of a prehistoric evolution, "ours is the fulfillment of things." One man says that because his is the oldest religion it is the best; another makes the same claim because his is the latest.

We have to recognize that each one of them has the same saving power as every other. The same God helps all, and it is not you or I or any body of men that is responsible for the safety and salvation of the least little bit of the soul. I do not understand how people declare themselves to be believers in God, and at the same time think that God has handed over to a little body of men all truth, and that they are the guardians of the rest of humanity.

Do not try to disturb the faith of any man. If you can give him something better, if you can get hold of a man where he stands and give him a push upward, do so; but do not destroy what he has. The only true teacher is he who can convert himself, as it were, into a thousand persons at a moment's notice. The only true teacher is he who can immediately come down to the level of the student and transfer his soul to the student's soul and see through the student's eyes and hear through his ears and understand through his mind. Such a teacher can really teach, and none else. All these negative, destructive teachers that are in the world can never do any good.

In the presence of my Master I found out that a man could be perfect even in this body. Those lips never cursed anyone, never even criticized anyone. Those eyes were beyond the possibility of seeing evil, that mind had lost the power of thinking evil. He saw nothing but good. That tremendous purity, that tremendous renunciation, is the one secret of spirituality. "Neither through wealth nor through progeny, but through renunciation alone, is immortality to be reached," say the Vedas. "Sell all that thou hast and give to the poor, and follow me," says Christ. So all great saints and prophets have expressed it and have carried it out in their lives. How can great spirituality come without that renunciation? Renunciation is the background of all religious thought, wherever it be; and you will always find that the more this idea of renunciation diminishes, the more the senses will creep into the field of religion and spirituality will decrease.

That man was the embodiment of renunciation. In our country it is necessary for a man who wants to realize God to give up all wealth and position; and this condition my Master carried out literally. There were many who would have felt themselves blest if he would only have accepted a present from them; who would gladly have given him thousands of rupees if he would have taken them; but these were the only men from whom he would turn away. He was a triumphant example, a living realization of the complete conquest of lust and of desire for money. He was beyond all ideas of either. Such men are necessary for this century. Such renunciation is necessary in these days when men have begun to think that they cannot live a month without what they call their "necessities," which they are increasing out of all proportion. It is necessary in a time like this that someone should arise to demonstrate to the skeptics of the world that there yet breathes a man who does not care a straw for all the gold or all the fame that is in the universe. And there are such men.

The third idea I learnt from my Master was intense love for others. The first part of his life was spent in acquiring spirituality, and the remaining years in distributing it.

Men came in crowds to hear him and he would talk twenty hours out of twenty-four, and that not for one day, but for months and months, until at last the body broke down under the pressure of this tremendous strain. His intense love for mankind would not let him refuse to help even the humblest of the thousands who sought his aid. Gradually, there developed a fatal throat disorder, and yet he could not be persuaded to refrain from these exertions. As soon as he heard that people were asking to see him, he would insist upon having them admitted and would answer all their questions. When expostulated with, he replied: "I do not care. I will give up twenty thousand such bodies to help one man. It is glorious to help even one man." There was no rest for him. Once a man asked him, "Sir, you are a great yogi; why do you not put your mind a little on your body and cure your disease?" At first he did not answer, but when the question had been repeated, he gently said: "My friend, I thought you were a sage, but you talk like other men of the world. This mind has been given to the Lord; do you mean to say that I should take it back and put it upon the body, which is but a mere cage of the soul?"

So he went on preaching to people. When the news spread that his body was about to pass away, people began to flock to him in greater crowds than ever. You cannot imagine the way they come to these great religious teachers in India, how they crowd round them and make gods of them while they are yet living. Thousands wait simply to touch the hem of their garments. It is through this appreciation of spirituality in others that spirituality is produced. Whatever man wants and appreciates, he will get; and it is the same with nations. If you go to India and deliver a political lecture, however grand it may be, you will scarcely find people to listen to you; but just go and teach religion, *live* it, not merely talk it, and hundreds will crowd just to look at you, to touch your feet. When the people heard that this holy man was likely to go from them soon, they began to come to him more than ever before, and my Master went on teaching them without the least regard for his health. We could not prevent this. Many of the people came from long distances, and he would not rest until he had answered their questions. "While I can speak, I must teach them," he would say, and he was as good as his word. One day he told us that he would lay down the body that day, and repeating the most sacred word of the Vedas he entered into samadhi and passed away.

His thoughts and his message were known to very few capable of giving them out. Among others, he left a few young boys who had renounced the world and were ready to carry on his work. Attempts were made to crush them; but they stood firm, having the inspiration of that great life before them. Having had the contact of that blessed life for years, they stood their ground. These young men lived as sannyasins, begged through the streets of the city where they were born, although some of them came from well-known families. At first they met with great antagonism, but they persevered and went on from day to day spreading all over India the message of that great man, until the whole country was filled with the ideas he had preached. This man, from a remote village of Bengal, without education, by the sheer force of his own determination, realized the truth and gave it to others, leaving only a few young boys to keep it alive.

Today the name of Sri Ramakrishna Paramahamsa is known all over India, with its millions of people. Nay, the power of that man has spread beyond India, and if there has ever been a word of truth, a word of spirituality, that I have spoken anywhere in the world, I owe it to my Master. Only the mistakes are mine.

This is the message of Sri Ramakrishna to the modern world: "Do not care for doctrines, do not care for dogmas or sects or churches or temples. They count for little compared with the essence of existence in each man, which is spirituality; and the more a man develops it, the more power he has for good. Earn that first, acquire that, and criticize no one; for all doctrines and creeds have some good in them. Show by your lives that religion does not mean words or names or sects, but that it means spiritual realization. Only those can understand who have felt. Only those who have attained to spirituality can communicate it to others, can be great teachers of mankind. They alone are the powers of light."

The more such men are produced in a country, the more that country will be raised; and that country where such men do not exist is simply doomed; nothing can save it. Therefore my Master's message to mankind is: "Be spiritual and realize truth for yourself." He would have you give up all for the sake of your fellow beings. He would have you cease talking about love for your brothers and set to work to prove your words. The time has come for renunciation, for realization, and then you will see the harmony in all the religions of the world. You will know that there is no need of any quarrel; and then only will you be ready to help humanity. To proclaim and make clear the fundamental

unity underlying all religions was the mission of my Master. Other teachers have taught special religions which bear their names, but this great
teacher of the nineteenth century made no claim for himself. He left
every religion undisturbed because he had realized that, in reality,
they are all part and parcel of one eternal religion.

Swami Vivekananda, London, 1896

5

Intimate Glimpses of Vivekananda

Reports in Newspapers

Boston Evening Transcript, "Hindus at the Fair," September 30, 1893

The most striking figure one meets in this anteroom [at the World's Fair Parliament of Religions] is Swami Vivekananda, the Brahmin monk. He is a large, well-built man, with the superb carriage of the Hindustanis, his face clean-shaven, squarely molded regular features, white teeth, and with well-chiseled lips that are usually parted in a benevolent smile while he is conversing. His finely poised head is crowned with either a lemon-colored or a red turban, and his cassock (not the technical name for this garment), belted in at the waist and falling below the knees, alternates in a bright orange and rich crimson. He speaks excellent English and replied readily to any questions asked in sincerity.

Along with his simplicity of manner there is a touch of personal reserve when speaking to ladies, which suggests his chosen vocation. When questioned about the laws of his order, he has said, "I can do as I please, I am independent. Sometimes I live in the Himalaya Mountains, and sometimes in the streets of cities. I never know where I will get my next meal; I never keep money with me; I come here by subscription." Then looking round at one or two of his fellow-countrymen who chanced to be standing near he added, "They will take care of me," giving the inference that his board bill in Chicago is attended to by others. When asked if he was wearing his usual monk's costume, he said, "This is a good dress; when I am home I am in rags, and I go bare-footed. Do I believe in caste? Caste is a social custom; religion has nothing to do with it; all castes will associate with me."

It is quite apparent, however, from the deportment, the general appearance of Mr. Vivekananda that he was born among high castes—years of voluntary poverty and homeless wanderings have not robbed him of his birth-right of gentleman; even his family name is unknown; he took that of Vivekananda in embracing a religious career, and "Swami" is merely the title of reverend accorded to him. He cannot be far along in the thirties, and looks as if made for this life and its fruition, as well as for meditation on the life beyond. One cannot help wondering what could have been the turning point with him.

"Why should I marry," was his abrupt response to a comment on all he had renounced in becoming a monk, "when I see in every woman only the divine mother? Why do I make all these sacrifices? To emanci-pate myself from earthly ties and attachments so that there will be no re-birth for me. When I die I want to become at once absorbed in the divine, one with God. I would be a Buddha."

Vivekananda does not mean by this that he is a Bud-dhist. No name or sect can label him. He is an outcome of the higher Brahminism, a product of the Hindu spirit, which is vast, dreamy, self-extinguishing, a Sannyasi or holy man....

Vivekananda's address before the Parliament was broad as the heavens above us, embracing the best in all religions, as the ultimate universal religion—charity to all mankind, good works for the love of God, not for fear of punishment or hope of reward. He is a great favorite at the Parliament, from the grandeur of his sentiments and his appearance as well. If he merely crosses the platform he is applauded, and this marked approval of thousands he accepts in a childlike spirit of gratification, without a trace of conceit....

At the Parliament of Religions they used to keep Vivekananda until the end of the program to make people stay till the end of the session.... The four thousand fanning people in the Hall of Columbus would sit smiling and expectant, waiting for an hour or two to listen to Vivekananda for fifteen minutes. The chairman knew the old rule of keeping the best until the last.

New York Herald

> He is undoubtedly the greatest figure in the Parliament of Religions. After hearing him we feel how foolish it is to send missionaries to this learned nation.

The Critic, October 7, 1893

> An orator by divine right, and his strong intelligent face in its picturesque setting of yellow and orange was hardly less interesting than these earnest words and the rich, rhythmical utterance he gave them.

Appeal-Avalanche, Tennessee, "The Hindoo Monk," January 16, 1894

> Swami Vive Kananda, the Hindoo monk, who is to lecture at the Auditorium [Memphis] tonight, is one of the most eloquent men who has ever appeared on the religious or lecture platform in this country. His matchless oratory, deep penetration into things occult, his cleverness in debate, and great earnestness captured the closest attention of the world's thinking men at the World's Fair Parliament of Religion, and the admiration

of thousands of people who have since heard him during his lecture tour through many of the states of the Union.

In conversation he is a most pleasant gentleman; his choice of words are the gems of the English language, and his general bearing ranks him with the most cultured people of Western etiquette and custom. As a companion he is a most charming man, and as a conversationalist he is, perhaps, not surpassed in the drawing-rooms of any city in the Western World. He speaks English not only distinctly, but fluently, and his ideas, as new as sparkling, drop from his tongue in a perfectly bewildering overflow of ornamental language....

He had always been a close student of the wonderful and mysterious works of nature as drawn from God's high conception, and ... [has] acquired a knowledge that has given him a worldwide reputation as one of the most thoughtful scholars of the age.

His wonderful first address before the members of the World's Fair Parliament stamped him at once as a leader in that great body of religious thinkers. During the session he was frequently heard in defense of his religion, and some of the most beautiful and philosophical gems that grace the English language rolled from his lips there in picturing the higher duties that man owed to man and to his Creator. He is an artist in thought, an idealist in belief and a dramatist on the platform.

Since his arrival in Memphis he has been guest of Mr. Hu L. Brinkley, where he has received calls day and evening from many in Memphis who desired to pay their respects to him.

Ada Record, Ohio, "Divinity of Man," February 28, 1894

The lecture on the Divinity of Man by Swami Vive Kananda, the Hindu monk, drew a packed house at the Opera last Friday evening [February 22].

He stated that the fundamental basis of all religions was belief in the soul which is the real man, and something beyond both mind and matter, and proceeded to demonstrate the proposition.... The speaker said: "I am a spirit and not matter. The religion of the West hopes to again live with their body. Ours teaches there cannot be such a state. We say freedom of the soul instead of salvation."

The lecture proper lasted but thirty minutes but the president of the lecture committee had announced that at the close of the lecture the speaker would answer any questions propounded him. He gave that opportunity and liberal use was made of the privilege. They came from preachers and professors, physicians and philosophers, from citizens and students, from saints and sinners, some were written but dozens arose in their seats and propounded their questions directly. The speaker responded to all—mark the word, please—in an affable manner and in several instances turned the laugh on the inquirer. They kept up the fusillade for nearly an hour; when the speaker begged to be excused from further labor there yet remained a large pile of unanswered questions. He was an artful dodger on many of the questions. From his answers we glean the following additional statements in regard to the Hindu belief and teachings: ... Worship is feeling the holiness of God. Our religion does not believe in missions and teaches that man should love God for love's sake and his neighbor in spite of himself. The people of the West struggle too hard; repose is a factor of civilization. We do not lay our infirmities to God. There is a tendency toward a union of religions.

Northampton Daily Herald, "An Evening with Our Hindu Cousins," April 16, 1894

But to see and hear Swami Vive Kananda is an opportunity which no intelligent fair-minded American ought to miss if one cares to see a shining light of the very finest product of the mental, moral and spiritual culture of a race which reckons its age by thousands where we count ours by hundreds and is richly worth the study of every mind. Sunday afternoon [April 15] the distinguished Hindu spoke to the students of Smith college at the vesper service, the Fatherhood of God and the Brotherhood of man being, virtually, his theme, and that the address made a deep impression is evinced by the report of every auditor, the broadest liberality of true religious sentiment and precept characterizing the whole trend of thought.

Washington Post, "All Religions Are Good," October 29, 1894

Mr. Kananda spoke yesterday at the People's Church on the invitation of Dr. Kent, pastor of the church. His talk in the morning was a regular sermon, dealing entirely with the spiritual side of religion, and presenting the, to orthodox sects, rather original proposition that there is good in the foundation of every religion, that all religions, like languages, are descended from a common stock, and that each is good in its corporal and spiritual aspects so long as it is kept free from dogma and fossilism....

After the meeting, to a *Post* reporter Mr. Kananda said: "I claim no affiliation with any religious sect, but occupy the position of an observer, and so far as I may, of a teacher to mankind. All religion to me is good."

Westminster Gazette, "An Indian Yogi in London," October 23, 1895

Indian philosophy has in recent years had a deep and growing fascination for many minds, though up to the present time its exponents in this country have been entirely Western in their thought and training, with the result that very little is really known of the deeper mysteries of the Vedanta wisdom, and that little only by a select few. Not many have the courage or the intuition to seek in heavy translations, made greatly in the interests of philologists, for that sublime knowledge which they really reveal to an able exponent brought up in all the traditions of the East.

It was therefore with interest and not without some curiosity, writes a correspondent, that I proceeded to interview an exponent entirely novel to Western people in the person of the Swami Vivekananda, an actual Indian Yogi, who has boldly undertaken to visit the Western world to expound the traditional teaching which has been handed down by ascetics and Yogis through many ages and who in pursuance of this object, delivered a lecture last night in the Princes' Hall.

The Swami Vivekananda is a striking figure with his turban (or miter-shaped black cloth cap) and his calm but kindly features.

On my inquiring as to the significance, if any, of his name, the Swami said: "Of the name by which I am now known (Swami Vivekananda), the first word is descriptive of a Sannyasin, or one who formally renounces the world, and the second is the title I assumed—as is customary with all Sannyasins—on my renunciation of the world, it signifies, literally, 'the bliss of discrimination.'"

"And what induced you to forsake the ordinary course of the world, Swami?" I asked.

"I had a deep interest in religion and philosophy from my childhood," he replied, "and our books teach renunciation as the highest ideal to which man can aspire. It only needed the meeting with a great Teacher—Ramakrishna Paramahamsa—to kindle in me the final determination to follow the path he himself had trod, as in him I found my highest ideal realised."

"Then did he found a sect, which you now represent?"

"No," replied the Swami quickly. "No, his whole life was spent in breaking down the barriers of sectarianism and dogma. He formed no sect. Quite the reverse. He advocated and strove to establish absolute freedom of thought. He was a great Yogi."

"Then you are connected with no society or sect in this country? Neither Theosophical nor Christian Scientist, nor any other?"

"None whatever!" said the Swami in clear and impressive tones. (His face lights up like that of a child, it is so simple, straightforward and honest.) "My teaching is my own interpretation of our ancient books, in the light which my Master shed upon them. I claim no supernatural authority. Whatever in my teaching may appeal to the highest intelligence and be accepted by thinking men, the adoption of that will be my reward." "All religions," he continued, "have for their object the teaching either of devotion, knowledge, or Yoga, in a concrete form. Now, the philosophy of Vedanta is the abstract science which embraces all these methods, and this it is that I teach, leaving each one to apply it to his own concrete form. I refer each individual to his own experiences, and where reference is made to books, the latter are procurable, and may be studied by each one for himself. Above all, I teach no authority proceeding from hidden beings speaking through visible agents, any more than I claim learning from hidden books or manuscripts. I am the exponent of no occult societies, nor do I believe that good can come of such bodies. Truth stands on its own authority, and truth can bear the light of day."

"Then you do not propose to form any society, Swami?" I suggested.

"None; no society whatever. I teach only the Self hidden in the heart of every individual and common to all. A handful of strong men knowing that Self and living in Its light would revolutionise the world, even today, as has been the case by single strong men before each in his day."

"Have you just arrived from India?" I inquired—for the Swami is suggestive of Eastern suns.

"No," he replied, "I represented the Hindu religion at the Parliament of Religions held at Chicago in 1893. Since then I have been travelling and lecturing in the United States. The American people have proved most interested audiences and sympathetic friends, and my work there has so taken root that I must shortly return to that country."

"And what is your attitude towards the Western religions, Swami?"

"I propound a philosophy which can serve as a basis to every possible religious system in the world, and my attitude towards all of them is one of extreme sympathy—my teaching is antagonistic to none. I direct my attention to the individual, to make him strong, to teach him that he himself is divine, and I call upon men to make themselves conscious of this divinity within. That is really the ideal—conscious or unconscious—of every religion."

"And what shape will your activities take in this country?"

"My hope is to imbue individuals with the teachings to which I have referred, and to encourage them to express these to others in their own way; let them modify them as they will; I do not teach them as dogmas; truth at length must inevitably prevail. The actual machinery through which I work is in the hands of one or two friends. On October 22, they have arranged for me to deliver an address to a British audience at Princes' Hall, Piccadilly, at 8:30 p.m. The event is being advertised. The subject will be on the key of my philosophy—'Self-Knowledge.' Afterwards I am prepared to follow any course that opens—to attend meetings in people's drawing-rooms or elsewhere, to answer letters, or discuss personally. In a mercenary age I may venture to remark that none of my activities are undertaken for a pecuniary reward."

I then took my leave from one of the most original of men that I have had the honour of meeting.

Appreciations by Great Thinkers

Nobel Laureate Romain Rolland

> He was energy personified, and action was his message to men. For him, as for Beethoven, it was the root of all the virtues.... When this quite unknown young man of thirty appeared in Chicago at the inaugural meeting of the Parliament of Religions, opened in September 1893, by Cardinal Gibbons, all his fellow-members were forgotten in his commanding presence. His strength and beauty, the grace and dignity of his bearing, the dark light of his eyes, his imposing appearance, and from the moment he began to speak, the splendid music of his rich deep voice enthralled the vast audience of American Anglo-Saxons, previously prejudiced again him on account of his color. The thought of this warrior prophet of India left a deep mark upon the United States.... Everybody recognized in him at sight the leader, the anointed of God, the man marked with the stamp of power to command.
>
> His words are great music, phrases in the style of Beethoven, stirring rhythms like the march of Handel choruses. I cannot touch these sayings of his, scattered as they are through the pages of books at thirty years' distance, without receiving a thrill through my body like an electric shock. And what shocks, what transports must have been produced when in burning words they issued from the lips of the hero!

American philosopher William James

> The paragon of all monistic systems is the Vedanta phi-
> losophy of Hindostan, and the paragon of Vedantists
> was Swami Vivekananda who visited our land some
> years ago.... I have just been reading some of
> Vivekananda's addresses in England, which I had not
> seen. That man is simply a wonder for oratorical
> power.... The Swami is an honor to humanity in any case.

Leo Tolstoy

> The most eminent of modern Indian thinkers is
> Vivekananda.

Indian philosopher and former president of India S. Radhakrishnan

> And if there is any call which Vivekananda made to us,
> it is to rely on our own spiritual resources.... He gave
> us fortitude in suffering, he gave us hope in distress,
> he gave us courage in despair.

Mahatma Gandhi

> I have gone through his works very thoroughly, and hav-
> ing gone through them, the love that I had for my coun-
> try became a thousandfold.

Nobel Laureate Rabindranath Tagore

> Vivekananda said that there was the power of Brahman
> [Ultimate Reality] in every man, that Narayana [the per-
> sonal God] wanted to have our service through the poor.
> This is what I call real gospel. This gospel showed the
> path of infinite freedom from man's tiny egocentric self
> beyond the limits of all selfishness. This was no sermon
> relating to a particular ritual, nor was it a narrow injunc-
> tion to be imposed upon one's external life....
> Vivekananda's gospel marked the awakening of man in
> his fullness and that is why it inspired our youth to

the diverse courses of liberation through work and sacrifice.

Merwin-Marie Snell, president of the scientific section of the 1893 Parliament of Religions

> Swami Vivekananda ... was beyond question the most popular and influential man in the Parliament. He frequently spoke both on the floor of the Parliament itself and in the meeting of the Scientific section over which I had the honor to preside, and on all occasions he was received with greater enthusiasm than any other speaker, Christian or "Pagan." The people thronged about him wherever he went and hung with eagerness on his every word. Since the Parliament he has been lecturing before large audiences in the principal cities of the United States and has received an ovation wherever he has gone. He has often been invited to preach in Christian pulpits and has, by all those who have heard him on any occasion and still more by those who have made his personal acquaintance, been always spoken of in terms of the highest admiration. The most rigid orthodox Christians say of him, "He is, indeed, a prince among men." America thanks India for sending him and begs her to send many more like him, if such there are, to teach by their example those of her own children who have not yet learned the lesson of universal fraternity and openness of mind and heart and by their precepts those who have not come to see divinity in all things and a oneness transcending all.

C. C. Everett, dean of Harvard Divinity School

> There are, indeed, few departments of study more attractive than the Hindu thought. It is a rare pleasure to see a form of belief that to most seems so far away and unreal as the Vedanta system, represented by an actually living and extremely intelligent believer. This system is

not to be regarded merely as a curiosity, as a speculative vagary. Hegel said that Spinozism is the necessary beginning of all philosophizing. This can be said even more emphatically of the Vedanta system. We occidentals busy ourselves with the manifold. We can, however, have no understanding of the manifold, if we have no sense of the One in which the manifold exists. The reality of the One is the truth which the East may well teach us; and we owe a debt of gratitude to Vivekananda that he has taught this lesson so effectively.

Sri Ramakrishna, nineteenth-century Godman, prophet of the harmony of religions, and spiritual Master of Swami Vivekananda

Narendra[1] belongs to a very high plane—the realm of the Absolute. He has a manly nature. So many devotees come here, but there is no one like him.

Every now and then I take stock of the devotees. I find that some are like lotuses with ten petals, some like lotuses with sixteen petals, some like lotuses with a hundred petals. But among lotuses Narendra is a thousand-petalled one.

Narendra and people of his type belong to the class of the ever-free. They are never entangled in the world. When they grow a little older they feel the awakening of inner consciousness and go directly toward God. They come to the world only to teach others.

One day I saw that, through samadhi, my mind was going up by a luminous path. Going beyond the gross world studded with the sun, the moon and the stars, it entered first of all into the subtle world of ideas. The more it began to ascend to subtler and subtler strata of that realm, the more did I see beautiful ideal forms of deities existing on both sides of the path. It came gradually to the last extremity of that region. I saw a barrier of light there separating the realm of the divisible from

---

[1] Narendra or Naren, the premonastic name of Swami Vivekananda.

that of the indivisible. Leaping over it, the mind entered by degrees the realm of the indivisible. I saw that there was no more any person or thing there having a form. As if, afraid to enter there, even the gods and goddesses possessing heavenly bodies exercised their authority only over realms far below. But the very next moment I saw seven wise rishis having bodies consisting of divine light only, seated there in samadhi. I felt that, in virtue and knowledge, love and renunciation they had excelled even the gods and goddesses, not to speak of human beings. Astonished, I was pondering over their greatness when I saw before me that a part of the homogeneous mass of light of the "Abode of the Indivisible," devoid of the slightest tinge of difference, became solidified and converted into the form of a divine child. Coming down to one of those rishis, and throwing its soft and delicate arms round his neck, the divine child embraced him and, afterwards, calling him with its ambrosial words, sweeter than the music of the vina, made great efforts to wake him up from his samadhi. The rishi woke up at the delicate and loving touch and looked on that wonderful child with half-shut eyes, free from winking. Seeing his bright face, full of delight at the sight of the child, I thought that the child was the treasure of his heart and that their familiarity was a matter of eternity. The extraordinary divine child then expressed infinite joy and said to him, "I am going, you must come with me." The rishi said nothing at that request, but his loving eyes expressed his hearty assent. Afterwards, looking on the child with loving eyes, he entered again into samadhi. Astonished, I then saw that a part of the mind and body of that rishi converted into the form of a bright light, came down to the earth along the reverse path. Hardly had I seen Narendra for the first time than I knew that he was that rishi.

Narendra will give up his body of his own will. When he realizes his true nature, he will refuse to stay on this earth. Very soon he will shake the world by his intellectual and spiritual powers. I have prayed to the Divine Mother to keep away from him the knowledge of the Absolute and cover his eyes with a veil of maya. There is much work to be done by him.

Holy Mother Sri Sarada Devi, wife and spiritual companion of Sri Ramakrishna

[Swami Vivekananda once wrote a letter from America urging the monks of the Ramakrishna Order to renounce everything in the service of God. When Holy Mother heard this, she said,] Naren is an instrument of the Master. It is the Master who writes through Naren about the future duties of his children and devotees for the good of the world. What he has written is all correct. You will see it bearing fruit in course of time.

[To Swami Vivekananda:] What you are doing now and what you will do in the future will be permanent. You are born just to accomplish this work. Thousands of people will hail you as a world teacher, a bestower of divine knowledge.

Students, friends, and admirers, London

The students of the Vedanta philosophy in London under your remarkably able instruction feel that they would be lacking in their duty and privilege if they failed to record their warm and heartfelt appreciation of the noble and unselfish work you have set yourself to do, and the great help you have been to them in their study of religion.

We feel the very deepest regret that you are so soon to leave England, but we should not be true students of the very beautiful philosophy you have taught us to regard so highly if we did not recognize that there are claims upon your work from our brothers and sisters in India. That you may prosper very greatly in that work is the united prayer of all who have come under the elevating influence of your teaching, and no less of your personal attributes, which, as a living example of Vedanta, we recognize as the most helpful encouragement to us one and all to become real lovers of God, in practice as well as in theory.

We look forward with great interest and keen anticipation to your speedy return to this country, but, at the same time, we feel real pleasure that India, which you have taught us to regard in an altogether new light, and we should like to add, to love, is to share with us the generous service which you are giving to the world.

In conclusion we would especially beg of you to convey our loving sympathy to the Indian people and to accept from us our assurance that we regard their cause as ours, realizing as we do from you that we are all One in God.

Reminiscences of Swami Vivekananda

From the reminiscences of Cornelia Conger

Before the Congress (or Parliament) of Religions met in Chicago at the time of the Columbian Exposition in 1893, members of various churches volunteered to ask into their homes as guests delegates to it. My grandmother, Mrs. John B. Lyon, was one of these, requesting, if possible, that a delegate who was broad-minded be sent to us, as my grandfather was much interested in philosophy but heartily disliked bigots.

Our home was 262 Michigan Avenue, a pleasant somewhat old-fashioned frame-house, painted olive green with boxes of red geraniums across the front. It was full of guests all that summer as my grandparents were naturally hospitable and this World's Fair was a very exciting and fascinating affair. So all our out-of-town relatives and friends were eager to come to

Chicago to see it. When word came that our delegate was to arrive on a certain evening, the house was so crowded that my grandmother had to send her elder son to a friend's house to have his room for our guest.

We had been given no idea who he would be, nor even what religion he was representing. A message came that a member of our Church—the First Presbyterian—would bring him after midnight. Everyone went to bed except my grandmother who waited up to receive them. When she answered the doorbell, there stood Swami Vivekananda in a long yellow robe, a red sash, and a red turban—a very startling sight to her, because she had probably never seen an East Indian before. She welcomed him warmly and showed him to his room. When she went to bed, she was somewhat troubled....

When my grandfather woke up, she told him of the problem and said he must decide whether it would be uncomfortable for Swami and for our Southern friends to be together. If so, she said he could put Swami up as our guest at the new Auditorium Hotel near us. My grandfather was dressed about half an hour before breakfast and went into the library to read his morning paper. There he found Swami and, before breakfast was served, he came to my grandmother and said, "I don't care a bit, Emily, if all our guests leave! This Indian is the most brilliant and interesting man who has ever been in our home, and he shall stay as long as he wishes." That began a warm friendship between them which was later summed up—much to my grandfather's embarrassment—by having Swami calmly remark to a group of my grandfather's friends one day at the Chicago Club: "I believe Mr. Lyon is the most Christlike man I ever met."

He seemed to feel especially close to my grandmother, who reminded him of his own mother. She was short and very erect, with quiet dignity and assurance, excellent common sense, and a dry humor that he enjoyed. My mother, who was a pretty and charming young widow, and I—who was only six years old—lived with them. My grandmother and my mother attended most of the meetings of the Congress of Religions and heard Swamiji[2] speak there and later at lectures he gave. I know he helped my sad young mother who missed her young husband so much. Mother read and studied Swamiji's books later and tried to follow his teachings.

My memories are simply of him as a guest in our home—of a great personality who is still vivid to me. His brilliant eyes, his charming voice with the lilt of a slight well-bred Irish brogue, his warm smile. He told me enchanting stories of India, of monkeys and peacocks, and flights of bright green parrots, of banyan trees and masses of flowers, and markets piled with all colors of fruits and vegetables. To me they sounded like fairytales, but now that I have driven over many hundreds of miles of Indian roads, I realize that he was simply describing scenes from the memories of his own boyhood.

I used to rush up to him when he came into the house and cry, "Tell me another story, Swami," and climb into his lap. Perhaps, so far from home and in so strange a country, he found comfort in the love and enthusiasm of a child. He was always wonderful to me! Yet—because a child is sensitive—I remember times when I would run into his room and suddenly know he did not want to be disturbed—when he was in meditation. He asked me many questions about what I learnt in school, and made me show him my schoolbooks, and pointed out India to me on the map—it was pink, I recall—and told me about his country. He seemed sad that little Indian girls did not have, in general, the chance to have as good an education as we American children. Imagine how interested I was when Swami

---

[2] Swami Vivekananda.

Shankarananda,[3] President, Belur Math, told me he founded a girls' school in Calcutta!

My grandmother was president of the Women's Hospital at home, and he visited it with lively interest and asked for all the figures in infant mortality, etc. So again it showed how much he was learning in our country to be used in helping his own people, because I was told that a maternity hospital was also founded later. How very happy that would have made my grandmother!

I was fascinated by his turban which struck me as a very funny kind of a hat, especially as it had to be wound up afresh every time he put it on! I persuaded him to let me see him wrap it back and forth around his head.

As our American food is less highly seasoned than India, my grandmother was afraid he might find it flat. He told us, on arrival, that he had been told to conform to all the customs and the food of his hosts, so he ate as we did. My grandmother used to make a little ceremony of making salad dressing at the table, and one of the condiments she used was Tabasco Sauce, put up by some friends of hers, the McIlhennys in Louisiana. She handed him the bottle and said, "You might like a drop or two of this on your meat, Swami." He sprinkled it on with such a lavish hand that we all gasped and said, "But you can't do that! It's terribly hot!" He laughed and ate it with such enjoyment that a special bottle of the sauce was always put at his place after that....

When he began to give lectures, people offered him money for the work he hoped to do in India. He had no purse. So he used to tie it up in a handkerchief and bring it back and—like a proud little boy!—pour it into my grandmother's lap to keep for him. She made him learn the different coins and to stack them up neatly

---

[3] Swami Shankarananda, the seventh president of the Ramakrishna Order from 1951 to 1962.

to count them. She made him write down the amount each time, and she deposited in her bank for him. He was overwhelmed by the generosity of his audience who seemed so happy to give to help people they had never seen so far away.

Once he said to my grandmother that he had had the greatest temptation of his life in America. She liked to tease him a bit and said, "Who is she, Swami?" He burst out laughing and said, "Oh, it is not a lady; it is organization!" He explained how the followers of Ramakrishna had all gone out alone and when they reached a village, would just quietly sit under a tree and wait for those in trouble to come to consult them. But in the States he saw how much could be accomplished by organizing work. Yet he was doubtful about just what type of organization would be acceptable to the Indian character, and he gave a great deal of thought and study how to adapt what seemed good to him in our Western world to the best advantage of his own people. I can see that Belur Math and his many charities are the result of this period in his life....

When Swamiji returned to Chicago a year or so later to give lectures ... he only stayed with us for a short time. He knew he could teach better if he lived in his own regime of food and of many hours for meditation. It also left him free to receive many who came to him for help. So my grandmother helped him find a simple but comfortable little flat, but I do not recall that I ever saw it.

Swamiji was such a dynamic and attractive personality that many women were quite swept away by him and made every effort by flattery to gain his interest. He was still young and, in spite of his great spirituality and his brilliance of mind, seemed to be very unworldly. This used to trouble my grandmother who feared he might be put in a false or uncomfortable position, and she tried to caution him a little. Her concern touched and amused him, and he patted her hand and said, "Dear Mrs. Lyon, you dear American mother of mine, don't be afraid for me! It is true I often sleep under a banyan tree with a bowl of rice given me by a kindly peasant, but it is equally true that I also am sometimes the guest in the palace of a great maharaja and a slave girl is appointed to wave a peacock feather fan over me all night long! I am used to temptation, and you need not fear for me!"

After having talked with Swami Shankarananda and been encouraged by him, I wished I had talked to my mother's younger sister, Katharine (Mrs. Robert W. Hamill) about her recollections of Swamiji. So when I reached home I asked her what she could add to my scattered memories. She was a bride and had her own home. She was not at her mother's and father's so very much. She recalled Swamiji much as I did, but never heard him lecture. However, she and her husband were "young intellectuals" and had a group of young professors from our university, young newspaper men, etc., around them. One Sunday evening she was telling them how remarkable Swamiji was, and they said that modern scientists and psychologists could "show up" his religious beliefs in no time. She said, "If I can persuade him to come here next Sunday evening, will you all come back and meet him?" They agreed, and Swamiji met them all at an informal supper party. My aunt does not recall just what subjects were brought up, but that the entire evening was a lively and interesting debate on all sorts of ideas—Aunt Katharine said that Swamiji's great knowledge of the Bible and the Koran as well as the various oriental religions, his grasp of science and of psychology were astounding. Before the evening was over, the "doubting Thomases" threw up their hands and admitted that Swamiji had held his own on every point and that they parted from him with warmest admiration and affection....

So here is my very tiny "facet" [of the life of Swami Vivekananda] offered in memory of someone I have loved for all these 62 years—not as a teacher, nor a great religious leader—but as a wonderful and vivid friend who lived in our home.

From the reminiscences of Martha Brown Fincke

Early in November 1935 I landed in Calcutta and set foot for the first time on the soil of India. As I left my home in the United States of America, journeying westward to encircle the globe, I thought of myself as a tourist in the different countries through which I passed. Only when I reached India did I in thought become a pilgrim. As a pilgrim I went the day after landing to the Belur Math on the farther side of the Ganges to bow my head in reverence before the tomb of the great Swami Vivekananda. In the upper room of the guesthouse I met Miss Josephine MacLeod, his devoted friend. I also met several of the resident swamis. When to each of them I said that I had once known Swami Vivekananda, their eagerness to hear of that far-off meeting surprised me. It was indeed to me one of the most vital influences of my life; but could it mean anything to others? Since they assured me that it was so, I am setting down my recollections of those two days, now 42 years ago, when I came under the influence of that great man.

In September 1893, at the World's Fair held in Chicago to commemorate the 400th anniversary of the discovery of America by Columbus, a Parliament of Religions was a part of the program. To this journeyed the then unknown young Hindu monk, Swami Vivekananda. His power over the audiences who heard him set forth his universal gospel and the magic of his personality are common knowledge.

At the close of the Parliament, in order to be independent of the personal benefactions of his admirers, the swami engaged with a Lecture Bureau to tour the States beginning with the East, and early in November he came to the town of Northampton, Massachusetts. This charming old town, halfway between New York and Boston, and since prominent as the home of Calvin Coolidge, is situated on low hills in the Connecticut Valley just before the river plunges into the gap between Mt. Tom and Mt. Holyoke. In the flood seasons the low-lying meadows about the town shine with the covering waters, and the purple outline of the Mt. Holyoke range forms the horizon to the south. Stately elm trees border the streets, and the place had then a slumberous aspect except when an eruption of students woke it to animation. For a women's college formed the center of its intellectual life, Smith College, founded in 1875 by Sophia Smith for the higher education of women.

To this College I went as a freshman in the fall of 1893, an immature girl of eighteen, undisciplined but reaching out eagerly for the things of the mind and spirit. Brought up in a sheltered atmosphere, in the strictest Protestant Christian orthodoxy, it was with some misgivings that my parents saw me leave the home and be exposed to the dangers of so called free thinking. Had not one of my friends gone the year before to Vassar College and was rumored to have "lost her faith"?

The College dormitories were not large enough to house all of the incoming class, so I with three other freshmen boarded in a square brown house near the campus. This was kept by a lady whose independent spirit and humorous outlook endeared her to us, despite her despotic rule. College lectures for the whole body of students with compulsory attendance were of frequent occurrence, and many well-known leaders of thought visited us.

On the bulletin for November was the name of Swami Vivekananda who was to give two evening lectures. That he was a Hindu monk we knew—nothing more; for the fame he had won in the recent Parliament of Religions had not reached our ears. Then an exciting piece of news leaked out; he was to live at our house, to eat with us, and we could ask him questions about India. Our hostess' breadth of tolerance may be seen in receiving into her house a man with dark skin, whom the hotel had doubtless refused to admit. As late as 1912 the great poet Tagore with his companion wandered through the streets of New York looking in vain for shelter!

The name of India was familiar to me from my earliest childhood. Had not my mother almost decided to marry a young man who went as a missionary to India, and did not a box from our Church Missionary Association go each year to the zenanas? India was a hot land where snakes abounded, and "the heathen in his blindness bows down to wood and stone." It is astonishing how little an eager reader like myself knew about the history or literature of the great country. The life of William Carey I had read, had heard of St. Francis Xavier of Goa, but it was all from the missionary standpoint. You must remember *Kim* had not yet appeared. To talk with a real Indian would be a chance indeed.

The day came, the little guestroom was ready, and a stately presence entered our home. The swami's dress was a black Prince Albert coat, dark trousers, and a yellow turban wound in intricate folds about a finely shaped head. But the face with its inscrutable expression, the eyes so full of flashing light, and the whole emanation of power, are beyond description. We were awed and silent. Our hostess, however, was not one to be awed, and she led an animated conversation. I sat next to the swami, and with my superfluity of reverence found not a word to say.

Of the lecture that evening I can recall nothing. The imposing figure on the platform in red robe, orange cord, and yellow turban, I do remember, and the wonderful mastery of the English language with its rich sonorous tones, but the ideas did not take root in my mind, or else the many years since then have obliterated them. But what I do remember was the symposium that followed.

To our house came the College president, the head of the philosophy department, and several other professors, the ministers of the Northampton churches, and a well-known author. In a corner of the living room we girls sat as quiet as mice and listened eagerly to the discussion which followed. To give a detailed account of this conversation is beyond me, though I have a strong impression that it dealt mainly with Christianity and why it is the only true religion. Not that the subject was the swami's choosing. As his imposing presence faced the row of black-coated and somewhat austere gentlemen, one felt that he was being challenged. Surely these leaders of thought in our world had an unfair advantage. They knew their Bibles thoroughly and the European systems of philosophy, as well as the poets and commentators. How could one expect a Hindu from far-off India to hold his own with these, master though he might be of his own learning? The reaction to the surprising result that followed is my purely subjective one, but I cannot exaggerate its intensity.

To texts from the Bible, the swami replied by other and more apposite ones from the same book. In upholding his side of the argument he quoted English philosophers and writers on religious subjects. Even the poets he seemed to know thoroughly, quoting Wordsworth and Thomas Gray (and not from the well-known *Elegy*). Why were my sympathies not with those of my own world? Why did I exult in the air of freedom that blew through the room as the swami broadened the scope of religion till it embraced all mankind? Was it that his words found an echo in my own longings, or was it merely the magic of his personality? I cannot tell; I only know that I felt triumphant with him.

In speaking with a swami at the Belur Math, he said that to him Swami Vivekananda personified love. To me that night he personified power. I think that I can explain this from my later knowledge. No doubt these great men of our college-world were narrow-minded, of closed convictions, "wise in their own conceits." How could they accept the saying "Whosoever comes to me [the Lord] through whatsoever form, I reach him"?[4] At Chicago the swami had recently felt the rancor of Christian missionaries, and undoubtedly his accents took on an austerity as he felt the same spirit in these representatives of Western learning. To them love would not appeal, but power can awe even when it does not force agreement. The discussion, beginning with the utmost courtesy, became less cordial, then bitterness crept in, a resentment on the part of the champions of Christianity as they felt that it was "thumbs down" for them. And truly it was. The repercussion of the triumph that filled me then is with me to this day.

Early the next morning loud splashings came from the bathroom, and mingling with them a deep voice chanting in an unknown tongue. I believe that a group of us huddled near the door to listen. At breakfast we asked him the meaning of the chant. He replied: "I first put the water on my forehead, then on my breast, and each time I chant a prayer for blessings on all creatures." This struck me forcibly. I was used to a morning prayer, but it was for myself first that I prayed, then for my family. It had never occurred to me to include all mankind in my family and to put them before myself.

After breakfast the Swami suggested a walk, and we four students, two on each side, escorted the majestic figure proudly through the streets. As we went, we shyly tried to open conversation. He was instantly responsive and smiled showing his beautiful teeth. I

---

[4] Bhagavad Gita.

only remember one thing he said. Speaking of Christian doctrines, he remarked how abhorrent to him was the constant use of the term "the *blood* of Christ." That made me think. I had always hated the hymn "There is a fountain filled with blood, drawn from Emmanuel's veins," but what daring to criticize an accepted doctrine of the Church! My "free-thinking" certainly dates from the awakening given me by that freedom-loving soul. I led the conversation to the Vedas, those holy books of India he had mentioned in his lecture. He advised me to read them for myself, preferably in the original. I then and there made a resolve to learn Sanskrit, a purpose which I regret to say I have never fulfilled. Indeed as far as outward result goes, I am a case of the good seed choked by thorns.

One rather humorous outcome of this advice about the Vedas should not be omitted. The following summer a pretty little Guernsey calf was added to the family livestock, and when my father gave it to me, I named it "Veda." Unfortunately the little one only lived a few months and my father said its name had killed it.

Of the succeeding lecture I can say nothing. The great Swami left us and I never saw him again. I even lost sight of his journeyings through our country and did not know that he made another visit to it two years later. And yet those two days of his mighty presence have certainly colored all the rest of my life. I wrote to my family a detailed account of this visit, expressing myself so strongly that my devoted but over-solicitous father became alarmed. He pictured me leaving the faith of my father and becoming a disciple of the Swami. He used argument and ridicule, and to spare him further anxiety—for I adored my father—I stopped talking of my new thoughts, and kept them to myself.

I often think of the time I have lost, of the roundabout way I have come, groping my way, when under such guidance I might have aimed directly for the goal.

But for an immortal soul it is wiser not to spend time in regrets, since to be on the way is the important thing.

One reads of the seeds found in Egyptian sarcophagi, buried thousands of years previously and yet retaining enough vitality to sprout when planted. Lying apparently lifeless in my mind and heart, the far-off memory of that great apostle from India has during the past year begun to send forth shoots. It has at last brought me to this country. During the intervening years—years of sorrow and responsibility and struggle mingled with joy—my inmost self has been trying out this and that doctrine to see if it was what I wanted to live by. Always some dissatisfaction resulted. Dogmas and rituals, made so important by orthodox believers, seemed to me so unimportant, so curbing that freedom of the spirit that I longed for.

I find in the universal Gospel that Swamiji preached the satisfaction of my longing. To believe that the Divine is within us, that we are from the very first a part of God, and that this is true of every man, what more can one ask? In receiving this, as I have on the soil of India, I feel that I have come Home.

From the reminiscences of Ida Ansell

All the superlatives in the language couldn't convey one's impressions of Swami Vivekananda when he introduced us, early in 1900, to a completely new conception of life and religion. I have been requested, as one who took notes of his lectures for her own use, with no thought of their ever being published, to give my impressions of him. How to do it? He seemed like a radiant being from a higher plane, and yet so understanding of every phase of humanity. He appealed to every grade of intelligence by his oratory, his humor, his mimicry, his scornful denunciation of any form of pettiness or intolerance, and by his compassion for every human need.

Startled at the loftiness of his conception compared with our little ideas, we knew, as we left the hall with the Swami's vibrant chanting of a Sanskrit *shloka* [verse] still ringing within, that he was ushering us, in the beginning of this twentieth century, into a new and larger conception of the meaning of life.... He was surely a Mahatma or a divine being, more than human. No one had ever been so sublimely eloquent or so deliciously humorous, such an entrancing storyteller, or such a perfect mimic....

Besides the public lectures, Swamiji had some morning classes for earnest students, in meditation.... First there would be a meditation and then a period of instruction, followed by questions and answers and practical suggestions as to exercise, rest, and diet.... Many questions were answered in these classes. Also, for those who arrived before class time, there was a little opportunity for getting acquainted personally with the Swami. We were invited into the dining room, where we enjoyed some informal talks. He would make fun of our habit of rushing here and there. He never hurried. That majestic calmness never left him. It amused him to see someone run for a street car. "Won't there be another one?" he would ask. It did not trouble him at all if he was late in beginning a class or a lecture, and there was no set time for its ending. He would continue until he finished his subject, even if it took more than double the allotted time. These early morning visits previous to the class were completely informal. Swamiji would wear a gray flannel robe, sit cross-legged in an arm-chair, smoke, answer questions, and tell jokes. When it was time for the class, he would appear two minutes later in the living room, clad in his ocher robe, his hair smooth, and the pipe missing. But the jokes continued to be interspersed among the serious subjects.

The same was true in his public lectures. He playfully ridiculed the question: What becomes of one's

Swami Vivekananda at Thousand Island Park, New York, 1895

individuality when one realizes his oneness with God? "You people in this country are so afraid of losing your in-di-vid-u-al-i-ty!" he would exclaim. "Why, you are not individuals yet. When you realize your whole nature, you will attain your true individuality, not before. In knowing God you cannot lose anything...."

He encouraged questions at the end of each lecture, and once when someone suggested that they were tiring him with too many questions, he said, "Ask all the questions you like, the more the better. That is what I am here for and I won't leave you until you understand. In India they tell me I ought not to teach Advaita (monistic) Vedanta to the people at large, but I say I can make even a child understand it. You cannot begin too early to teach the highest spiritual truths."

From the reminiscences of Mary C. Funke, who writes of her experience at Thousand Island Park, N.Y., 1895

So here we are—in the very house with *Vivekananda*, listening to him from 8 o'clock in the morning until late at night. Even in my wildest dreams I could not imagine anything so wonderful, so perfect.... Oh, the sublime teaching of Vivekananda! No nonsense, no talk of "astrals," "imps," etc., but God, Jesus, Buddha. I feel that I shall never be quite the same again for I have caught a glimpse of the Real.

Just think what it means to listen to a Vivekananda at every meal, lessons each morning and the nights on the porch, the eternal stars shining like "patinas of bright gold"! In the afternoon, we take long walks and the Swami literally, and so simply, finds "books in the running brooks, sermons in stones, and good in everything." And this same Swami is so merry and fun-loving. We just go *mad* at times....

Swami tells us to forget that there is any Detroit[5] for the present—that is, to allow no personal thoughts to

---

[5] Mary C. Funke was from Detroit.

occupy our minds while taking this instruction. We are taught to see God in *everything* from the blade of grass to man—"even in the diabolical man." ...

We are trying to take notes of all that he says but *I* find myself lost in listening and forget the notes. His *voice* is wondrously beautiful. One might well lose one-self in its divine music.... Sometimes I ask him rather daring questions, for I am so anxious to know just how he would react under certain conditions. He takes it so kindly when I in my impulsive way sometimes "rush in where angels fear to tread." Once he said to someone, "Mrs. Funke rests me, she is so naïve." Wasn't that dear of him?

One evening, when it was raining and we were all sitting in the living room, the Swami was talking about pure womanhood and told us the story of Sita. How he can tell a story! You *see* it, and all the characters become real. I found myself wondering just how some of the beautiful society queens of the West would appear to him—especially those versed in the art of allurement—and before I took time to think, out popped the question, and immediately I was covered with confusion. The Swami, however, looked at me calmly with his big, serious eyes and gravely replied, "If the most beautiful woman in the world were to look at me in an immodest or unwomanly way, she would immediately turn into a hideous green frog, and one does not, of course, admire frogs!" ...

And he was so sweet, so gentle and benign all that evening, just like an indulgent father who had given his children beautiful gifts, although many of us were much older than he.

The Swami has accepted Christine as one fitted for his work in India. She is so happy. I was very disappointed, because he would not encourage me to go to India. I had a vague idea that to live in a cave and wear a yellow robe would be the proper thing to do if one wished to develop spiritually. How foolish of me and how wise Swamiji was! He said, "You are a householder. Go back to Detroit, find God in your husband and family. *That* is your path at present." ...

This morning we went to the village and Swami had tin-types taken of himself at our request. He was so full of fun, so merry. I am trying to write you in class as there is literally no other time. I am sitting near the Swami, and he is saying these very words. "The guru is like a crystal. He reflects perfectly the consciousness of all who come to him. He thus understands how and in what way to help." He means by this that a guru must be able to see what each person needs and he must meet them on their own plane of consciousness.

Now he has closed class for the morning, and he has turned to me, "Mrs. Funke, tell me a funny story. We are going to part soon, and we must talk funny things, isn't it?" ...

We take long walks every afternoon, and our favorite walk is back of the cottage down a hill and then a rustic path to the river. One day there was olfactory evidence of a polecat in the vicinity, and ever since Swami will say, "shall we walk down Skunk Avenue?"

Sometimes we stop several times and sit around on the grass and listen to Swami's wonderful talks. A bird, a flower, a butterfly, will start him off, and he will tell us stories from the Vedas or recite Indian poetry....

The last day has been a very wonderful and precious one. This morning there was no class. He asked Christine and me to take a walk, as he wished to be alone with us. (The others had been with him all summer, and he felt we should have a last talk.) We went up a hill about half a mile away. All was woods and solitude. Finally he selected a low-branched tree, and we sat under the low-spreading branches. Instead of the expected talk, he suddenly said, "Now we will meditate. We shall be like Buddha under the Bo-tree." He seemed to turn to bronze, so still was he. Then a thunderstorm came up, and it poured. He never noticed it. I raised my umbrella and protected him as much as possible. Completely absorbed in his meditation, he was oblivious of everything. Soon we heard shouts in the distance. The others had come out after us with raincoats and umbrellas. Swamiji looked around regretfully, for we *had* to go, and said, "Once more am I in Calcutta in the rains."

He was so tender and sweet all this last day. As the steamer rounded the bend in the river, he boyishly and joyously waved his hat to us in farewell, and he had departed indeed! ...

Ah, those blessed halcyon days at Thousand Island Park! The nights all glowing with the soft mystery of moonlight or golden starlight. And yet the Swami's arrival amongst us held no mystery, apparently. He came in simple guise.

We found later that anything which smacked of the mystery-monger was abhorrent to him. He came to make manifest the Glory and Radiance of the Self. Man's limitations are of his own making. "Thine only is the hand that holds the rope that drags thee on." This was the motif running through the Swami's teachings.

With infinite pains he tried to show us the path he himself had trod. After thirty-one years Swamiji stands out in my consciousness a colossal figure—a cleaver of bondage, knowing when and where not to spare. With his two-edged flaming sword came this Man "out of the East"—this Man of Fire and Flame, and some there were who received him, and to those who received him he gave Power.

From the reminiscences of Sister Christine, who writes of her days at Thousand Island Park

Of the wonderful weeks that followed, it is difficult to write. Only if one's mind were lifted to that high state

of consciousness in which we lived for the time, could
one hope to recapture the experience. We were filled
with joy. We did not know at that time that we were
living in his radiance. On the wings of inspiration, he
carried us to the height which was his natural abode.
He himself, speaking of it later, said that he was at his
best in Thousand Islands. Then he felt that he had
found the channel through which his message might
be spread, the way to fulfill his mission, for the guru
had found his own disciples. His first overwhelming
desire was to show us the path to *mukti* (freedom), to
set us free. "Ah," he said with touching pathos, "If I
could only set you free with a touch!" His second
object, not so apparent perhaps, but always in the
under-current, was to train this group to carry on the
work in America. "This message must be preached by
Indians in India, and by Americans in America," he
said. On his own little veranda, overlooking the tree
tops and the beautiful St. Lawrence, he often called
upon us to make speeches. His object was, as he said,
to teach us to think upon our feet. Did he know that if
we could conquer our self-consciousness in his presence,
could speak before him who was considered one of the
great orators of the world, no audience anywhere would
dismay us? It was a trying ordeal. Each in turn was
called upon to make an attempt. There was no escape.
Perhaps that was why certain of our group failed to
make an appearance at these intimate evening gather-
ings, although they knew that often he soared to the
greatest heights as the night advanced. What if it was
two o'clock in the morning? What if we had watched
the moon rise and set? Time and space had vanished
for us.

There was nothing set or formed about these nights
on the upper veranda. He sat in his large chair at the
end, near his door. Sometimes he went into a deep
meditation. At such times we too meditated or sat in

profound silence. Often it lasted for hours and one after the other slipped away. For we knew that after this he would not feel inclined to speak. Or again the meditation would be short, and he would encourage us to ask questions afterwards, often calling on one of us to answer. No matter how far wrong these answers were, he let us flounder about until we were near the truth, and then in a few words, he would clear up the difficulty. This was his invariable method in teaching. He knew how to stimulate the mind of the learner and make it do its own thinking. Did we go to him for confirmation of a new idea or point of view and begin, "I see it is thus and so," his "Yes?" with an upper inflection always sent us back for further thought. Again we would come with a more clarified understanding, and again the "Yes?" stimulated us to further thought. Perhaps after the third time, when the capacity for further thought along that particular line was reached, he would point out the error—an error usually due to something in our Western mode of thought.

And so he trained us with such patience, such benignity. It was like a benediction. Later, after his return to India, he hoped to have a place in the Himalayas for further training of Eastern and Western disciples together....

The first morning we learnt that there is a state of consciousness higher than the surface consciousness—which is called *samadhi*. Instead of the two divisions we are accustomed to, the conscious and the unconscious—it would be more accurate to make the classification, the subconscious, the conscious, and the superconscious. This is where confusion arises in the Western way of thinking, which divides consciousness into the subconscious or unconscious and the conscious. They cognize only the normal state of mind, forgetting that there is a state beyond consciousness—a superconscious state, inspiration. How can we know that this is a higher state? To quote Swami literally, "In the one case a man goes in and comes out as a fool. In the other case he goes in a man and comes out a God." And he always said, "Remember the superconscious never contradicts reason. It transcends it, but contradicts it never. Faith is not belief, it is the grasp on the Ultimate, an illumination."

Truth is for all, for the good of all. Not secret but sacred. The steps are: hear, then reason about it, "let the flood of reason flow over it, then meditate upon it, concentrate your mind upon it, make yourself one with it." Accumulate power in silence and become a dynamo of spirituality. What can a beggar give? Only a king can give, and he only when he wants nothing himself.

"Hold your money merely as a custodian for what is God's. Have no attachment for it. Let name and fame and money go; they are a terrible bondage. Feel the wonderful atmosphere of freedom. You are free, free, free! Oh blessed am I! Freedom am I! I am the Infinite! In my soul I can find no beginning and no end. All is my Self. Say this unceasingly."

He told us that God was real, a reality which could be experienced just as tangibly as any other reality; that there were methods by which these experiences could be made which were as exact as laboratory methods of experiment. The mind is the instrument. Sages, yogis, and saints from prehistoric times made discoveries in this science of the Self. They have left their knowledge as a precious legacy not only to their immediate disciples but to seekers of Truth in future times....

For the first time we understood why all religions begin with ethics. For without truth, non-injury, continence, non-stealing, cleanliness, austerity, there can be no spirituality.... Beyond a few directions in meditation there was very little set instruction, yet in course of these few days our ideas were revolutionized, our outlook enormously enlarged, our values changed. It was a re-education. We learnt to think clearly and fearlessly. Our conception of spirituality was not only clarified but transcended. Spirituality brings life, power, joy, fire, glow, enthusiasm—all the beautiful and positive things, never inertia, dullness, weakness. Then why should one have been so surprised to find a man of God with a power in an unusual degree. Why have we in the West always associated emaciation and anemic weakness with spirituality? Looking back upon it now one wonders how one could ever have been so illogical. Spirit is life, *shakti,* the divine energy.

It is needless to repeat the formal teaching, the great central idea. These one can read for himself. But there was something else, an influence, an atmosphere charged with the desire to escape from bondage—call it what you will—that can never be put into words, and yet was more powerful than any words. It was this which made us realize that we were blessed beyond words. To hear him say, "This indecent clinging to life," drew aside the curtain for us into the region beyond life and death, and planted in our hearts the desire for that glorious freedom. We saw a soul struggling to escape the meshes of maya [ignorance, delusion], one to whom the body was an intolerable bondage, not only a limitation, but a degrading humiliation. "*Azad, Azad,* the Free," he cried, pacing up and down like a caged lion. Yes, like the lion in the cage who found the bars not of iron but of bamboo. "Let us not be caught this time" would be his refrain another day. "So many times maya has caught us, so many times have we exchanged our freedom for sugar dolls which melted when the water touched them. Let us not be caught this time." So in us was planted the great desire for freedom. Two of the three requisites we already had—a human body and a guru, and now he was giving us the third, the desire to be free.

"Don't be deceived. Maya is a great cheat. Get out. Do not let her catch you this time," and so on and so on. "Do not sell your priceless heritage for such delusions. Arise, awake, stop not till the goal is reached." Then he would rush up to one of us with blazing eyes and fingers pointing and would exclaim, "Remember, God is the only Reality." Like a madman, but he was mad for God. For it was at this time that he wrote "The Song of the Sannyasin." We have not only lost our divinity, we have forgotten that we ever had it. "Arise, awake, Ye Children of Immortal Bliss." Up and down, over and over again. "Don't let yourself be tempted by dolls. They are dolls of sugar, or dolls of salt, and they will melt and become nothing. Be a king and know you own the world. This never comes until you give it up and it ceases to bind. Give up, give up."

The struggle for existence, or the effort to acquire wealth and power, or the pursuit of pleasure, takes up the thought, energy, and time of human beings. We seemed to be in a different world. The end to be attained was Freedom—freedom from bondage in which maya has caught us, in which maya has enmeshed all mankind. Sooner or later the opportunity to escape will come to all. Ours had come. For these days every aspiration, every desire, every struggle was directed toward this one purpose—consciously by our Teacher, blindly, unconsciously by us, following the influence he created.

With him it was a passion. Freedom not for himself alone, but for all—though he could help only those in whom he could light the fire to help them out of maya's chains:

"Strike off thy fetters! Bonds that bind thee down,
Of shining gold, or darker, baser ore; ...
                        Say—'Om Tat Sat, Om.'"

From the reminiscences of Josephine MacLeod

On the twenty-ninth of January 1895, I went with my sister to 54 West 33rd Street, New York, and heard the Swami Vivekananda in his sitting room where were assembled fifteen or twenty ladies and two or three gentlemen. The room was crowded. All the arm chairs were taken; so I sat on the floor in the front row. Swami stood in the corner. He said something, the particular words of which I do not remember, but instantly to me that was truth, and the second sentence he spoke was truth, and the third sentence was truth. And I listened to him for seven years and whatever he uttered was to me truth. From that moment life had a different import. It was as if he made you realize that you were in eternity. It never altered. It never grew. It was like the sun that you will never forget once you have seen.

I heard him all that winter, three days a week, mornings at eleven o'clock. I never spoke to him, but as we were so regular in coming, two front seats were always kept for us in this sitting room of the Swamiji. One day he turned and said, "Are you sisters?" "Yes," we answered. Then he said, "Do you come very far?" We said, "No, not very far—about thirty miles up the Hudson." "So far? That is wonderful." Those were the first words I ever spoke to him.

I always felt that after Vivekananda, Mrs. Roethlisberger was the most spiritual person I ever met. It was she who took us to him. Swamiji had a great place for her also. One day she and I went to the Swami and said, "Swami, will you tell us how to meditate?" He said, "Meditate on the word 'OM' for a week and come again and tell me." So after a week we went back and Mrs. Roethlisberger said, "I see a light." He said, "Good, keep on." "O no, it is more like a glow at the heart." And he said to me, "Good, keep on." That is all he ever taught me. But we had been meditating before we ever met him, and we knew the Gita by heart. I think that prepared us for recognition of this tremendous life force which he was. His power lay, perhaps, in the courage he gave others. He did not ever seem to be conscious of himself at all. It was the other man who interested him. "When the book of life begins to open, then the fun begins," he would say. He used to make us realize there was nothing secular in life; it was all holy. "Always remember, you are incidentally an American, and a woman, but always a child of God. Tell yourself day and night who you are. Never forget it." That is what he used to tell us. His presence, you see, was dynamic. You cannot pass that power on unless you have it, just as you cannot give money away unless you have it. You may imagine it, but you cannot do it....

In the June of that year Swami went up to Camp Percy, Christine Lake, N.H., to be the guest of Mr. Leggett at his fishing camp. We also went. There my sister's engagement to Mr. Leggett was announced, and Swami was invited to go abroad and be the witness at the wedding. While he was at the Camp, Swami would go out under those beautiful white birch trees and meditate for hours. Without telling us anything about it, he made two beautiful birch bark books, written in Sanskrit and English, which he gave to my sister and me.

Then when my sister and I went to Paris to buy her trousseau, Swami went to Thousand Island Park and for six weeks gave those wonderful talks called *Inspired Talks*, which to me are the most beautiful words that were written, because they were given to a group of intimate disciples. *They* were disciples, whereas I was never anything but a friend. But that quality that he gave them! Nothing I think revealed his heart as those days did.

He came over to Paris with Mr. Leggett in August. There, my sister and I stayed at the Holland House, and the Swami and Mr. Leggett stayed at a different hotel; but we saw them every day. At that time, Mr. Leggett had a courier who always called Swami *'Mon Prince!'* And Swami said to him, "But I am not a prince. I am a Hindu monk." The courier answered, "You may call yourself that, but I am used to dealing with princes, and I know one when I see one." His dignity impressed everyone. Yet, when someone once said to him, "You are so dignified, Swami," he replied, "It isn't me, it's my walk." ...

Swamiji's knowledge was prodigious. Once when my niece, Alberta Sturges, later Lady Sandwich, was with him in Rome, showing him the sights, she was amazed at his knowledge of where the great monuments were. And when she went to St. Peter's with him, she was still more amazed to see him so reverential to the symbols of the Roman Church—to all the jewels, all the beautiful draperies, put upon the saints. She said, "Swami, you don't believe in a personal God; why do you honor this so much?" He answered, "But Alberta, if you do believe in a personal God, surely you give it your best."

That autumn he went from Switzerland to India with Mr. and Mrs. Sevier and Mr. J. J. Goodwin, where a great ovation awaited him by the entire nation. This can be read about in the discourses called *Lectures from Colombo to Almora*. Mr. Goodwin was the stenographer who had been engaged at 54 West 33rd Street to take down the lectures of Swami Vivekananda. Mr. Goodwin was a court-stenographer, which meant two hundred words a minute, and he was very expensive; but as we did not want to lose any of Vivekananda's words, we engaged him. After the first week Mr. Goodwin refused any money; when they said to him, "What do you mean?" he said, "If Vivekananda gives his life, the least I can do is to give my service." He followed Swami around the world, and we have seven volumes hot from his lips that Mr. Goodwin took down.

I never wrote to Swami after he went to India, waiting to hear from him. Finally I had a letter, "Why don't

you write?" Then I sent back, "Shall I come to India?"
And his answer was, "Yes, come, if you want filth and
degradation and poverty and many loin cloths talking
religion. Don't come if you want anything else. We cannot bear one more criticism." Naturally I went over by
the first ship; I sailed on the twelfth of January with Mrs.
Ole Bull and Swami Saradananda. We stopped in London. Then on to Rome. We arrived in Bombay on the
twelfth of February where Mr. Alasinga met us, who
wore the vertical red marks of the Vaishnavite sect. Later
on, once when I was sitting with Swami on our way to
Kashmir, I happened to make the remark, "What a pity
that Mr. Alasinga wears those Vaishnavite marks on his
forehead!" Instantly Swami turned and said with great
sternness, "Hands off! What have you ever done?" I did
not know what I had done then. Of course I never
answered. Tears came to my eyes and I waited. I learnt
later that Mr. Alasinga Perumal was a young Brahmin
teaching philosophy in a college in Madras earning 100
rupees a month, supporting his father, mother, wife,
and four children, and who had gone from door to door
to beg the money to send Vivekananda to the West
Perhaps without him we never would have met
Vivekananda. Then one understood the anger with
which Swamiji met the slightest attack on Mr.
Alasinga....

In a day or two we went up to see Swami at his tem-
porary monastery at Belur, at Nilambar Mukherjee's gar-
den-house. During the afternoon Swami said, "I must
take you to the new monastery that we are buying." I
said, "O, but Swami, isn't this big enough?" It was a
lovely little villa he had, with perhaps an acre or two of
land, a small lake and many flowers. I thought it was big
enough for anyone. But he evidently saw things in a different scale. So he took us across little gullies to the place
where is now the present monastery. Mrs. Ole Bull and
I, finding this old riverside house empty, said, "Swami,

can't we use this house?" "It isn't in order," he answered. "But we'll put it in order," we told him. With that he gave us permission. So we had it all newly whitewashed and went down to the bazaars, bought old mahogany furniture and made a drawing room half of which was Indian style and half of which was Western style. We had an outside dining room, our bedroom with an extra room for Sister Nivedita who was our guest until we went to Kashmir. We stayed there quite two months. It was perhaps the most beautiful time we ever had with Swamiji. He came every morning for early tea which he used to take under the great mango tree. That tree is still in existence. We never allowed them to cut it down, though they were keen to do it. He loved our living at that riverside cottage; and he would bring all those who came to visit him, to see what a charming home we had made of this house he had thought uninhabitable. In the afternoons we used to give tea-parties in front of the house, in full view of the river, where always could be seen loads of boats going up-stream, we receiving as if we were in our own drawing rooms. Swamiji loved all that intimate use we made of things which they took as a matter of course. One night there came one of those deluges of rain, like sheets of water. He paced up and down our outside dining room verandah, talking of Krishna and the love of Krishna and the power that love was in the world. He had a curious quality that when he was a bhakta, a lover, he brushed aside karma and raja and jnana yogas as if they were of no consequence whatever. And when he was a karma-yogi, then he made that the great theme. Or equally so, the jnana. Sometimes, weeks, he would fall in one particular mood utterly disregardful of what he had been, just previous to that. He seemed to be filled with an amazing power of concentration; of opening up to the great cosmic qualities that are all about us. It was probably that power of concentration that kept him so young and so fresh. He never seemed to repeat himself. There would be an incident of very little consequence which would illuminate a whole new passage for him. And he had such a place for us Westerners whom he called "Living Vedantins." He would say, "When you believe a thing is true, you do it, you do not dream about it. That is your power." ...

In July 1899 Swami came to England again with Sister Nivedita, where Sister Christine and Mrs. Funke met him. From there he came to America and he came to us at Ridgely Manor in September of that year where we gave him his own cottage with two of his monks, Turiyananda and Abhedananda.... In the evening, sitting around the great fire in the hall of Ridgely Manor, he would talk, and once after he came out with some of his thoughts a lady said, "Swami, I don't agree with you there." "No? Then it is not for you," he answered. Someone else said, "O, but that is where I find you true." "Ah, then it was for you," he said, showing that utter respect for the other man's views....

Swami lectured a great number of times at the Home of Truth [Los Angeles] and in various halls, but perhaps the most outstanding lecture I ever heard was his talk on "Jesus of Nazareth," when he seemed to radiate a white light from head to foot, so lost was he in the wonder and the power of Christ. I was so impressed with this obvious halo that I did not speak to him on the way back for fear of interrupting, as I thought, the great thoughts that were still in his mind. Suddenly he said to me, "I know how it is done." I said, "How what is done?" "How they make mulligatawny soup! They put a bay leaf in it," he told me. That utter lack of self-consciousness, of self-importance, was perhaps one of his outstanding characteristics. He seemed to see the strength and the glory and the power of the other man who felt that courage enter into him, until everyone who came near him went away refreshed and invigorated and sustained. So when people have said to me, "What is your test of spirituality?" I have always said, "It is the courage that is given by the presence of a holy man." Swamiji used to say, "The saviors should take on the sins and tribulations of their disciples and let the disciples go on their way rejoicing and free. There is the difference! The saviors should carry the burdens." ...

At Belur Math one day, while Sister Nivedita was distributing prizes for some athletics, I was standing in Swamiji's bedroom at the Math, at the window, watching, and he said to me, "I shall never see forty." I, knowing he was thirty-nine, said to him, "But Swami, Buddha did not do his great work until between forty and eighty." But he said, "I delivered my message and I must go." I asked, "Why go?" and he said, "The shadow of a big tree will not let the smaller trees grow up. I must go to make room." ...

On the second of July [1902], Sister Nivedita saw him for the last time. She went to inquire whether she should teach a certain science in her school. Swami answered, "Perhaps you are right, but my mind is given to other things. I am preparing for death." So she thought he was indifferent. Then he said, "But you must have a meal." Sister Nivedita always ate with her fingers, à la Hindu; and after she had eaten, Swami poured water over her hands. She said, very much the disciple, "I cannot bear you to do this." He answered, "Jesus Christ washed the feet of his disciples." Sister Nivedita had it on the tip of her tongue to say, "But that was the last time they ever met." It was the last time she ever saw him. That last day he spoke to her of me and of many people, but when he spoke of me he said, "She is pure as purity, loving as love itself." So I always took that as Swamiji's last message to me. In two days he died having said, "The spiritual impact that has come here to Belur will last fifteen hundred years—and this will be a great university. Do not think I imagine it, I see it."

Letters of Swami Vivekananda
Breezy Meadows, Metcalf, Massachusetts, 20 August, 1893

Dear Alasinga [Alasinga Perumal, a disciple of Swami Vivekananda],

... Gird up your loins, my boys! I am called by the Lord for this.... The hope lies in you—in the meek, the lowly, but the faithful. Feel for the miserable and look up for help—it shall come. I have traveled twelve years with this load in my heart and this idea in my head. I have gone from door to door of the so-called rich and great. With a bleeding heart I have crossed half the world to this strange land, seeking help. The Lord is great. I know he will help me. I may perish of cold and hunger in this land, but I bequeath to you young men this sympathy, this struggle for the poor, the ignorant, the oppressed.... Go down on your faces before him and make a great sacrifice, the sacrifice of a whole life for them, for whom he comes from time to time, whom he loves above all—the poor, the lowly, the oppressed. Vow, then, to devote your whole lives to the cause of these three hundred millions, going down and down every day....

Glory unto the Lord! We will succeed. Hundreds will fall in the struggle—hundreds will be ready to take it up. Faith—sympathy, fiery faith and fiery sympathy! Life is nothing, death is nothing—hunger nothing, cold nothing. Glory unto the Lord! March on, the Lord is our general. Do not look back to see who falls—forward—onward!...

Yours,
Vivekananda

541 Dearborn Avenue, Chicago, 1894

Dear Alasinga,

... What India wants is a new, electric power to stir up a fresh vigor in the national veins. This was ever, and always will be, slow work. Be content to work and above all be true to yourself. Be pure, staunch, and sincere to the very backbone and everything will be all right. If you have marked anything in the disciples of Sri Ramakrishna, it is this—they are sincere to the backbone. My task will be done and I shall be quite content to die if I can bring up and launch one hundred such men over India. He, the Lord, knows best. Let ignorant men talk nonsense. We neither seek aid nor avoid it—we are the servants of the Most High. The petty attempts of small men should be beneath our notice. Onward! Through the struggle of ages character is built. Be not discouraged. One word of truth can never be lost; for ages it may be hidden under rubbish, but it will show itself sooner or later. Truth is indestructible, virtue is indestructible, purity is indestructible. Give me a genuine man; I do not want masses of converts. My son, hold fast! Do not look for anybody to help you. Is not the Lord infinitely greater than all human help? Be holy—trust in the Lord, depend on him always, and you are on the right track; nothing can prevail against you....

Let us pray, "Lead, Kindly Light"—a beam will come through the dark and a hand will be stretched forth to lead us. I always pray for you: you must pray for me. Let each one of us pray day and night for the downtrodden millions in India, who are held fast by poverty, priestcraft, and tyranny—pray day and night for them. I care more to preach religion to them than to the high and the rich. I am no metaphysician, no philosopher, nay, no saint. But I am poor, I love the poor. I see what they call the poor of this country and how many there are who feel for them. What an immense difference in India! Who feels there for the two hundred millions of men and women sunken forever in poverty and ignorance? Where is the way out? Who feels for them? They cannot find light or education. Who will bring the light to them—who will travel from door to door bringing education to them? Let these people be your God—think of them, work for them, pray for them incessantly—the Lord will show you the way. Him I call a mahatma whose heart bleeds for the poor; otherwise he is a duratma. Let us unite our wills in continued prayer for their good. We may die unknown, unpitied, unbewailed, without accomplishing anything—but not one thought will be lost. It will take effect, sooner or later. My heart is too full to express my feeling; you know it, you can imagine it. So long as the millions live in hunger and ignorance, I hold every man a traitor who, having been educated at their expense, pays not the least heed to them. I call those men—who strut about in their finery, having got all their money by grinding the poor—wretches, so long as they do not do anything for those two hundred millions who are now no better than hungry savages. We are poor, my brothers, we are nobodies, but such have always been the instruments of the Most High. The Lord bless you all!

With all love,
Vivekananda

Washington, D.C., 27 October, 1894

Dear Alasinga,

... You have asked me often to send over to you all about my movements in this country and all my lecture reports. I am doing here exactly what I used to do in India—always depending on the Lord and making no plans ahead.... Moreover you must remember that I have to work incessantly in this country and that I have no time to put together my thoughts in the form of a book—so much so, that this constant rush has worn my nerves, and I am feeling it. I cannot express my obligation to you, and all my friends in Madras, for the most unselfish and heroic work you did for me. I am not an organizer; my nature tends towards scholarship and meditation. I think I have worked enough. Now I want rest and to teach a little to those that have come to me from my Gurudeva. You have known now what you can do, for it is really you young men of Madras that have done all. I am only the figurehead. I am a tyagi;[6] I only want one thing. I do not believe in a religion or God which cannot wipe the widow's tears or bring a piece of bread to the orphan's mouth. However sublime be the theories, however well spun may be the philosophy, I do not call it religion so long as it is confined to books and dogmas. The eye is in the forehead and not in the back. Move onward and carry into practice that which you are very proud to call your religion, and God bless you!

Look not to me, look to yourselves. I am happy to have been the occasion of rousing an enthusiasm. Take advantage of it, float along with it, and everything will come right. Love never fails, my son. Today or tomorrow or ages after, truth will conquer. Love shall win the victory. Do you love your fellow men? Where should you go to seek for God? Are not all the poor, the miserable, the weak, Gods? Why not worship them first? Why go dig a well on the bank of the Ganges? Believe in the omnipotent power of love. Who cares for these tinsel puffs of fame? I never keep watch of what the newspapers are saying. Have you love? If so, you are omnipotent. Are you perfectly unselfish? If so, you are irresistible. It is character that pays everywhere. It is the Lord who protects his children in the depths of the sea. Your country requires heroes—be heroes!

---

[6] One who has renounced the world.

Everybody wants me to come over to India. They think they will be able to do more if I come over. They are mistaken, my friend. The present enthusiasm is only a little patriotism; it means nothing. If it is true and genuine, you will find in a short time hundreds of heroes coming forward and carrying on the work. Therefore know that you have really done all, and go on. Look not for me. Here is a grand field. What have I to do with this "ism" or that "ism"? I am the servant of the Lord, and where on earth is there a better field than here for propagating all high ideas?—here, where if one man is against me, a hundred hands are ready to help me—here, where man feels for man, and women are goddesses! Even idiots may stand up to hear themselves praised, and cowards assume the attitude of the brave when everything is sure to turn out well, but the true hero works in silence. How many Buddhas die before one finds expression! My son, I believe in God and I believe in man. I believe in helping the miserable, I believe in going even to hell to save others. Talk of the Westerners—they have given me food, shelter, friendship, protection—even the most orthodox Christians! What do our people do when any of their priests go to India? You do not touch them even, they are mlechchas! No man, no nation, my son, can hate others and live. India's doom was sealed the very day they invented the word *mlechcha* and stopped from communion with others. Take care how you foster that idea. It is good to talk glibly about the Vedanta, but how hard to carry out even its least precepts!

Ever yours with blessings,
Vivekananda

P. S. Take care of these two things—love of power and jealousy. Cultivate always "faith in yourself."

Swami Vivekananda, Madras, India, 1897

1894

Dear Brothers [Brother Disciples],

... If you want any good to come, just throw your ceremonials over-board and worship the living God, the man-God, every being that wears a human form, God in his universal as well as individual aspect. The universal aspect of God means this world, and worshipping it means serving it—this indeed is work, not indulging in ceremonials. Neither is it work to cogitate as to whether the rice-plate should be placed in front of the God for ten minutes or for half an hour—that is called lunacy. Millions of rupees have been spent only that the temple doors at Varanasi or Vrindavan may play at opening and shutting all day long!... And all this, while the living God is dying for want of food, for want of education! The banias of Bombay are erecting hospitals for bugs—while they would do nothing for men even if they die!... Let some of you spread like fire, and preach this worship of the universal aspect of the Godhead—a thing that was never undertaken before in our country. No quarrelling with people, we must be friends with all....

Yours affly,
Vivekananda

17 February, 1896

Dear Alasinga,

... The work is terribly hard, and the more it is growing the harder it is becoming. I need a long rest very badly. Yet a great work is before me in England ... Have patience, my son—it will grow beyond all your expectations.... Every work has got to pass through hundreds of difficulties before succeeding. Those that persevere will see the light sooner or later....

I have succeeded in rousing the very heart of the American civilization, New York. But it has been a terrific struggle.... I have spent nearly all I had on this New York work and in England. Now things are in such a shape that they will go on.

To put the Hindu ideas into English and then make out of dry philosophy and intricate mythology and queer, startling psychology a religion which shall be easy, simple, popular, and at the same time meet the requirements of the highest minds—is a task that only those can understand who have attempted it. The abstract Advaita must become living—poetic—in everyday life; out of hopelessly intricate mythology must come concrete moral forms; and out of bewildering yogi-ism must come the most scientific and practical psychology—and all this must be put in such a form that a child may grasp it. That is my life's work. The Lord only knows how far I shall succeed. To work we have the right, not to the fruits thereof.

It is hard work, my boy, hard work! To keep oneself steady in the midst of this whirl of kama-kanchana [lust and greed], and hold on to one's own ideals until disciples are molded to conceive the ideas of realization and perfect renunciation, is indeed difficult work. Thank God, already there is great success. I cannot blame the missionaries and others for not understanding me—they hardly ever saw a man who did not care about women and money. At first they could not believe it— how could they? You must not think that the Western nations have the same ideas of chastity and purity as the Indians. Their equivalents are honesty and courage.... People are now flocking to me. Hundreds have become convinced that there are men who can really control their bodily desires, and reverence and respect for these principles are growing. All things come to him who waits.

May you be blessed for ever and ever!

Yours,
Vivekananda

63 St. George's Road, London, 7 June, 1896

Dear Miss Noble [Sister Nivedita],

My ideal indeed can be put into a few words and that is: to preach unto mankind their divinity, and how to make it manifest in every moment of life.

This world is in chains of superstition. I pity the oppressed, whether man or woman, and I pity more the oppressors.

One idea that I see clear as daylight is that misery is caused by *ignorance* and nothing else. Who will give the world light? Sacrifice in the past has been the law—it will be, alas, for ages to come. The earth's bravest and best will have to sacrifice themselves for the good of many, for the welfare of all. Buddhas by the hundred are necessary with eternal love and pity.

The religions of the world have become lifeless mockeries. What the world wants is character. The world is in need of those whose life is one burning love—selfless. That love will make every word fall like a thunderbolt.

It is no superstition with you, I am sure. You have the making in you of a world-mover, and others will also come. Bold words and bolder deeds are what we want. Awake, awake, great one! The world is burning with misery. Can you sleep? Let us call and call till the sleeping gods awake, till the god within answers to the call. What more is in life? What greater work? The details come to me as I go. I never make plans. Plans grow and work themselves. I only say, awake, awake!

May all blessings attend you for ever!

Yours affectionately,
Vivekananda

Almora, 9 July, 1897

Dear Sister [Miss Mary Hale],

... It would have made your heart glad to see how my boys are working in the midst of famine and disease and misery—nursing by the mat-
bed of the cholera-stricken pariah and feeding the starving chandala,
and the Lord sends help to me, to them, to all....

I feel my task is done—at most three or four years more of life are
left. I have lost all wish for my salvation. I never wanted earthly enjoyments. I must see my machine in strong working order, and then, knowing for sure that I have put in a lever for the good of humanity, in India
at least, which no power can drive back, I will sleep—without caring
what will be next.

And may I be born again and again, and suffer thousands of miseries, so that I may worship the only God that exists, the only God I
believe in, the sum total of all souls. And above all, my God the wicked,
my God the miserable, my God the poor of all races, of all species, is
the especial object of my worship.

He who is in you and outside of you, who works through every
hand, who walks through every foot—whose body you are—him worship and break all other idols.

He who is the high and the low, the saint and the sinner, the god
and the worm—him worship, the visible, the knowable, the real, the
omnipresent. Break all other idols.

In whom there is neither past life nor future birth, nor death, nor
going nor coming, in whom we always have been and always will be
one—him worship. Break all other idols.

Ay, fools, who are neglecting the living God and his infinite reflections, of which the world is full, and running after imaginary shad-

ows, leading to quarrels and fights—him worship, the only visible one. Break all other idols....

Yours ever affectionately,
Vivekananda

Poems by Swami Vivekananda

The Song of the Free
(Composed February 15, 1895, in New York)

The wounded snake its hood unfurls,
The flame stirred up doth blaze,
The desert air resounds the calls
Of heart-struck lion's rage.

The cloud puts forth its deluge strength
When lightning cleaves its breast;
When the soul is stirred to its inmost depth
Great ones unfold their best.

Let eyes grow dim and heart grow faint
And friendship fail and love betray;
Let Fate its hundred horrors send
And clotted darkness block the way—

All nature wear one angry frown
To crush you out—still know, my soul,
You are divine. March on and on,
Nor right nor left, but to the goal.

Nor angel I, nor man nor brute,
Nor body, mind, nor he nor she;
The books do stop in wonder mute
To tell my nature: I am He.

Before the sun, the moon, the earth,
Before the stars or comets free,
Before e'en time had had its birth,
I was, I am, and I will be.

The beauteous earth, the glorious sun,
The calm, sweet moon, the spangled sky,
Causation's laws do make them run;
They live in bonds, in bonds they die.

And mind its mantle, dreamy net,
Casts o'er them all and holds them fast:
In warp and woof of thought are set
Earth, hells, and heavens, or worse or best.

Know these are but the outer crust—
All space and time, effect and cause;
I am beyond all sense, all thought,
The Witness of the universe.

Not two or many, 'tis but One;
And thus in me all me's I have.
I cannot hate, I cannot shun
Myself from me—I can but love.

From dreams awake, from bonds be free.
Be not afraid! This mystery,
My shadow, cannot frighten me.
Know once for all that I am He.

Peace
(Composed September 21, 1899, at Ridgely Manor,
Stone Ridge, New York)

Behold, it comes in might,
The power that is not power,

The light that is in darkness,
The shade in dazzling light.

It is joy that never spoke,
And grief unfelt, profound,
Immortal life unlived,
Eternal death unmourned.

It is not joy nor sorrow,
But that which is between,
It is not night nor morrow,
But that which joins them in.

It is sweet rest in music
And pause in sacred art,
The silence between speaking;
Between the fits of passion
It is the calm of heart.

It is beauty never lovèd
And love that stands alone;
It is song that lives unsung
And knowledge never known.

It is death between two lives
And lull between two storms,
The void whence rose creation
And that where it returns.

To it the tear-drop goes
To spread the smiling form.
It is the goal of life,
And peace, its only home.

To a Friend
(Translated from the original Bengali)

Where darkness is beheld as light,
And sorrow understood as joy;
Where sickness masquerades as health,
And but the new-born infant's cry
Tells one it lives—O wise one, say,
Seekest thou satisfaction here?
Where strife and battle never cease,
And even the father, pitiless,
Turns out his son, and the sole note
Is self and ever self alone,
How dost thou hope, O sage, to find
The mine of everlasting peace?

Who can escape this wretched world,
A very heaven and hell in one?
Say, where can the poor slave, constrained
With karma's fetters round his neck,
Find out at length his freedom here?
Practice of yoga, sense-delight,
Householder's and monastic life,
Prayer, hoarded wealth, austerity,
Dispassion, vows, asceticism—
These I have fathomed through and through,
And so at last have come to know
That not a grain of joy is here;
Embodied life is mockery;
The nobler grows thy heart, be sure,
The more thy share of pain must be.

O selfless lover, great of heart,
Know thou, within this sordid world
There is no room at all for thee:
Could a frail marble bust endure
The blow an anvil's mass will bear?
Be as one slothful, mean, and vile,
With honeyed tongue but poisoned heart,

Empty of truth and self-enslaved—
Then thou wilt find thy place on earth.

For knowledge staking even my life,
I have devoted half my days;
For love, like one insane have I
Clutched often at mere lifeless shades;
And, for religion, countless creeds
Have sought; along the Ganges' banks,
In burning-grounds, by sacred streams,
Or deep in mountain caves have dwelt;
And many a day have passed on alms,
Friendless and clad in common rags,
Begging for food from door to door
To fill my belly, and with frame
Broken by harsh austerities.
But what the treasure I have earned?

Friend, let me speak my heart to thee.
One lesson I have learnt in life:
This dreadful world is tossed with waves,
And one boat only fares across.
Study of scripture, sacred words,
Restraint of breath, conflicting schools,
Dispassion, science, philosophy,
Sense-pleasure, are but freaks of mind.
Love! Love!—that is the only jewel!
In soul and Brahman, man and God,
In ghosts and spirits without shape,
In angels, beasts, birds, insects, worms,
Dwells Love, deep in the hearts of all.

Say, who else is the God of gods?
Say, who else moves this universe?
The mother dies to save her young;
The robber steals; yet are these twain
By the same power of Love impelled.
Beyond both speech and mind concealed,
In grief and happiness Love dwells;

It is that Love Divine that comes
As Kali, death's embodiment,
Worshipped as Mother by us all.
Grief, sickness, pinching poverty,
Vice, virtue, fruits of deeds alike
Both good and ill, Love's worship are
In varying guise. Say, what is man?
And what can he accomplish here?

Foolish is he who seeks alone
His own delight; mad equally
Whoever racks his flesh with pain.
Insane is he who longs for death;
Eternal life—a hopeless quest!
However far and far you speed,
Mounting the chariot of the mind,
The selfsame ocean of the world
Spreads out, its waves of bitterness
And pleasure ever plunging on.

Hearken, thou bird bereft of wings!
That way lies no escape for thee.
Times without number beaten back,
Why seek this fruitless task again?
Rely no more on wisdom, prayer,
Offerings to God, or strength of will;
For the sole jewel is selfless Love.
Behold, the insects teach us so
As they embrace the shining flame:
The tiny moth is blinded quite,
Charmed with the beauty of its rays;
So, too, thy heart is mad for Love.
O lover, cast upon the fire
The dross of all thy selfishness!

Say, can a beggar live content?
What good is gleaned from pity's glance?
Give, if within thy heart resides

The slightest treasure fit to share:
Look not behind for recompense!
Ay, to the Infinite born heir
Art thou: within thy bosom swells
The ocean of unbound Love.
Give! Give! Whoever asks return—
His ocean dwindles to a drop.
From highest Brahman to the worm,
Even to the atom's inmost core,
All things with Love are interfused.
Friend, offer body, mind, and soul
In constant service at their feet.
Thy God is here before thee now,
Revealed in all these myriad forms:
Rejecting them, where seekest thou
His presence? He who freely shares
His love with every living thing
Proffers true service unto God.

The Song of the Sannyasin
(Composed July 1895, at Thousand Island Park, New York)

Wake up the note! the song that had its birth
Far off, where worldly taint could never reach;
In mountain caves and glades of forest deep,
Whose calm no sigh for lust or wealth or fame
Could ever dare to break; where rolled the stream
Of knowledge, truth, and bliss that follows both.
Sing high that note, sannyasin bold! Say,
    "Om Tat Sat, Om!"[7]

Strike off thy fetters! bonds that bind thee down,
Of shining gold or darker, baser ore—

---

[7] "Om That Supreme Reality!"

Love, hate; good, bad; and all the dual throng.
Know slave is slave, caressed or whipped, not free;
For fetters, though of gold, are not less strong to bind.
Then off with them, sannyasin bold! Say,
  "Om Tat Sat, Om!"

Let darkness go, the will-o'-the-wisp that leads
With blinking light to pile more gloom on gloom.
This thirst for life, for ever quench; it drags
From birth to death, and death to birth, the soul.
He conquers all who conquers self. Know this
And never yield, sannyasin bold! Say,
  "Om Tat Sat, Om!"

"Who sows must reap," they say, "and cause must bring
The sure effect: good, good; bad, bad; and none
Escape the law—but whoso wears a form
Must wear the chain." Too true; but far beyond
Both name and form is Atman, ever free.
Know thou art That, sannyasin bold! Say,
  "Om Tat Sat, Om!"

They know not truth who dream such vacant dreams
As father, mother, children, wife, and friend.
The sexless Self—whose father He? whose child?
Whose friend, whose foe, is He who is but One?
The Self is all in all—none else exists;
And thou art That, sannyasin bold! Say,
  "Om Tat Sat, Om!"

There is but One: the Free, the Knower, Self,
Without a name, without a form or stain.
In Him is maya, dreaming all this dream.
The Witness, He appears as nature, soul.
Know thou art That, sannyasin bold! Say,
  "Om Tat Sat, Om!"

Where seekest thou? That freedom, friend, this world
Nor that can give. In books and temples, vain

Thy search. Thine only is the hand that holds
The rope that drags thee on. Then cease lament.
Let go thy hold, sannyasin bold! Say,
　　"Om Tat Sat, Om!"

Say: "Peace to all! From me no danger be
To aught that lives. In those that dwell on high,
In those that lowly creep—I am the Self in all.
All life, both here and there, do I renounce,
All heavens and earths and hells, all hopes and fears."
Thus cut thy bonds, sannyasin bold! Say,
　　"Om Tat Sat, Om!"

Heed then no more how body lives or goes.
Its task is done: let karma float it down.
Let one put garlands on, another kick
This frame: say naught. No praise or blame can be
Where praiser, praised, and blamer, blamed are one.
Thus be thou calm, sannyasin bold! Say,
　　"Om Tat Sat, Om!"

Truth never comes where lust and fame and greed
Of gain reside. No man who thinks of woman
As his wife can ever perfect be;
Nor he who owns the least of things, nor he
Whom anger chains, can ever pass through maya's gates.
So give these up, sannyasin bold! Say,
　　"Om Tat Sat, Om!"

Have thou no home. What home can hold thee, friend?
The sky thy roof, the grass thy bed, and food
What chance may bring—well cooked or ill, judge not.
No food or drink can taint that noble Self
Which knows Itself. Like rolling river free
Thou ever be, sannyasin bold! Say,
　　"Om Tat Sat, Om!"

Few only know the truth. The rest will hate
And laugh at thee, great one; but pay no heed.

Go thou, the free, from place to place, and help
Them out of darkness, maya's veil. Without
The fear of pain or search for pleasure, go
Beyond them both, sannyasin bold! Say,
    "Om Tat Sat, Om!"

Thus, day by day, till karma's powers, spent,
Release the soul for ever. No more is birth,
Nor I, nor thou, nor God, nor man. The "I"
Has All become, the All is "I" and Bliss.
Know thou art That, sannyasin bold! Say,
    "Om Tat Sat, Om!"

Chronology of Swami Vivekananda's Life

1863   January 12, born Narendranath Datta, in the city of Calcutta, India.

1879   Enters Presidency College, Calcutta.

1880   Joins Scottish Church College, Calcutta; studies Western logic, philosophy, and history; first hears of Sri Ramakrishna from Professor William Hastie, principal of the college.

        Begins searching for someone who has directly experienced God.

1881   First meeting with Sri Ramakrishna (1836–1886), the prophet of the harmony of religions; for six years, his spiritual life is molded by his Master, Sri Ramakrishna.

1885   Sri Ramakrishna falls ill and is taken to Cossipore Garden House, where Vivekananda and his brother disciples stay with their Master and devote themselves to his service.

        Sri Ramakrishna designates Vivekananda as his spiritual heir and instructs Vivekananda to lead the disciples and carry out his spiritual mission.

1886   August 16, Sri Ramakrishna passes away.

Under the leadership of Vivekananda, the disciples of Sri Ramakrishna establish a monastery at Baranagore; on Christmas Eve, they take the monastic vows of chastity and poverty, dedicating themselves to the realization of God and service of God in all.

1890   Sets off on pilgrimage—without a companion, without a name, with only a staff and begging-bowl—traveling the length and breadth of the Indian subcontinent and visiting sites of pilgrimage, cities, towns, and villages.

1892   Reaches the southernmost tip of India at Cape Comorin; recalls all he has seen with his own eyes—the pitiable condition of the Indian masses—and realizes his spiritual mission: to dedicate himself to the service of God revealed through humanity.

Decides to go to America to take part in the World's Parliament of Religions in Chicago to present to America the spiritual wisdom of India and bring back to India the knowledge of science and technology for the uplift of the Indian people.

1893   First visit to the West. September 11–27, Delegate at the World's Colombian Exposition, Parliament of Religions, Chicago; introduces the teachings of Vedanta to the West; acclaimed by newspapers as "undoubtedly the greatest figure in the Parliament of Religions."

Joins a lecture bureau and tours America to help his philanthropic and religious work in India; travels to Iowa City, Des Moines, St. Louis, Indianapolis, Minneapolis, Detroit, Buffalo, Hartford, Boston, Cambridge, New York, Baltimore, Washington D.C., and other major cities.

Meets, among other notables, the famous orator and agnostic Robert Ingersoll, the scientist Nikola Tesla, leading representatives of Western science William Thomson (afterward Lord Kelvin) and Professor Helmholtz, actress Sarah Bernhardt, and opera singer Madame Emma Calvé.

1894 Founds the Vedanta Society of New York.

1895 Completes *Raja-Yoga*, his translation and exposition of the *Yoga Aphorisms* of Patanjali.

June–August, seven-week stay at Thousand Island Park, N.Y., with a number of sincere spiritual seekers; daily classes recorded and later published as *Inspired Talks*.

Sails for Europe; travels to London and Paris; returns to America.

Delivers the *Karma-Yoga* lectures in New York.

1896 Delivers lectures in New York at Hardman Hall, the People's Church, and the *Bhakti-Yoga* lectures in Madison Square Garden; lectures at Harvard University and Columbia University and is offered the Chair of Eastern Philosophy at Harvard and a similar position at Columbia, both of which he declines.

Returns to Europe; travels to London, Oxford, Geneva, Berlin, Amsterdam, Naples, Milan, Florence, Rome, and other cities.

Delivers the *Jnana-Yoga* lectures.

Meets the famous Orientalists Max Müller and Paul Deussen, and other notables.

Establishes the English-language monthly journal *Prabuddha Bharata: Awakened India.*

1897 Returns to India, receiving unprecedented public acclaim and honor in cities and towns throughout India.

In a series of lectures in Madras, outlines his plan for the future material and spiritual revival of India.

May 1, in Calcutta, calls a meeting of the monastic and lay devotees of Sri Ramakrishna, at which the Ramakrishna Mission Association comes into existence.

Progress of the Vedanta work in America appreciated in a letter signed by Lewis G. Janes, president of the Brooklyn Ethical Association; C. C. Everett, dean of Harvard Divinity School; William James and Josiah Royce, professors of philosophy at Harvard University; Mrs. Sara C. Bull, and others.

1898   Devotes himself mainly to the training of his disciples, both Indian and Western, and to the consolidation of his work already in progress.

1899   Establishes the Belur Math, the present headquarters of the Ramakrishna Order.

Establishes Advaita Ashrama at Mayavati in the Himalayas.

1899–
1900   Second visit to America. Lectures in Los Angeles, Pasadena, Oakland, San Francisco, New York, and other cities.

1900   Founds Vedanta Society in San Francisco.

Third visit to Europe. Participates in the Congress of the History of Religions at the World's Fair (Exposition Universelle), Paris.
Returns to India.

1901   Stays at the Belur Math and visits cities and holy places in India.

Until the very end, guides the details of the daily life of the Belur monastery.

1902   July 4, at the Belur Math, enters into deep meditation and passes away before his 40th birthday.

Credits

Grateful acknowledgment is given for permission to use material from the following sources:

From *Complete Works of Swami Vivekananda*, vols. 1–3, 5–6, 2003, 2002, 2001, 2001, and 2003; *Reminiscences of Swami Vivekananda*, by His Eastern and Western Admirers, 2004, used by permission of the publisher, Advaita Ashrama, Calcutta, West Bengal, India.

From *Sri Ramakrishna, the Great Master*, vol. 2, by Swami Saradananda, translated by Swami Jagadananda, 2001, used by permission of the publisher, Sri Ramakrishna Math, Chennai, India.

From *Vivekananda: The Yogas and Other Works*, edited by Swami Nikhilananda, © 1953, used by the permission of the publisher, Ramakrishna-Vivekananda Center of New York.

About the Editor

Swami Adiswarananda, a senior monk of the Ramakrishna Order of India, is the Minister and Spiritual Leader of the Ramakrishna-Vivekananda Center of New York. Born in 1925 in West Bengal, India, Swami received his undergraduate and Master's degrees from the University of Calcutta. He joined the monastic order of Sri Ramakrishna in 1954 and was ordained a monk in 1963. Before being sent by the Ramakrishna Order to its New York center in 1968, he taught religious subjects in one of the premier colleges of the Order and was later editor of *Prabuddha Bharata: Awakened India*, the English-language monthly journal on religion and philosophy published by the Order. Swami is a frequent lecturer at colleges, universities, and other religious, educational, and cultural institutions, and his writings appear regularly in many scholarly journals on religion and philosophy. He is the author of *The Four Yogas: A Guide to the Spiritual Paths of Action, Devotion, Meditation and Knowledge; The Spiritual Quest and the Way of Yoga: The Goal, the Journey and the Milestones; The Vedanta Way to Peace and Happiness* and *Meditation and Its Practices: A Definitive Guide to Techniques and Traditions of Meditation in Yoga and Vedanta* (all SkyLight Paths). He is also the editor of *Sri Ramakrishna, the Face of Silence* and *Sri Sarada Devi, The Holy Mother: Her Teachings and Conversations* (both SkyLight Paths).

Global Spiritual Perspectives

Spiritual Perspectives on America's Role as Superpower
by the Editors at SkyLight Paths

Are we the world's good neighbor or a global bully? From a spiritual perspective, what are America's responsibilities as the only remaining superpower? Contributors:

Dr. Beatrice Bruteau • Dr. Joan Brown Campbell • Tony Campolo • Rev. Forrest Church • Lama Surya Das • Matthew Fox • Kabir Helminski • Thich Nhat Hanh • Eboo Patel • Abbot M. Basil Pennington, ocso • Dennis Prager • Rosemary Radford Ruether • Wayne Teasdale • Rev. William McD. Tully • Rabbi Arthur Waskow • John Wilson

5½ x 8½, 256 pp, Quality PB, 978-1-893361-81-2 **$16.95**

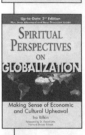

Spiritual Perspectives on Globalization, 2nd Edition
Making Sense of Economic and Cultural Upheaval
by Ira Rifkin; Foreword by Dr. David Little, Harvard Divinity School

What is globalization? Surveys the religious landscape. Includes a new Discussion Guide designed for group use.

5½ x 8½, 256 pp, Quality PB, 978-1-59473-045-0 **$16.99**

Hinduism / Vedanta

The Four Yogas
A Guide to the Spiritual Paths of Action, Devotion, Meditation and Knowledge
by Swami Adiswarananda 6 x 9, 320 pp, HC, 978-1-59473-143-3 **$29.99**

Meditation & Its Practices
A Definitive Guide to Techniques and Traditions of Meditation in Yoga and Vedanta
by Swami Adiswarananda 6 x 9, 504 pp, Quality PB, 978-1-59473-105-1 **$19.99**

The Spiritual Quest and the Way of Yoga: The Goal, the Journey and the Milestones
by Swami Adiswarananda 6 x 9, 288 pp, HC, 978-1-59473-113-6 **$29.99**

Sri Ramakrishna, the Face of Silence
by Swami Nikhilananda and Dhan Gopal Mukerji
Edited with an Introduction by Swami Adiswarananda; Foreword by Dhan Gopal Mukerji II

Classic biographies present the life and thought of Sri Ramakrishna.
6 x 9, 352 pp, HC, 978-1-59473-115-0 **$29.99**

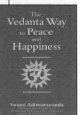

Sri Sarada Devi, The Holy Mother
Her Teachings and Conversations
Translated with Notes by Swami Nikhilananda; Edited with an Introduction by Swami Adiswarananda
6 x 9, 288 pp, HC, 978-1-59473-070-2 **$29.99**

The Vedanta Way to Peace and Happiness *by Swami Adiswarananda*
6 x 9, 240 pp, HC, 978-1-59473-034-4 **$29.99**

Vivekananda, World Teacher: His Teachings on the Spiritual Unity of Humankind
Edited and with an Introduction by Swami Adiswarananda
6 x 9, 272 pp, Quality PB, 978-1-59473-210-2 **$21.99**

Sikhism

The First Sikh Spiritual Master
Timeless Wisdom from the Life and Teachings of Guru Nanak *by Harish Dhillon*

Tells the story of a unique spiritual leader who showed a gentle, peaceful path to God-realization while highlighting Guru Nanak's quest for tolerance and compassion. 6 x 9, 240 pp, Quality PB, 978-1-59473-209-6 **$16.99**

Spirituality & Crafts

The Knitting Way: A Guide to Spiritual Self-Discovery
by Linda Skolnik and Janice MacDaniels
7 x 9, 240 pp, Quality PB, 978-1-59473-079-5 **$16.99**

The Quilting Path
A Guide to Spiritual Discovery through Fabric, Thread and Kabbalah
by Louise Silk
7 x 9, 192 pp, Quality PB, 978-1-59473-206-5 **$16.99**

Spiritual Practice

Divining the Body
Reclaim the Holiness of Your Physical Self *by Jan Phillips*
A practical and inspiring guidebook for connecting the body and soul in spiritual practice. Leads you into a milieu of reverence, mystery and delight, helping you discover your body as a pathway to the Divine.
8 x 8, 256 pp, Quality PB, 978-1-59473-080-1 **$16.99**

Finding Time for the Timeless: Spirituality in the Workweek
by John McQuiston II
Simple, refreshing stories that provide you with examples of how you can refocus and enrich your daily life using prayer or meditation, ritual and other forms of spiritual practice. 5½ x 6¾, 208 pp, HC, 978-1-59473-035-1 **$17.99**

The Gospel of Thomas
A Guidebook for Spiritual Practice *by Ron Miller; Translations by Stevan Davies*
An innovative guide to bring a new spiritual classic into daily life.
6 x 9, 160 pp, Quality PB, 978-1-59473-047-4 **$14.99**

Earth, Water, Fire, and Air: Essential Ways of Connecting to Spirit
by Cait Johnson 6 x 9, 224 pp, HC, 978-1-893361-65-2 **$19.95**

Labyrinths from the Outside In: Walking to Spiritual Insight—A Beginner's Guide
by Donna Schaper and Carole Ann Camp
6 x 9, 208 pp, b/w illus. and photos, Quality PB, 978-1-893361-18-8 **$16.95**

Practicing the Sacred Art of Listening: A Guide to Enrich Your Relationships
and Kindle Your Spiritual Life—The Listening Center Workshop
by Kay Lindahl 8 x 8, 176 pp, Quality PB, 978-1-893361-85-0 **$16.95**

Releasing the Creative Spirit: Unleash the Creativity in Your Life
by Dan Wakefield 7 x 10, 256 pp, Quality PB, 978-1-893361-36-2 **$16.95**

The Sacred Art of Bowing: Preparing to Practice
by Andi Young 5½ x 8½, 128 pp, b/w illus., Quality PB, 978-1-893361-82-9 **$14.95**

The Sacred Art of Chant: Preparing to Practice
by Ana Hernández 5½ x 8½, 192 pp, Quality PB, 978-1-59473-036-8 **$15.99**

The Sacred Art of Fasting: Preparing to Practice
by Thomas Ryan, CSP 5½ x 8½, 192 pp, Quality PB, 978-1-59473-078-8 **$15.99**

The Sacred Art of Forgiveness: Forgiving Ourselves and Others through God's Grace
by Marcia Ford 8 x 8, 176 pp, Quality PB, 978-1-59473-175-4 **$16.99**

The Sacred Art of Listening: Forty Reflections for Cultivating a Spiritual Practice
by Kay Lindahl; Illustrations by Amy Schnapper
8 x 8, 160 pp, b/w illus., Quality PB, 978-1-893361-44-7 **$16.99**

The Sacred Art of Lovingkindness: Preparing to Practice
by Rabbi Rami Shapiro; Foreword by Marcia Ford
5½ x 8½, 176 pp, Quality PB, 978-1-59473-151-8 **$16.99**

Sacred Speech: A Practical Guide for Keeping Spirit in Your Speech
by Rev. Donna Schaper 6 x 9, 176 pp, Quality PB, 978-1-59473-068-9 **$15.99**
HC, 978-1-893361-74-4 **$21.95**

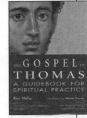

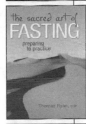

Sacred Texts—SkyLight Illuminations Series
Andrew Harvey, Series Editor

Offers today's spiritual seeker an accessible entry into the great classic texts of the world's spiritual traditions. Each classic is presented in an accessible translation, with facing pages of guided commentary from experts, giving you the keys you need to understand the history, context and meaning of the text. This series enables you, whatever your background, to experience and understand classic spiritual texts directly, and to make them a part of your life.

CHRISTIANITY

The End of Days: Essential Selections from Apocalyptic Texts—Annotated & Explained *Annotation by Robert G. Clouse*
Introduces you to the beliefs and values held by those who rely on the promises found in the Book of Revelation. 5½ x 8½, 192 pp, Quality PB, 978-1-59473-170-9 **$16.99**

The Hidden Gospel of Matthew: Annotated & Explained
Translation & Annotation by Ron Miller
Takes you deep into the text cherished around the world to discover the words and events that have the strongest connection to the historical Jesus.
5½ x 8½, 272 pp, Quality PB, 978-1-59473-038-2 **$16.99**

The Lost Sayings of Jesus: Teachings from Ancient Christian, Jewish, Gnostic and Islamic Sources—Annotated & Explained
Translation & Annotation by Andrew Phillip Smith; Foreword by Stephan A. Hoeller
This collection of more than three hundred sayings depicts Jesus as a Wisdom teacher who speaks to people of all faiths as a mystic and spiritual master.
5½ x 8½, 240 pp, Quality PB, 978-1-59473-172-3 **$16.99**

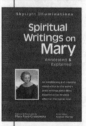

Philokalia: The Eastern Christian Spiritual Texts—Selections Annotated & Explained *Annotation by Allyne Smith; Foreword by Bishop Kallistos Ware*
The first approachable introduction to the wisdom of the Philokalia, which is the classic text of Eastern Christian spirituality.
5½ x 8½, 240 pp, Quality PB, 978-1-59473-103-7 **$16.99**

Spiritual Writings on Mary: Annotated & Explained
Annotation by Mary Ford-Grabowsky; Foreword by Andrew Harvey
Examines the role of Mary, the mother of Jesus, as a source of inspiration in history and in life today. 5½ x 8½, 288 pp, Quality PB, 978-1-59473-001-6 **$16.99**

The Way of a Pilgrim: Annotated & Explained
Translation & Annotation by Gleb Pokrovsky; Foreword by Andrew Harvey
This classic of Russian spirituality is the delightful account of one man who sets out to learn the prayer of the heart, also known as the "Jesus prayer."
5½ x 8½, 160 pp, Illus., Quality PB, 978-1-893361-31-7 **$14.95**

MORMONISM

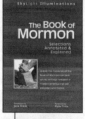

The Book of Mormon: Selections Annotated & Explained
Annotation by Jana Riess; Foreword by Phyllis Tickle
Explores the sacred epic that is cherished by more than twelve million members of the LDS church as the keystone of their faith.
5½ x 8½, 272 pp, Quality PB, 978-1-59473-076-4 **$16.99**

NATIVE AMERICAN

Native American Stories of the Sacred: Annotated & Explained
Retold & Annotated by Evan T. Pritchard
Intended for more than entertainment, these teaching tales contain elegantly simple illustrations of time-honored truths.
5½ x 8½, 272 pp, Quality PB, 978-1-59473-112-9 **$16.99**

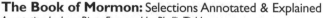

Sacred Texts—cont.

GNOSTICISM

The Gospel of Philip: Annotated & Explained
Translation & Annotation by Andrew Phillip Smith; Foreword by Stevan Davies
Reveals otherwise unrecorded sayings of Jesus and fragments of Gnostic mythology.
5½ x 8½, 160 pp, Quality PB, 978-1-59473-111-2 **$16.99**

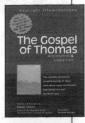

The Gospel of Thomas: Annotated & Explained
Translation & Annotation by Stevan Davies Sheds new light on the origins of Christianity and portrays Jesus as a wisdom-loving sage. 5½ x 8½, 192 pp, Quality PB, 978-1-893361-45-4 **$16.99**

The Secret Book of John: The Gnostic Gospel—Annotated & Explained
Translation & Annotation by Stevan Davies The most significant and influential text of the ancient Gnostic religion. 5½ x 8½, 208 pp, Quality PB, 978-1-59473-082-5 **$16.99**

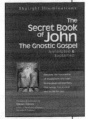

JUDAISM

The Divine Feminine in Biblical Wisdom Literature
Selections Annotated & Explained
Translation & Annotation by Rabbi Rami Shapiro; Foreword by Rev. Cynthia Bourgeault, PhD
Uses the Hebrew books of Psalms, Proverbs, Song of Songs, Ecclesiastes and Job, Wisdom literature and the Wisdom of Solomon to clarify who Wisdom is.
5½ x 8½, 240 pp, Quality PB, 978-1-59473-109-9 **$16.99**

Ethics of the Sages: *Pirke Avot*—Annotated & Explained
Translation & Annotation by Rabbi Rami Shapiro Clarifies the ethical teachings of the early Rabbis. 5½ x 8½, 192 pp, Quality PB, 978-1-59473-207-2 **$16.99**

Hasidic Tales: Annotated & Explained
Translation & Annotation by Rabbi Rami Shapiro
Introduces the legendary tales of the impassioned Hasidic rabbis, presenting them as stories rather than as parables. 5½ x 8½, 240 pp, Quality PB, 978-1-893361-86-7 **$16.95**

The Hebrew Prophets: Selections Annotated & Explained
Translation & Annotation by Rabbi Rami Shapiro; Foreword by Zalman M. Schachter-Shalomi
Focuses on the central themes covered by all the Hebrew prophets.
5½ x 8½, 224 pp, Quality PB, 978-1-59473-037-5 **$16.99**

Zohar: Annotated & Explained *Translation & Annotation by Daniel C. Matt*
The best-selling author of *The Essential Kabbalah* brings together in one place the most important teachings of the Zohar, the canonical text of Jewish mystical tradition.
5½ x 8½, 176 pp, Quality PB, 978-1-893361-51-5 **$15.99**

EASTERN RELIGIONS

Bhagavad Gita: Annotated & Explained *Translation by Shri Purohit Swami*
Annotation by Kendra Crossen Burroughs Explains references and philosophical terms, shares the interpretations of famous spiritual leaders and scholars, and more.
5½ x 8½, 192 pp, Quality PB, 978-1-893361-28-7 **$16.95**

Dhammapada: Annotated & Explained *Translation by Max Müller and revised by*
Jack Maguire; Annotation by Jack Maguire Contains all of Buddhism's key teachings.
5½ x 8½, 160 pp, b/w photos, Quality PB, 978-1-893361-42-3 **$14.95**

Rumi and Islam: Selections from His Stories, Poems, and Discourses—
Annotated & Explained *Translation & Annotation by Ibrahim Gamard*
Focuses on Rumi's place within the Sufi tradition of Islam, providing insight into the mystical side of the religion. 5½ x 8½, 240 pp, Quality PB, 978-1-59473-002-3 **$15.99**

Selections from the Gospel of Sri Ramakrishna: Annotated & Explained
Translation by Swami Nikhilananda; Annotation by Kendra Crossen Burroughs
Introduces the fascinating world of the Indian mystic and the universal appeal of his message. 5½ x 8½, 240 pp, b/w photos, Quality PB, 978-1-893361-46-1 **$16.95**

Tao Te Ching: Annotated & Explained *Translation & Annotation by Derek Lin*
Introduces an Eastern classic in an accessible, poetic and completely original way.
5½ x 8½, 192 pp, Quality PB, 978-1-59473-204-1 **$16.99**

About SKYLIGHT PATHS Publishing

SkyLight Paths Publishing is creating a place where people of different spiritual traditions come together for challenge and inspiration, a place where we can help each other understand the mystery that lies at the heart of our existence.

Through spirituality, our religious beliefs are increasingly becoming a part of our lives—rather than *apart* from our lives. While many of us may be more interested than ever in spiritual growth, we may be less firmly planted in traditional religion. Yet, we do want to deepen our relationship to the sacred, to learn from our own as well as from other faith traditions, and to practice in new ways.

SkyLight Paths sees both believers and seekers as a community that increasingly transcends traditional boundaries of religion and denomination—people wanting to learn from each other, *walking together, finding the way.*

For your information and convenience, at the back of this book we have provided a list of other SkyLight Paths books you might find interesting and useful. They cover the following subjects:

Buddhism / Zen	Gnosticism	Mysticism
Catholicism	Hinduism /	Poetry
Children's Books	Vedanta	Prayer
Christianity	Inspiration	Religious Etiquette
Comparative	Islam / Sufism	Retirement
Religion	Judaism / Kabbalah /	Spiritual Biography
Current Events	Enneagram	Spiritual Direction
Earth-Based	Meditation	Spirituality
Spirituality	Midrash Fiction	Women's Interest
Global Spiritual	Monasticism	Worship
Perspectives		

Or phone, fax, mail or e-mail to: SKYLIGHT PATHS Publishing
Sunset Farm Offices, Route 4 • P.O. Box 237 • Woodstock, Vermont 05091
Tel: (802) 457-4000 • Fax: (802) 457-4004 • www.skylightpaths.com
Credit card orders: (800) 962-4544 (8:30AM–5:30PM ET Monday–Friday)
Generous discounts on quantity orders. SATISFACTION GUARANTEED. Prices subject to change.